Conjunctures and Continuities in Southeast Asian Politics

Conjunctures and Continuities in Southeast Asian Politics

EDITED BY
N. GANESAN

ISEAS

INSTITUTE OF SOUTHEAST ASIAN STUDIES
SINGAPORE

First published in Singapore in 2013 by
ISEAS Publishing
Institute of Southeast Asian Studies
30 Heng Mui Keng Terrace
Pasir Panjang
Singapore 119614

E-mail: publish@iseas.edu.sg
Website: <http://bookshop.iseas.edu.sg>

ISEAS Library Cataloguing-in-Publication Data

Conjunctures and continuities in Southeast Asian politics / edited by
    N. Ganesan.
    1. Southeast Asia—Politics and government.
    I. Ganesan, N. (Narayanan), 1954–
DS526.7 C751   2013

ISBN 978-981-4379-946 (soft cover)
ISBN 978-981-4379-953 (e-book, PDF)

Typeset by Superskill Graphics Pte Ltd
Printed in Singapore by Markono Print Media Pte Ltd

CONTENTS

ACKNOWLEDGEMENTS

This edited volume is the outcome of a project that owes its origins to a workshop held in Kuala Lumpur in October 2009. The workshop that was entitled "Recent Historical Conjunctures in Southeast Asian Politics" was generously funded by the Swedish International Development Cooperation Agency (Sida) through the Asian Political and International Studies Association (APISA). I am especially indebted to Dr Hari Singh, the General Secretary of APISA for the funding and Ms Patricia Marin for assisting with the administration of the workshop.

Thanks are also due to the three discussants at the workshop who robustly engaged the paper writers and challenged them. They are Dr Nguyen vu Tung who is currently with the Vietnamese Embassy in Washington DC, Dr Lam Peng Er from the East Asian Institute and Dr Benjamin Wong from the National Institute of Education in Singapore.

At the publication stage I am indebted to the anonymous academic adviser at the Nordic Institute for Asian Studies (NIAS) who provided useful feedback on how to restructure the manuscript. Similarly, the suggestions of a second anonymous reviewer at the Institute of Southeast Asian Studies (ISEAS) in Singapore provided valuable feedback for a second round of revisions. And finally Mrs Triena Ong and Ms Rahilah Yusuf at ISEAS provided the necessary support to publish the manuscript expeditiously. All of them have made the manuscript stronger in its final form. Nonetheless the normal caveat that remaining shortcomings are attributable to me alone obtains.

The chapter written by Ehito Kimura entitled "Changing the Rules: Historical Conjuncture and Transition in Indonesia" was previously published in *Asia Pacific Viewpoint* 51, no. 3 (December 2010): 248–61.

ABBREVIATIONS

ACMES	Ayeyawady Chao Phraya Mekong Economic Cooperation Strategy
ASEAN	Association of Southeast Asian Nations
BA	Barisan Alternatif (Malaysia)
BCP	Communist Party of Burma/Burma Communist Party
BIMSTEC	Bay of Bengal Initiative for Multi-Sectoral Technical and Economic Cooperation
BN	Barisan Nasional (Malaysia)
BSPP	Burma Socialist Programme Party
CGDK	Coalition Government of Democratic Kampuchea
CPK	Communist Party of Kampuchea
CPP	Cambodian People's Party
CPP	Communist Party of the Philippines
CSA	Civil Society Agent (Malaysia)
CSO	civil society organizations
DAP	Democratic Action Party (Malaysia)
DK	Democratic Kampuchea
DRV	Democratic Republic of Vietnam
EC	Election Commission (Malaysia)
FDI	foreign direct investment
FRU	Federal Reserve Unit (Malaysia)
FUNCINPEC	Front de Union Nationale Pour un Cambodge Independent, Pacifique, Neutrale et Co-operatif (Cambodia)
GOLKAR	Golongan Karya (Indonesia)
HINDRAF	Hindu Rights Action Force (Malaysia)
IMF	International Monetary Fund
ISA	Internal Security Act (Malaysia)
JIM	Jakarta Informal Meeting

KIA	Kachin Independence Army (Myanmar)
KIO	Kachin Independence Organization (Myanmar)
KMP	Kilusan ng Magbubukid sa Pilipinas (Movement of Farmers in the Philippines)
KNU	Karen National Union (Myanmar)
KNUFNS	Kampuchean National Front for National Salvation
KPNLF	Khmer People's National Liberation Front (Cambodia)
LDC	least developed country
MB	Menteri Besar (Malaysia)
MCA	Malaysian Chinese Association
MIC	Malaysian Indian Congress
NATO	North Atlantic Treaty Organization
NC	National Convention (Myanmar)
ND	National Democratic (Philippines)
NGC	National Government of Cambodia
NLD	National League for Democracy (Myanmar)
NLF	National Liberation Front
NPA	New People's Army (Philippines)
NPKC	National Peace-Keeping Council
PAD	People's Alliance for Democracy (Thailand)
PAS	Parti Islam Se-Malaysia
PCC	Paris Conference on Cambodia
PCHR	Philippine Committee on Human Rights
PDIP	Indonesian Democratic Party – Struggle
PDK	Party of Democratic Kampuchea
PKN	Parti Keadilan Nasional (Malaysia)
PKR	People's Justice Party (Malaysia)
PPP	People's Progressive Party (Malaysia)
PRK	People's Republic of Kampuchea
RAM	Reform the Armed Forces Movement (Philippines)
RGNUC	Royal Government of National Union of Cambodia
RIT	Rangoon Institute of Technology (Myanmar)
ROV	Republic of Vietnam
SAARC	South Asian Association for Regional Cooperation
SAPP	Sabah Progressive Party
SLORC	State Law and Order Restoration Council (Myanmar)
SNC	Supreme National Council (Cambodia)
SOC	State of Cambodia

SOE	state-owned enterprise
SPDC	State Peace and Development Council (Myanmar)
SSA	Shan State Army (Myanmar)
TOL	Temporary Occupation Lease (Malaysia)
UDD	United Front for Democracy Against Dictatorship (Thailand)
UMFCCI	Union of Myanmar Federation of Chambers of Commerce and Industry
UMNO	United Malays National Organisation (Malaysia)
UNAMIC	United Nations Advance Mission in Cambodia
UNTAC	United Nations Transitional Authority in Cambodia
UPKO	United Pasokmomogun Kadazandusun Murut Organization (Malaysia)
USDA	Union Solidarity and Development Association (Myanmar)
USSR	Union of Soviet Socialist Republics
UTPP	United Thai People's Party
UWSA	United Wa State Army (Myanmar)
VCP/CPV	Vietnamese Communist Party (Viet Nam Cong San Dang)/Communist Party of Vietnam (Đảng Cộng sản Việt Nam)

CONTRIBUTORS

N. Ganesan is Professor of Southeast Asian Politics at the Hiroshima Peace Institute in Japan where he has been since 2004. He concurrently serves as Visiting Professor at the National Graduate Institute for Policy Studies (GRIPS) in Tokyo. His research interest focuses on sources of intrastate and interstate tensions and conflict in Southeast Asia.

Ramses Amer is Senior Research Fellow at the Department of Oriental Languages, Stockholm University, Stockholm and Research Associate, Swedish Institute of International Affairs, Stockholm. Major areas of research include (a) security issues and conflict resolution in Southeast Asia and the wider Pacific Asia and (b) the role of the United Nations in the international system. His most recent books are *Conflict Management and Dispute Settlement in East Asia* (Farnham and Burlington: Ashgate, 2011) (co-edited with Keyuan Zou) and *The Security-Development Nexus: Peace, Conflict and Development* (London: Anthem Press, 2012) (co-edited with Ashok Swain and Joakim Öjendal).

Lisandro E. Claudio is Assistant Professor in the Department of Political Science, Ateneo de Manila University. He obtained his doctorate from the School of Historical and Philosophical Studies, the University of Melbourne.

Rommel A. Curaming is Programme Leader and Lecturer in History and Southeast Asian Studies Programme at the University of Brunei Darussalam (UBD). Prior to joining UBD, he was Postdoctoral Fellow at the National University of Singapore (NUS) and Postdoctoral Research Fellow under Endeavour Awards (2008) at La Trobe University. He completed his PhD in Southeast Asian Studies at the Australian National University (ANU) with a thesis on state-scholar relations in Indonesia and the Philippines.

His recent research and publications focus on history and memory of political violence, Filipino Malayness, and politics and ethics of knowledge production.

Federico Ferrara is Assistant Professor in the Department of Asian and International Studies of the City University of Hong Kong. He is the author of *Thailand Unhinged: The Death of Thai-Style Democracy* (2011) and numerous articles on comparative elections and party systems.

Ehito Kimura is Assistant Professor of Political Science at the University of Hawai'i at Manoa. His research interests include contemporary Indonesian and Southeast Asia politics. He is the author of *Political Change and Territoriality in Indonesia: Provincial Proliferation* (2012) as well as articles in journals such as *Asian Survey, Southeast Asia Research, Indonesia,* and *Asia Pacific Viewpoint.*

Johan Saravanamuttu is Visiting Senior Research Fellow at the Institute of Southeast Asian Studies, Singapore and was formerly Professor of Political Science at Universiti Sains Malaysia (USM) in Penang where he served as Dean of the School of Social Sciences (1994–1996). In 1997 he was the Visiting Chair in ASEAN and International Studies at the University of Toronto. His publications include *New Politics in Malaysia* (ISEAS, 2003) (edited with Francis Loh) and *March 8: Eclipsing May 13* (ISEAS, 2008) (with Ooi Kee Beng and Lee Hock Guan). His latest books are *Islam and Politics in Southeast Asia* (editor) (Routledge, 2010) and *Malaysia's Foreign Policy, the First 50 Years: Alignment, Neutralism, Islamism* (ISEAS, 2010).

Tin Maung Maung Than, a Myanmar national, is a Senior Research Fellow at the Institute of Southeast Asian Studies (ISEAS) Singapore. He is the author of *State Dominance in Myanmar: The Political Economy of Industrialization* (ISEAS, 2007); and more recently "Myanmar's 2010 Elections, Continuity and Change", in *Southeast Asian Affairs 2011* (ISEAS, 2011). His research interests include political economy of development, democratization and civil-military relations in developing countries, human security, nuclear proliferation, Myanmar politics and economics.

Ta Minh Tuan is Director General and Assistant to the Deputy Prime Minister, Vietnam. He also holds an Associate Professorship at the

Diplomatic Academy of Vietnam. His research and teaching includes U.S. foreign policy, security in the Asia-Pacific, Vietnam's politics and foreign policy, nuclear non-proliferation and Vietnam's nuclear energy policy. Dr Tuan was a Fulbright fellow at the University of South Carolina (2004), a fellow at the Asia-Pacific Center for Security Studies in Hawaii (2006), and a fellow at the Center for Northeast Asia Policy Studies, the Brookings Institution (2011). He is a member of CSCAP Study Group on Countering the Proliferation of WMD in the Asia Pacific and a member of CSCAP Vietnam. Dr Tuan earned his PhD in political science from the Polish Academy of Sciences, Poland in 2002.

1

CONJUNCTURES AND CONTINUITIES IN SOUTHEAST ASIAN POLITICS

N. Ganesan

In their evolution of political structures and life, countries often undergo significant conjunctures or what is sometimes referred to as historical junctures. For parsimony, the term conjuncture which appears to better reflect a confluence of forces has been chosen. A conjuncture involves "interaction effects between distinct causal sequences that become joined at particular points in time".[1] During such moments "relatively long periods of institutional stability and reproduction are punctuated occasionally by brief periods of institutional flux".[2] At the formative level, such conjunctures are likely to be important starting points in the historical evolution of a society or country. Just like ethnic nations, these formative episodes are likely to involve an important event, declaration or document. The American Civil War in the 1800s and the Magna Carta in the United Kingdom constitute such episodes. Subsequently, and deriving their legitimacy from these formative events, structures, rituals and practices that acquire symbolic and mythical value evolve over time. Whereas such practices naturally undergo changes over time to reflect both the popular will as well as administrative refinements, there is a certain permanence about these foundational norms. For example, in the United Kingdom, as democracy evolved, power gradually shifted from the upper House of Lords to the lower House of Commons. Notwithstanding the changes in the configuration of power between both Houses, it can be argued that the structures have remained intact. In fact, the transfer of power from the Lords to the Commons quite simply reflected the democratic value that state sovereignty should be vested with the citizenry rather than the elite aristocracy.

Foundational conjunctures are likely to determine structural and cultural norms that order political life. Such events typically identify the rules of engagement and provide both opportunities and constraints to regulate politics. Changes then occur incrementally while the basic principles or rules of engagement become reified. However, from time to time states and societies undergo major events that reorder political structures and norms. These events mark a major point of departure from the past and introduce new structures and norms that subsequently become ensconced. In the literature in comparative politics the study of conjunctures falls within the historical institutionalist approach. The approach places great emphasis on the importance of time and the availability of options at the time of the conjuncture. It is also concerned with the concept of "increasing returns", a term borrowed from economics to describe how a specific decision ordains path dependency and perpetuates it over time. It is this dependency that in turn precludes other possible trajectories over time. Conjunctures are moments in time that offer the possibility of evolving path-dependent decisions.

This chapter provides the background to a number of important conjunctures that have occurred in Southeast Asia in the last two decades. In line with the technical definition of a conjuncture, it is likely concerned with developments that have served to dislodge previous structures and practices and replace them with new ones that have in turn acquired their own legitimacy and volition over time. It will also identify the nature of the break with the immediate past and the new structures and norms that obtain. Admittedly the older these conjunctures are the easier it is to identify the changes. Where such conjunctures are of recent vintage the best that can be hoped for is an intelligent guess on the likely trajectory of future developments as path dependency locks in future developments. In this regard it should be noted from the outset that conjunctures require some time for new norms and practices to crystallize.

CONJUNCTURES AND RELATED CONCEPTS

Conjunctures are those that can be best described as major watersheds in political life. Such conjunctures establish "certain directions of change and foreclose others in a way that shapes politics for years to come".[3] Traditionally, such studies emphasized either "deeply embedded antecedent conditions" or "societal conditions or crises" that lead to such junctures. This notion of critical junctures is extremely important in historical institutional analysis and "characterized by a situation in which the structural (that is economic, cultural, ideological, organizational) influences on political action are significantly relaxed for a relatively short period with two main consequences: the range of plausible choices open to powerful political actors expands substantially and the consequences of their decisions for the outcome of interest are potentially much more momentous".[4] Sometimes the emphasis is on the conjunctures themselves. Whatever the focus, the important point to note is that such conjunctures mark a critical departure from previously established practices and heralds a new era in terms of the calibration of politics. This likely structural as well as procedural change has in turn a significant impact on aspects of domestic politics and structures in the state experiencing the conjuncture. Importantly, early decisions made during conjunctures have lasting impact and "lock in" certain developments while dramatically negating the possibility of others. The establishment of a specific equilibrium in the power equation makes it resistant to change leading in turn to its embeddedness over time.[5] A central paradox deriving from this development is that path dependency may well lead to the creation over time of an inefficient mechanism that simply replicates itself. Owing to increasing returns, it then becomes difficult to undo the decision and return to a different method or solution.

There are a number of important features that identify the onset of a conjuncture. The first and perhaps most important development is that a conjuncture brings together a unique set of circumstances and issues that in turn provide a window of opportunity for significant changes to obtain. This confluence of factors and forces could not have been foreseen or anticipated. Additionally and importantly, authors on conjunctures note the importance of contingency in such a situation. In other words, when a conjuncture occurs, it opens up a number of possibilities and choices. It is generally thought that conjunctures are characterized by a period of openness where a range of decisions can be made. And in order to demonstrate this openness, it must be possible to explore alternative decisions that could have been made during the conjuncture. Importantly, it must also be possible to track the developments that would have arisen if a different decision was taken.

This treatment of counterfactuals proves the existence of a conjuncture and contingent conditions. Contingency presupposes that similar opportunities were not available during prior historical conditions.[6] The plotting of alternative scenarios is generally thought to be the test of a conjuncture in that it avails different possibilities. And the availability of different possibilities in turn confirms the existence of a conjuncture. The selection of a different alternative must clearly lead to a dramatically different outcome to demonstrate how specific choices blocked off other possibilities and created path-dependent conditions. Contingency also means that small decisions taken at specific times during the conjuncture have outcomes that are disproportionate to the decision itself. All in all a conjuncture constitutes an "analysis of decision-making under conditions of uncertainty".[7] Working backwards ex post facto then allows a researcher to undertake process tracing and identify the decision and decision-maker/s that were central to the narrative of the conjuncture and the introduction of path dependency.

The second way to identify a conjuncture is through what James Mahoney calls "the study of reactive sequences".[8] These are chains of events that are "temporally ordered and causally connected". The reaction is in relation to some aspect of an antecedent condition. In such a methodology, the final event tends to be the outcome under study and the total chain of events actually lead up to the event. And in order for such reactive tracing to identify a conjuncture, the preliminary decision that was made must suggest contingent conditions. In other words, the end of the reactive chain must have offered different possibilities when the decision was made. Mahoney also argues for another important condition to this method that he calls "inherent sequencing". By this he means that the trajectory of events must be properly sequenced to provide acceptable results. Importantly, reactive sequences differ substantially from reproductive increasing returns since they constitute a backlash that transforms and perhaps reverses an earlier sequence. In this regard, reactive sequencing involves the study of tightly linked negative responses to early events during a conjuncture.[9]

The historical institutionalist method is especially keen to capture the dynamics of time associated with a conjuncture. It is thought that a conjuncture spans a fraction of the time associated with changes that it has brought about. It is rather difficult to be much more specific than this description since conjunctures can vary in length. This non-discrete description however opens up the possibility of mistaking evolutionary change for a conjuncture. It also includes the additional problem of not defining how far back path-dependent tracing should go. Critical conjunctures are naturally expected to have some variance across countries in that similar antecedents or outcomes may not obtain. In this regard, there is some analytic difficulty in utilizing the comparative historical method in identifying conjunctures. Whereas allowance has to be made for differences across time and space, there must be some consistency in classifying a conjuncture for methodological rigour to obtain. It is for this reason that antecedent conditions and the changes obtained are important since they are likely to validate or nullify a claim.

Another major issue concerns the unit of analysis in question as well as the profundity of the changes. Most writings on conjunctures appear to suggest economic, structural, cultural or organizational changes in the makeup of the state. Alternatively, it may be a specific structure or feature of a state that is being studied. It is however important to realize that a conjuncture for a certain aspect of political economy or state-society relations does not trigger an institutional or national crisis. In other words, selected institutional features or practices may be studied using the historical institutional method. For example, Capoccia and Kelemen suggest how a critical juncture for a country's party system may have little bearing on a country's regime type or system of interest mediation.[10] In fact, even during national difficulties, many institutional aspects of politics are likely to remain unchanged or unchallenged. The use of this methodology is equally useful for the study of state-society relations or, for that matter, the political economy of the state. Conjunctures help to identify the conditions that spawned the opportunity for certain decisions to be made. And since the nature of the decisions taken yield increasing returns, there is a very real sense in which the early decisions create path-dependent conditions in turn. So, for example, states that were formed during times of civil war invariably created a sufficiently broad tax base to provide the necessary resources to deal with military conflicts.

Owing to the relative specificity of the changes, conjunctures create path-dependent conditions that tend in the direction of discontinuities. Especially important in this regard are the beginnings or early decisions that led to path dependency. Paul Pierson refers to "the powerful inertia or 'stickiness'" that characterize early decisions that subsequently lock in a particular trajectory of developments.[11] He goes on to provide the example of enduring consequences that obtain from certain institutional arrangements. The importance of such early decisions also lies in the fact that the outcomes deriving from them are replicated even in the absence of "the recurrence of the original event or process".[12] In order for such early decisions to obtain, it is equally important to examine agency choices and decisions. After all, the available choices need to be acted on in order to trigger the path-dependent conditions. The difference between such an opportunity and the normal historical development of interest setting lies in the manner in which early decisions during conjunctures foreclose other possibilities to create path-dependent conditions.

It is entirely possible however that a conjuncture did not yield any major changes. In other words, although the conditions for major change existed, the opportunity was not utilized, leading to a return of the previous condition and trajectory of developments. The emphasis on "structural fluidity and heightened contingency" does not preclude a return to the status quo in the aftermath of a conjuncture.[13] It is also generally thought that the longer the conjuncture, the greater the probability of structural impediments interfering with contingency and path-dependent decision-making. Both of these observations appear to apply in the case of Burma/Myanmar where the collapse of the BSPP government created a window of opportunity that lapsed over time and eventually led to the reinstatement of a military authoritarian regime. Alternatives that were previously available are likely to become closed off over time. So, for example, the downfall of the Soeharto regime in Indonesia constituted such a conjuncture. The conditions following the government's downfall made it clear that the military would become disengaged from the political process.[14] It also became apparent shortly afterwards that democratic norms were being considered and seriously implemented. Such broad-based changes undergirded a series of reforms and changes that characterized post–New Order governments.

Collier and Collier argue that in order to be able to identify a conjuncture, it is first important to identify antecedent conditions. These conditions would then serve as the baseline against which changes are measured. The baseline also serves the useful purpose of identifying continuities from the previous period and falsifying rival claims to the contrary. Continuities may also suggest that the origins of the historical conjuncture derive from the previous period and do not therefore constitute a significant break from the past. Nonetheless, it would be fair to note that even in instances where there appears to be a clear break from the past, certain systemic or more likely social continuities may obtain. It is therefore incumbent on the analysis to distinguish between continuities that have undergone a significant change and those that have not. The conjuncture must also have a clear cleavage or crisis that precipitates it. Social norms are often expressed in different ways, especially if they form a constitutive part of the social fabric and involve rights and obligations. The authors also argue for the elimination of the "constant causes" or evolutionary hypothesis that would negate the legacy of a conjuncture.

An important and early question for critical conjunctures is whether they were internally or externally triggered. In other words, were the factors responsible for the conjuncture domestic or foreign in origin? If the trigger was external, it is likely that the event had rippling effects over more than just one country. And if the event served to trigger a conjuncture in more than one country, it can be studied for variance which is likely to be interactive with antecedent conditions in the manner which the conjuncture played itself out. Systemic and sub-systemic shocks are therefore likely to be more easily identified owing to their typically broad-based impact. So, for example, the Asian financial crisis, as a major regional disturbance, had a wide-ranging impact on Indonesia, South Korea and Thailand. The next major question involves the length of the conjuncture. In some cases where there is clear revolutionary change the conjuncture is likely to be short-lived albeit with major structural and associated changes. However, a conjuncture may also span a significant period of time and come about on the basis of sustained application of policies to bring about change. Such evolutionary change is sometimes much harder to identify since it is easily confused with continuity and provides evidence to disprove the onset of a conjuncture. The rule of thumb is that the conjuncture typically constitutes a fraction of the time in relation to the changes that obtain and their subsequent reinforcement.

Another important question pertains to the lead-up to the conjuncture that forms part of the antecedent conditions. Were there important cleavages in state-society relations that eventually resulted in the conjuncture? In other words, were there what Collier and Collier call "generative cleavages" that eventually led to a rupture of the structures and social fabric as previously constituted that in turn created the openness associated with contingency?

If such cleavages existed then it becomes important to discern why the cleavage was so deeply embedded and what its linkage is in turn to the conjuncture as well as the changes obtained. If sufficiently nested to create and trigger a conjuncture, a cleavage must have some enduring impact on the legacy deriving from the conjuncture. Similarly, the conjuncture must demonstrate a clear fissure with past historical developments and stand out as sufficiently unique to warrant its classification. For example, structural-functional changes are easily identified but, without sufficient enforcement or compliance mechanisms, are of little value. In other words, structural changes must have a clear bearing on some aspect of state-society relations that change them for the better or worse. And more importantly, such changes must demonstrate a clear break from the past, as previously mentioned.

Another major consideration in appraising a conjuncture is that the new politics must demonstrate a clear break from the past. After all, if there was no such breach then it will be sufficient to frame the discourse in terms of continuities and, more importantly, incremental changes. The analysis should also be able to isolate specific tendencies or policy strands that assist in the process of yielding increasing returns. And finally, it is important to distinguish the early decisions themselves and their subsequent impact and self-reinforcement or increasing returns. The conjuncture, despite coming into being on the basis of a crisis or cleavage, may "crystallize" or become fully formed over time. This staggered formation of the conjuncture is not to be confused with incremental changes from the previous situation.

OTHER THEORETICAL CONSIDERATIONS AND CONCERNS

The focus of this book essentially examines significant changes to the tone and temper of domestic politics. Such changes may include the calibration of domestic politics as in the case of Cambodia after the United Nations–sponsored Peace Accords and subsequent settlement of the civil war. It may also indicate regime change as in the case of Thailand after the September 2006 military coup against the Thaksin government. Alternatively, political recalibration may involve major changes to the structuration of politics as in the case of Malaysia where the political opposition secured victories in five states in the March 2008 general election. It is also entirely possible that conjunctures affected a significant aspect of the country's political economy as in the case of Vietnam after the introduction of the economic renovation policy in 1986. Alternatively, as mentioned earlier, the conjuncture may have had little impact on the constitution of the regime in power as was the case with Myanmar in 1988 after the student-led uprising and again in 1990 after the opposition National League for Democracy (NLD) secured an overwhelming victory. In this regard it should be noted from the outset that the case studies were strictly chosen on the basis that significant conjunctures appeared to have obtained in them at the time when the project was conceptualized. Whereas some of the case studies like Thailand and Indonesia may be predisposed towards regime change, that was certainly not the thrust of the project. Similarly, it should not be assumed that this is a study about the onset and progress of democratization in Southeast Asia. In this regard, there are no ideological considerations that have conceptually driven this book. In fact, it is abundantly evident that countries like Thailand and Myanmar have actually regressed in terms of democratic development.

The second observation that should be made is that this book does not assume that change occurs in a linear and positive fashion. It is not a Whig reading of history as Thomas Kuhn notes in his book on scientific revolutions.[15] Consequently, the cases chosen were not considered for the outcome of the conjunctures and were value free at the time the choices were made. In fact, the authors of the country chapters were given sufficient latitude to determine when conjunctures had occurred in their countries of expertise. In some cases like Cambodia and Thailand, simply identifying the conjuncture generated animated discussions. Naturally, in countries where changes obtained as a result of conjunctures, a fair question would be who did the changes affect? The authors, all country specialists, were tasked to identify the conjuncture and the path chosen during a period of contingency. Subsequently, they were asked to identify the nature of the impact on the country writ large. Specifically, they have been asked to identify the structures and constituencies that have been most affected by the conjuncture.

Arising from the assertion that this is not a Whig study of history, it should be noted that authors were allowed to make the judgment call whether a conjuncture had led or did not lead to a path-dependent outcome. In other words, did the initial momentum from the conjuncture simply peter out? If so, it would merely have led to a relapse of what previously existed. And the Myanmar situation certainly appears to augur the possibility of just such a development. A more difficult question is whether a conjuncture has been wrongly identified. Since conjunctures sometimes resemble evolutionary changes when they span a long period of time, the two may well be difficult to distinguish. The rule that the conjuncture lasts only a fraction of the time compared to the path-dependent changes essentially constitutes a judgment call. Similarly, path dependency and increasing returns has the potential to become a norm after some time. How does the analyst decide when such a transformation occurs?

Finally, it should be noted that the theme of this book is on conjunctures as well as continuities. If conjunctures augur the potential to lead to an abrupt change that is in turn path dependent, presumably it performs a dislocation function. Yet we intuitively know that many social phenomena often transform themselves in the face of challenges. Consequently, it may be useful to think of conjunctures and continuities as more than just polar opposites. A seemingly abrupt dislocation may well yield patterns and practices that do not readily lend themselves to scrutiny or judgment. Hence, the two developments may well form part of a conceptual and larger whole, as Joel Migdal regards his "state in society" approach to the study of state-society relations.[16]

THE CASE STUDIES

The 1986 "People Power" uprising that occurred in the Philippines constituted a defining moment in Philippine political history. Yet authors Curaming and Claudio are quick to warn their readers that the utility of the uprising has to be measured against the antecedent conditions and in particular the various meanings attributed to the Marcos regime. The demonization of the martial law government instituted by Ferdinand Marcos in the post-EDSA period also complicates the process of viewing this conjuncture within the framework of socio-political considerations. The authors argue that although EDSA represented a sharp break with the past in terms of the elite in power and the new structural characteristics of the system that obtained, there are a large number of continuities as well. Such continuities include the self-serving demonization of the Marcos regime that was perpetuated by previously displaced elite that were anxious to secure their share of the spoils in the post-Marcos period. Also, notwithstanding the structural changes to the Philippine political system, the changes had little bearing on the structuration of power and the dispersion of resources since it merely implied the displacement of a segment of the elite by another with little filtration of power downwards as expected in a democracy. The authors allude to important continuities that obtained especially in the areas of land reform and human rights. Nevertheless, embedded within the discourse is also an altruistic component that seeks to displace authoritarianism from Philippine politics in the future. Similarly, the authors think that the exuberance in the Philippine case in 1986 derived in part from the global hegemony of the discourse on democratization in academia and international relations.

The EDSA event itself was triggered at the outset by dissension within the ranks of the military.[17] Subsequently, other social groups like the clergy and students and intellectuals became involved in it. The successful uprising also meant that an incumbent president had to leave office and, interestingly, it was the United States that arranged for his political exile, not unlike the case with the Shah of Iran in 1979 when the Islamic Revolution occurred. Therefore, in terms of ending a longstanding practice and regime type, the 1986 event clearly fulfils the conditions of a conjuncture. All presidents after Marcos were democratically elected, although a case can be made that Gloria Arroyo's first term of office in replacement of Joseph "Erap" Estrada was not necessarily constitutional. The important question remains whether street protests leading to regime change is also a part of the Philippine legacy of the conjuncture since it has been subsequently invoked. Nonetheless, there appears to be general agreement that the country has reverted to being a democracy and aspirants for political office have generally abided by this practice notwithstanding the number of coup attempts that plagued the government of Corazon Aquino.[18] The strong compact between the state and the military was also broken after the Marcos government and serves as another legacy albeit members of the military establishment have found alternative political avenues within the local political structures. Civilian supremacy has obtained in the aftermath of the uprising and even Fidel Ramos who assumed the Presidency after Corazon Aquino was retired from the military before his election into office. In fact his presidency both placated and pacified the military and in turn further strengthened civilian supremacy over the military. The introduction of a term limit on the office of the president was an important feature of the conjuncture. After Marcos, all presidents have been subjected to a six-year term limit in office. The exception to the rule, Gloria Arroyo, ascended to the first term on the basis of the uprising against Estrada for a first four-year term and was subsequently elected for a second six-year term that expired in 2010. Interestingly, the newly elected president, Benigno (Noynoy) Aquino, is the son of Corazon Aquino with little previous political involvement. The interesting question that arises is whether the personalities associated with the conjuncture are being reproduced or a pre-existing elite has simply capitalized on the conjuncture again. In this regard, it might be useful to remind ourselves that the Aquino family is part of the powerful Cojuangco clan notwithstanding the "moralization" of Philippine politics that has enabled another Aquino to come to power.

The Vietnamese introduction of *doi moi* or a renovation policy was also an important historical conjuncture although the antecedent conditions and the manner in which it came to be implemented do suggest an evolutionary conjuncture. Ta Tuan points to a series of initiatives loosening state control over agricultural production that were gradually implemented from 1980 following poor harvests and an ensuing socio-economic crisis. The latter was however precipitated by a number of external developments as well. These included the Vietnamese decision to invade and occupy Cambodia that cost the country dearly and disrupted agricultural production in the border areas. The Chinese punitive expedition in turn in 1979 also led to the loss of economic aid and these two hostilities led in turn to the displacement of ethnic Hoa who performed an important economic role in the country. Finally, the American-led economic embargo against Vietnam also took its transactional toll in the domestic and international markets.

Although *doi moi* did not replace the government or alter the rules of political contestation like the other case studies, it involved a major restructuring of state-society relations and the transformation of the country's political economy. Private companies became involved in commodity production and the government disbanded its attempts to collectivize the production process after the failure of its agricultural reform policies in the post-1976 period. Private enterprises and collectives began to play a role alongside the government in commodity production. The change in state-society relations involved a significant loosening of state controls over the process of production and distribution of resources. The market was allowed to determine prices and the availability of goods and services in a way that it had never done before following the communist victory in the civil war in 1975. This change led to a significant loosening of control over resources and their prices. As a result, a parallel market economy began to emerge alongside the command economy and, over time, there was also a liberalization of public political space that had been previously monopolized by the Communist Party. The abolishment of collectivization and continuation of private enterprise transformed the economic growth of the country. In the 1990s Vietnam achieved one of the highest rates of growth in Southeast Asia and significantly reduced poverty in the countryside. *Doi moi* clearly had a path-dependent trajectory in the form of state directives loosening control over price and resource allocations albeit the VCP retained its monopoly on political power.

The case of Myanmar provides a far clearer important historical conjuncture. The 1988 collapse of the Burma Socialist Programme Party (BSPP) government ended a particular type of political economy of the state that began in 1962 after Ne Win led a military coup against the elected government. The 1988 government's collapse effectively ended that socialist legacy and sought far greater economic and political liberalization. The first and most visible of these structural changes was the emergence of a set of counter-elites that sought to capitalize on the seeming political space by launching the "Four Eights" protest movement. Although the movement was eventually crushed, its enduring legacy was the continuation of the counterclaim in 1990 by the political opposition led by the NLD and Aung San Suu Kyi that won the 1990 election.

The collapse of the Communist Party of Burma (BCP) in 1988 further added to the significance of the conjuncture. The negotiation of ceasefire agreements with the ethnic insurgent armies to secure the border areas and reduce the domestic opposition within the country to the military's political plans arose from this collapse. This began at the outset with the Wa and the Kokang ethnic groups that were the sword arms of the BCP. Subsequently the military government went on to seal similar deals with twenty such groups and established a framework that ended almost five decades of internal conflict.[19] The structural legacy continues to obtain until today and includes the Karen National Union (KNU) as one of the major groups to finally ratify a ceasefire accord in 2012. The terms of the arrangement were liberal at the outset and allowed for the armies to retain control over contiguous territory and weapons in exchange for a cessation of hostilities. The military government also had to serve prior notice if it entered these areas. This arrangement was clearly a significant development that brought to an end a major source of internal conflict within the country. The military government expects that these armies will be integrated in the future as part of a larger border security guard force although the largest groups like the Kachin Independence Organization (KIO), Shan

State Army (SSA), United Wa Development Association (UWSA) and the Karen National Union (KNU) have already indicated their disagreement with such a plan. Key areas of disagreement include the composition of the armies and the command and control structures.

The military government's decision to hold elections in 1990 to replace the caretaker government from 1988 was an extension of the conjuncture. The widespread demonstrations against the military and calls for democracy that followed the collapse of the BSPP government unleashed social forces that wanted major changes in the structuration of government. The immediate response of the government was the violent suppression of the protests that eroded its own legitimacy. However, it was forced to concede that political legitimacy had to be regained to stave off both domestic and external pressures. Although it eventually refused to abide by the outcome of the elections that handed a major victory to the political opposition headed by the NLD and Aung San Suu Kyi, the process itself could no longer be reversed. The government was forced to convene a constitutional convention that took many years to eventuate and subsequently ran a referendum of the Constitution in 2008. Suu Kyi who had her house arrest extended by eighteen months till November 2010 was unable to compete in it although opposition candidates and parties competed under restrictive arrangements, at least to eke out a place for themselves within the new structural opportunities presented. In fact it is the feared loss of this "legitimate" counterclaim that led to the NLD's recent decision not to expel Suu Kyi for criminal convictions from the Party under the terms of the new constitution promulgated in 2008 as well as the decision not to contest the 2010 election. Hence, even as the military government in power seeks to entrench itself through the constitution and has steered the election and outcome in its favour, the requirement for a new set of rules and legitimacy remains a constant. Additionally, the previous compact achieved between the military and the state is likely to undergo some major transformation. The one-party dominant state is also likely to relinquish some of its power to a nascent political opposition. In this regard, this second structural aspect of the conjuncture has taken quite some time to play itself out and indeed is likely to be part of a longer ongoing process for some time to come. Additionally, since the election in 2010, Prime Minister Thein Sein has announced a large number of seemingly liberal initiatives. These include engaging Suu Kyi, postponement of the Myitsone Dam project that had led to skirmishes with the Kachin Independence Army (KIA), a call for exiles to return in exchange for amnesty, and the release of over 6,000 prisoners announced in October 2011. These policy initiatives have surprised both local and foreign observers and given some cause for optimism.

A third major aspect of the legacy in the Myanmar case is the changed political consciousness and the willingness of the public to demonstrate against the government even in the face of overwhelming odds against it. The August 1988 student-led protest movement was simply the harbinger of similar events to come. The 1990 elections and the mobilization involved was also unparalleled in recent political history. And since then, there have been a number of episodes to indicate that this legacy has not come to a complete close. The May 2003 violence in Depayin between the supporters of Suu Kyi and the military-sponsored Union Solidarity Development Association (USDA) again demonstrated public political will and action, although the event itself triggered the house arrest of Suu Kyi in 2003. There was another large outbreak of resistance to the government in August 2007 when fuel prices were suddenly raised astronomically and proved too difficult to cope with at the ground level. Similarly, the monks-led uprising against the military government in September 2007 that in turn led to a crackdown against the sangha was only another demonstration of an existing trend. And the most recent continuation of this trend occurred in May 2008 after the government's slow and poorly coordinated attempts to deal with the aftermath of Cyclone Nargis that left some 130,000 people dead. Again, there were very visible gestures of assistance from the public and local NGOs and scathing criticisms of the government's response. A number of the harshest critics from the Four Eights movement were subsequently detained by the government. This string of protests against the government again marks a clear break with the past during the tenure of the BSPP government and appears to be part of an ongoing legacy.

The final major historical legacy is the change in Burma/Myanmar's foreign policy after 1988. During the tenure of the BSPP government, Burma practised a policy of self-imposed isolationism in order to obtain political neutrality and stay clear of the dynamics of the Cold War. After 1988, it has practiced a much more engaging and high profile foreign policy. This engagement is certainly true of its enhanced ties with China and to a lesser extent India. More recently, it has also sought to cultivate close ties with Russia.[20] Whereas the cultivation of such ties served the useful purpose of deflecting pressures from the West, in particular the United States and the

European Union and the sanctions that they had imposed and periodically enlarged and extended against Myanmar, it still reflected a major change from previous policy output. The previous policy of isolationism has clearly been changed to one of engagement with selected countries to aid in economic and infrastructural development. This new policy also helped manage some of the debilitating impact of the international sanctions regime and avoid further international sanctions.

The Myanmar case presents an interesting contrast to some of the other countries, like Indonesia and the Philippines. The conjuncture and its discontinuities that serve as a major watershed in domestic politics are clear to see. However, since the military government that has been in place since 1990 is anxious to retain political power and thwart efforts by the opposition to make significant inroads in politics, more structural and real path-dependent developments are not yet forthcoming. Since the incumbent government remains generally unwilling to share power and leave political legitimacy entirely to the electorate, this thwarted trajectory of the conjuncture is likely to endure for some time to come. Nonetheless, it is equally unable to reverse some of the legacies that have been established thus far despite the important continuity of the military's continued domination of the country's political economy.

The 1992–93 UN-sponsored national election in Cambodia ranks clearly as a historical conjuncture. Nonetheless, Ramses Amer has argued that a number of other previous developments also led to significant path-dependent developments. He goes on to identify these developments as the 1970 overthrow of Norodom Sihanouk, the situation in 1975 that subsequently set the stage for the Vietnamese invasion, and the occupation of Cambodia in 1978/79 prior to the national election.

The 1970 overthrow of Sihanouk is regarded as important since it occurred within the framework of anti-Vietnamese rhetoric and policies. Vietnamese attempts to repatriate those discriminated against was successful in the first instance but much less later on. Importantly, the involvement of Vietnamese forces in eastern Cambodia and the government's failed attempts to stop them subsequently dragged Cambodia into the Vietnam War. Sihanouk's royalist forces then continued the resistance against Cambodian forces with the assistance of China and Vietnam.

The 1975 situation which allowed the Khmer Rouge to come into power is viewed as another conjuncture that led in turn to anti-Vietnamese and Chinese policies. The Cham ethnic minority also suffered a similar fate. Over and above these developments, the genocidal policies of the government then led to the mass starvation and death of a large number of Cambodians. The anti-Vietnamese policies became more aggressive over time and eventually resulted in open military clashes at the Vietnam-Cambodia border. These developments then led to the Vietnamese military intervention in 1978/79. The invasion and intervention in Cambodia is regarded as a conjuncture for its failure to deal a military defeat to the Khmer Rouge that then resulted in a prolonged internal military conflict. The second major aspect of the intervention is the failure of Vietnam to gain international recognition for the government that it had helped install in Cambodia. This second development had major ramifications in that international diplomatic recognition and assistance was not forthcoming on account of this condition.

The 1992/93 election brought to an end a state of civil war that previously existed in the country. This development was made possible on the basis of a number of antecedent conditions. The first of these was the intervention of the five permanent members of the United Nations Security Council and the second was the agreement by the disputing Cambodian parties to set up a Supreme National Council (SNC) to represent the country in international fora. There was also agreement to allow the constituted government to remain in power until the election and for all parties to be disarmed and go into cantonment before the election. And finally, it was agreed that Norodom Sihanouk would head the SNC. Although the Khmer Rouge refused to disarm and had to be defeated over time, all the other major factions — the Cambodian People's Party (CPP), Khmer People's National Liberation Front (KPNLF) and Front de Union Nationale Pour un Cambodge Independent, Pacifique, Neutrale et Co-operatif (FUNCINPEC) — agreed to a joint prime ministership scheme, to abide by the terms of the settlement and to ensure at least a transitional period of national reconciliation. Both the elections and the structural arrangements that followed marked a clear break from the previous reality on the ground.

The resulting changes from the conjuncture, although it would take some time to fully crystallize, were the introduction of a new constitution and a parliamentary-styled government with the necessary administrative structures to support it. The introduction of political parties and periodic elections to entrench democracy were also part of the more evolutionary changes. The demobilization and amnesty offered to a large number of guerrilla fighters as well as refugees to return the country to a modicum of normalcy and allow for the establishment of normal political life and activities constituted measures ensuring the longevity of the changes. Amer reiterates in his concluding comments how previous developments that he regards the equivalent of conjunctures have had a cascading effect on subsequent developments and produced path-dependent trajectories of their own. In this regard it might well be worth asking whether the 1970 overthrow of Norodom Sihanouk was a conjuncture that played itself out over a lengthy period of time. The answer would have been easier were it not for the fact that at critical turning points in the country's political evolution, external powers were involved as well. These included China, Vietnam and the United States. Nonetheless, Amer concludes his chapter by flagging the pivotal agency role of Norodom Sihanouk in all of the conjunctures and the choices that obtained from them.

Ehito Kimura argues that the collapse of Soeharto's New Order government in Indonesia in 1998 also clearly constituted a historical conjuncture. The most important structural change that the collapse brought about was the end of military authoritarian rule and the close compact achieved between the military and the ruling political party Golongan Karya (GOLKAR). Soeharto's cultivation of an Islamic constituency in the 1990s under his *keterbukaan* (openness) policy was also meant to perpetuate his power rather than liberalize the political environment. Similarly, it may be argued that Soeharto allowed for elections every five years but it ought to be remembered that the rules of contestation typically meant that there were no challengers to his position and that he had the leeway to pick the deputy president. Kimura argues that it was the increasingly authoritarian tendencies of the Soeharto government that paved the way for the conjuncture to occur, although the template had already been set with the widespread and relatively organized resistance to his rule in the 1990s. Importantly, however, the trigger that overthrew the regime came in the form of the Asian financial crisis and the swift and debilitating manner in which it undercut the developmental legitimacy and legacy of the incumbent government. Whereas an opportunity existed for the Soeharto government to extricate itself from the situation through substantive reforms, Kimura argues that the reactive behaviour of Soeharto who simply sought superficial changes while retaining his loyalists and cronies set the stage in turn for the regime's eventual collapse.

The collapse of the New Order government effectively changed many of the previous practices of the predecessor regime so as to constitute a clear break from the past. The most visible of these changes was the institutionalization of democratic elections and the entrenchment of political parties. Kimura's argument is that reformative and incremental policy changes provided the background to path-dependent developments that entrenched democratic practices. Reforms involving political parties and representation to accommodate the major cleavages in Indonesian politics and society are viewed as key developments that have had a lasting legacy. Administrative and fiscal decentralization formed the second important pillar of the reforms that in turn accommodated the various pulls that tended in the direction of separatism and violence. The important outcome of this second set of reforms was regional pacification and development that strengthened the country territorially. The wide dispersal of power that derived from both these reforms has had a stabilizing effect on politics as well as territoriality and has instilled a secular tendency on political developments.

Notwithstanding these major political changes that derive from the 1998 conjuncture in the country, Kimura also points to a number of continuities in the Indonesian political system. One such continuity is the retention of the army's territorial command structure and function that has allowed the military to retain a measure of power, independence and autonomy. Another important continuity is the number of Soeharto-era politicians who have remained in power and led the new political parties that have evolved. Additionally, the fragmentation of power and authority has allowed for the emergence of local strongmen who have been able to negotiate their situation through linkages with national elites.

In the case of Thailand, the September 2006 military coup against the elected Thaksin Shinawatra government clearly reversed the democratic gains and consolidation that the country had seen since the failed coup of 2001 led by Suchinda Krapayoon. What is surprising in the Thai case is that the military coup that ousted the Thaksin government was broadly welcomed in the urban areas and was viewed as a good coup that had ousted a rogue prime minister. Federico Ferrara argues that the importance of the coup lies in the fact that Thaksin, during his tenure, had transformed the Thai political system by aggregating an unstructured party system into a predominant one that was unassailable. The power that derived from such predominance allowed Thaksin to undertake policies that would previously have been impossible. The opportunities that availed themselves to such accumulation of power obtained in turn from the developments that were triggered in the aftermath of the Asian financial crisis of 1997. It was these antecedent conditions that in turn allowed for the political evolution of Thaksin and his Thai Rak Thai party.

The background against which Thaksin rose was strewn with military coups and self-serving politicians and governments. Political parties were merely vehicles for elite capture and retention of power and resources. They were heavily influenced and determined by personalities and factions that thrived to secure spoils. These developments led to an essentially unstable political party system that was highly prone to restructuring. The new Constitution that was drafted in 1997 was significantly more democratic than previous ones, with its emphasis on elections and an enlarged parliament with 500 seats. However, in the middle of this important structural transformation of the polity, the Asian financial crisis significantly reduced the financial and political standing of the existing elite. And it was at this time that Thaksin with his massive resource base entered the fray to build his predominant political party. He attracted attention with his nationalist rhetoric and promise of populist policies that would deliver the rural poor from their misery. In the process he won the support of rural community organizations that subsequently undergirded his political appeal and power.

The success of his party in the 2001 election was truly spectacular and that in 2005 even more so. After the first victory, Thaksin crafted a party that was organizationally and administratively tight unlike any other in the country. And the rhetoric and populist policies that included debt moratoriums, cash grants and a highly subsidized health care system meant that for the first time, provincial politics became nationalized and Thaksin was able to effectively mobilize the provinces like no previous political party. Ferrara also argues that the situation was such that the positive feedback associated with Thaksin's initial advantage triggered path-dependent equilibria that worked and benefitted him disproportionately. And as the party and the platform grew larger, Thaksin was able to capitalize on these disproportionate returns with the power and followers that it attracted. These advantages in turn enabled Thaksin to tweak structural political features and practices to his decisive gain. Critical to his sustenance though was the creation of a predominant political party rather than the minimalist coalitions that previous premiers had sought to cobble together. Nonetheless, there was less enthusiasm regarding some of his policies, like the extra-judicial killing of alleged drug traffickers and his hard-line security policies that inflamed passions and stoked violence in the predominantly Muslim southern states.

In the case of Malaysia, the 2008 national election marked a historical turning point in the country's political evolution.[21] The outcome was the loss of the ruling government's two-third majority in parliament as well as the loss of five state governments. These losses, together with the loss of half of all votes cast, constituted the most significant loss of seats and power for the incumbent coalition government that has ruled the country since political independence in 1957. The loss of its two-thirds majority in turn deprived the government of its ability to alter the Constitution at will to safeguard its rule and interest. The results indicated a cultural change in political life as well, since the opposition secured victory in seven out of nine by-elections that were called after the national election. Johan Saravanamuttu argues that the current situation is akin to a two-party or two-coalition system and a major departure from the predominant coalition system that existed previously. Additionally, he argues that the dominant mode of voting along ethnic lines has since been replaced by inter-ethnic voting patterns, suggesting a serious shift in the country's political culture. In fact the situation has now come to the point where the ruling government openly contemplates not fielding candidates in by-elections as a face-saving gesture. In this regard the legacy appears to include sociological change as well.

Another feature of the structural change is the evolution of a political party and social movement that is dedicated to challenging the community's representation at the elite level within the coalition government.[22] A final feature of the legacy is the crystallization of a trend that was begun some time ago in Malaysian politics. The opposition united itself under a broad-based coalition to challenge the incumbent government at the polls. Such a strategy has been a feature of opposition politics since Anwar Ibrahim led the opposition as part of a grand strategy to wrest power from the incumbent government and is perhaps best viewed as the crystallization of an ongoing recalibration of the system at the larger level.

The cross-ethnic voting pattern is described as part of a new political process that is unfolding and the subsequent by-election victories are viewed as a pattern of increasing returns from earlier voting patterns. The new trend is said to reflect a movement in the direction of more participatory and universalist politics that also constitutes a rejection of the government's ethnic model of political and policy calibration. The antecedent condition that triggered this new politics is said to be the *Reformasi* social movement that emerged after the detention of Anwar Ibrahim in 1998 and the agents of change are described as entirely domestically generated.

These then are the summary findings of the authors of the case studies selected for this volume. Naturally, the cases themselves lead on to larger theoretical and methodological considerations. These observations are noted in the conclusion that then brings the entire discussion full circle and to an appropriate close.

Notes

1. Paul Pierson, *Politics in Time: History, Institutions and Social Analysis* (Princeton: Princeton University Press, 2004), p. 12.
2. See Giovanni Capoccia and R. Daniel Kelemen, "The Study of Critical Junctures: Theory, Narrative and Counterfactuals in Historical Institutionalism", *World Politics* 59 (April 2007): 341. It should be noted here that the authors of this article prefer the term "critical junctures" as opposed to conjunctures. Whereas the descriptions of both situations have similar connotative value, juncture appears to suggest a shorter time frame and moment than conjunctures.
3. See for example "Framework: Critical Junctures and Historical Legacies", in *Shaping the Political Arena*, edited by Collier and Collier (Princeton, NJ: Princeton University Press, 1991), pp. 27–39.
4. Capoccia and Kelemen, p. 343.
5. See Paul Pierson, "Increasing Returns, Path Dependence, and the Study of Politics", *American Political Science Review* 94, no. 2 (June 2000): 263.
6. See James Mahoney, "Path Dependence in Historical Sociology", *Theory and Society* 29 (2000): 507–48.
7. Capoccia and Kelemen, p. 354.
8. Mahoney, p. 509.
9. Ibid., pp. 526–27.
10. Ibid., p. 349.
11. Pierson, *Politics in Time*, p. 11.
12. Ibid.
13. Capoccia and Kelemen, p. 352.
14. Jusuf Habibie commented that Prabowo Subianto, Soeharto's son-in-law and Kopassus (Special Forces) commander, attempted to usurp power and confronted him outside the presidential palace shortly after Soeharto's resignation. Presumably he was trying to emulate Soeharto who came into power on the basis of an executive order that transferred power from Sukarno to him in March 1966 called *Supersemar*. It was the acronym for *Surat Pemerintah Sepuluh Maret* (Executive Order of 10th March). The character *Semar* is the equivalent of the court jester in Indonesian *wayang kulit* (shadow play) and regarded as the most powerful adviser to the prince.
15. See Thomas S. Kuhn, *The Structure of Scientific Revolutions*, 2nd ed. (Chicago: University of Chicago Press, 1970).

16. Joel S. Migdal, *State in Society: Studying How States and Societies Transform and Constitute One Another* (Cambridge: Cambridge University Press, 2001).
17. The Defence Minister, Juan Ponce Enrile, was one of the first to defect from the regime. Other dissidents included elements from Reform the Armed Forces Movement (RAM) led by Colonel "Gringo" Honasan.
18. There were a total of nine coup attempts against the Aquino government led by RAM and the one in December 1989 almost succeeded. American fighter aircraft had to take to the skies to prevent rebel aircraft from attacking Malacanang Palace then.
19. The twenty groups that had officially negotiated peace settlements with the government by 2004 include the Kachin Independence Organization (KIO), New Democratic Army (Kachin), Palaung State Liberation Organization, Myanmar National Democracy Alliance (Kokang), Kachin Defense Army, Myanmar National Solidarity Party (Wa), National Democracy Alliance Army — Military Local Administration Committee (Shan/Akhar), Shan State Army, Pa-O National Organization, Shan State Nationalities People's Organization, Mong Tai Army (MTA), Kayan National Guard, Kayinni National Progressive Party, Kayan New Land Party, Kayinni National People's Liberation Front and New Mon State Party. The KNU that concluded a first round of peace talks delayed the ratification of the agreement following the detention of General Khin Nyunt in 2004 and the demise of Saw Bo Mya in 2006. The ceasefire eventually came into effect in 2012.
20. See Tin Maung Maung Than, "Myanmar's Relations with China: From Dependence to Interdependence?" in *East Asia Facing a Rising China*, edited by Lam Peng Er, N. Ganesan and Colin Duerkop (Seoul: KAS, 2010).
21. See for example Johan Saravanamuttu, "Malaysia: Political Transformation and Intrigue in an Election Year", *Southeast Asian Affairs 2009* (Singapore: Institute of Southeast Asian Studies, 2009), pp. 173–92.
22. This challenge was the clearest within the Indian community that sought representation outside the Barisan-sanctioned Malaysian Indian Congress. The social movements that arose out of unhappiness with the government were the Hindu Rights Action Force (HINDRAF) that metamorphosed into the Malaysian Indian Democratic Action Front (MINDRAF) and the Malaysian Maakal Sakti Party (Malaysian People Power Party) that began as a social movement in the state of Perak.

References

Capoccia, Giovanni and R. Daniel Kelemen. "The Study of Critical Junctures: Theory, Narrative and Counterfactuals in Historical Institutionalism". *World Politics* 59 (2007): 341.

Collier, Ruth Berins and David Collier, eds. "Framework: Critical Junctures and Historical Legacies". In *Shaping the Political Arena*. Princeton, NJ: Princeton University Press, 1991.

Kuhn, Thomas S. *The Structure of Scientific Revolutions*, 2nd ed. Chicago: University of Chicago Press, 1970.

Mahoney, James. "Path Dependence in Historical Sociology". *Theory and Society* 29 (2000): 507–48.

Migdal, Joel S. *State in Society: Studying How States and Societies Transform and Constitute One Another*. Cambridge: Cambridge University Press, 2001.

Pierson, Paul. *Politics in Time: History, Institutions and Social Analysis*. Princeton, NJ: Princeton University Press, 2004.

Sarvanamuttu, Johan. "Malaysia: Political Transformation and Intrigue in an Election Year". *Southeast Asian Affairs 2009*. Singapore: Institute of Southeast Asian Studies, 2009.

Tin Maung Maung Than. "Myanmar's Relations with China: From Dependence to Interdependence?" In *East Asia Facing a Rising China*, edited by Lam Peng Er, N. Ganesan and Colin Duerkop. Seoul: KAS, 2010.

2

(RE)ASSESSING THE EDSA "PEOPLE POWER" (1986) AS A CRITICAL CONJUNCTURE

Rommel Curaming and Lisandro Claudio

Having paved the way for restoring democracy after over a decade of Marcos' authoritarianism, popular views take EDSA People Power as a critical turning point in Philippine political history. This chapter seeks to take another look at this idea by evaluating the socio-political and discursive contexts within which it developed. Exploring two pathways, it shows, firstly, that the extent to which the EDSA revolt may be considered as a critical conjuncture depends significantly on the assessment of, and meanings attached to, the Marcos years. In other words, that this event looms large as a critical turning point notwithstanding the "return to good old days" in Philippine politics that it ushered in, is a reflection of two parallel and mutually reinforcing developments: (1) the hegemony of global discourse on democratization and (2) the strong anti-Marcos sentiments in the post-EDSA years that segments of the elite, civil society and international players promoted for their interests, both altruistic and self-serving. Secondly, this chapter argues that EDSA cannot be assessed simply in terms of its immediate effects on formal economic and political structures. One has to look at the democratization process "from below", which necessarily takes time, and away from formal democratic institutions, to see the spaces it opened and the political energies it strengthened. A set of broader analytic lenses — ones that consider discursive resonances, that de-centre analysis from central state institutions, and that consider long-term changes in political culture — must be deployed in order to uncover the changes set in train by this event.

The EDSA "People Power" revolt of 1986 stands out in political iconography and ideography of democratization, both within and beyond the Philippines. Hailed as a paragon of peaceful political change, it is touted as having inspired through "demonstration effect" the struggles for democracy elsewhere in the region and beyond.[1] The outpouring of sympathy for the death of Corazon Aquino in 2009, the victory of her son, Noynoy, in the May 2010 presidential elections, and the continuing effusive paean harped on her and Ninoy juxtaposed against the mounting contempt for Gloria Arroyo, Joseph Estrada and the Marcoses, all seem to indicate the still pre-eminent status of EDSA as a galvanizing political metaphor in the public imagination.[2] While efforts by segments of the elite to enflame the "spirit" of the "yellow revolution"[3] appear contrived to some observers, the possibility cannot be discounted that a significant section of Philippine society, and of course for various and possibly competing reasons, still holds EDSA as a pivotal historical moment to which it looks back with a mixture of pride, triumph, ambivalence and both wistful and wishful rumination.

That EDSA People Power of 1986 was a defining moment in recent Philippine political history cannot be doubted. Its watershed character, however, may not be assumed to be straightforward or unproblematic. The reason is simple: an event as critical as EDSA did not happen, and its meanings may not be grasped, in a social vacuum. The emphasis thus given by this chapter on the discursive in addition to the realpolitik contexts emanates from three considerations: first, the persistent and highly contentious character of the political arena within which EDSA took place and from which an analyst can only pretend to be above or apart; second, the nation state, which is often collapsed to what is happening in the capital or to what the elites in Congress and Malacanang (the district where the presidential palace is located) are doing, is simply too convenient and simplified a level of analysis to capture the complex, multidimensional reality that was EDSA; finally, and more importantly, the political behaviour of contemporary Filipinos appears to be influenced more by the "discursive EDSA" than the "real" one, assuming that such a clear-cut distinction is tenable. Given these considerations, the following set of questions should also be raised, in addition to those that call for ascertaining the "true nature" of EDSA as a conjuncture: in what particular sense, for whom, to whom and for what is it considered a watershed? And to what extent may it be so?

As a conjuncture, EDSA may not stand alone as an analytic unit. Given the sizeable literature emphasizing the "restorationist" (the return of the "good old days") character[4] of EDSA vis-à-vis the "traditional" in Philippine politics, EDSA might make sense only primarily in reference to Marcos' declaration of martial law on 21 September 1972, which marked the shift to dictatorial martial rule. They constitute the two sides of the same historical coin when considering critical conjunctures in the post–World War II political history of the Philippines. The two-peas-in-a-pod character of these events emanated from at least two mutually reinforcing sources. The first is the historic condition that saw EDSA People Power largely as a logical response to the authoritarianism that accompanied martial law. The second is the historically contingent relationships that gave rise to the still contestable but nevertheless hardening political iconography that pits one as a moral (not just political) antinomy of the other. In other words, without the declaration of martial law that ushered in Marcos' dictatorial rule, and without the continuing demonization of this era as a nightmarish detour from the otherwise unmolested march to a purer form of democracy, not only was it unlikely that the EDSA revolt would have taken place, it would have also assumed, if it did take place, a metaphorical significance different from what EDSA holds today. The extent to which the EDSA revolt may be considered as a critical juncture, thus, depends significantly on the assessment of, and meanings attached to, the Marcos years. Conversely, the ways in which images of the Marcos era evolve will be greatly influenced by the changes in how the public views EDSA. Be that as it may, this chapter also seeks to explore the possibility that by itself, without reference to the Marcos years, EDSA may be appreciated for opening up genuinely new pathways in the development of Philippine politics.

EDSA PEOPLE POWER

The events leading to the EDSA People Power are well documented. The key actors in this narrative include Defence Minister Juan Ponce Enrile, military Vice Chief of Staff Fidel Ramos, and members of the Reform the Armed Forces Movement (RAM), who attempted to stage a military coup against the Marcos government. When this plan fizzled, the rebels retreated to two military camps along EDSA to defend themselves against Marcos' counter-attack. In a desperate move, the rebels called on the people to surround the two camps in order to protect them. Manila Archbishop Jaime Cardinal Sin, who called on the people to support the rebels, heeded this call. The people — many of whom were supporters of Corazon Aquino's campaign for the presidency — arrived in droves, decidedly altering the power equation in favour of the rebels. The U.S. withdrawal of its support for Marcos reinforced the chain of events that culminated in the overthrow of the regime.[5]

The EDSA revolution, however, cannot simply be read as a spontaneous outburst of emotion over the course of four days. It is common in Philippine media and popular discourse to trace the beginnings of EDSA to the assassination of Marcos' political arch-rival, former Senator, Ninoy Aquino in 1983. The Senator's assassination mobilized the once dormant "middle forces" (the moderate and religious middle class of the Philippines) and set off a string of protests that developed into an organized challenge against the regime in the form of the Aquino campaign. On 16 September 1983, barely a month after the slaying, the "well-heeled" office workers of Makati — Manila's main financial district — held a rally for the late Senator. *Mr. and Ms.*, a weekly news magazine critical of the Marcos administration described the event as such:

> Makati never had a protest rally and when it did Sept. 16 Friday afternoon, it was the biggest ever complete with ticker tape raining down on Ayala and Paseo de Roxas avenues, [sic] Yellow confetti was ingeniously [sic][6] made out of telephone directory books and cast down by the hundreds by employees from any one of the high rise buildings along the rally route. Such style.[7]

On 30 September, the fortieth day after Aquino's death, at least two thousand mourners attended a mass at Forbes Park — the most prominent of Manila's elite gated communities.[8] Thus, while Aquino's death resonated with the masses, it is largely remembered for politicizing the elites and the middle class. This same section of society would constitute the supporters of the Aquino campaign, who eventually joined the Church and the rebel soldiers in overthrowing Marcos. The way Aquino dealt with these groups largely informed the policies of her administration.

The Aquino regime sought to de-"Marcosify" the political infrastructures and "restore democracy". The first to go was the 1973 Constitution and the Batasang Pambansa, the parliament. A constitutional commission was formed to draft a new constitution, which took effect in 1987. In the interim, she operated on the so-called Freedom Constitution, which granted her enormous power — power which she could have used but did not, to the consternation of many, to institute truly substantive and lasting reforms. The judiciary was also reorganized and the courts were made more amenable to the present dispensation. Soon, a plebiscite to ratify the newly framed Constitution was held; so were elections for the new legislature. At the local level, a purge of local officials ensued and they were replaced by those not associated with the previous regime. In due time, local elections were held with all the usual fanfare characteristic of previous eras. The vibrant and colourful pre–martial law electoral politics — often equated with democracy — was restored.

It was also a restoration in a different sense of the word. The Marcoses had barely left Malacanang when the old oligarchs sidelined by Marcos returned in droves and in style. Symbolic of this revival was the regaining of control of electricity hegemon Meralco and media empire ABS-CBN by the Lopez family. In the 1987 elections, three-fourths of those who won seats in Congress were either members of, or connected to, families who were prominent during the pre-martial law years. The good-old-days mood in Philippine politics was palpable.[9] The atmosphere was captured well by Benjamin Muego, a known student leader-activist in the Philippines in the late 1960s, who left for the United States in 1970. He was astounded upon returning to Manila in 1987 after seventeen years of absence. Expecting to see changes that the "EDSA Revolution" and martial law years were supposed to have brought forth, he was astonished at what he found:

> ...it was an uncanny feeling returning to an old familiar place seventeen years later, only to see the same things, listen to the same platitudes and shibboleths, see the same old political personalities in the evening news saying the same thing they were saying seventeen years earlier. The only difference was that while many of them used to unabashedly praise Marcos, now they are damning him to the heavens.[10]

POST-AUTHORITARIAN PHILIPPINES: A RESTORED OLD ORDER?

In order to assess EDSA's conjunctural role, it is necessary to examine not only the visible changes in political infrastructures, policies and practices, but also whether or not these changes altered the dynamics of political interaction and negotiation between the state and the civil society at large. In what follows, we discuss two areas that commentators often use as bases for assessing the Aquino administration: the economy and human rights. The economy is an important issue because one must determine whether regime change brought by EDSA altered the elite-driven economy of the country and created lasting change. As for human rights, the martial law period, as mentioned earlier, significantly increased the role and the power of the Philippine military, which used these new powers to commit various atrocities. If EDSA allowed for greater protection of human rights and if it paved the way for people to better access economic resources, then one is justified in claiming it constitutes a break from the recent past of martial law.

Those critical of Aquino's economic policy posit that the Aquino regime merely restored an elite order that deepened inequality in the country. Coronel, for instance, argues that neoliberal economic policies during the Aquino presidency served to cater to the demands of the elite and middle class:

> During the first three years of the Aquino presidency, a brisk economic growth rate, averaging 5.8 per cent, only reinforced the disparities. Posh condominiums and shopping centres reshaped the Manila skyline during those early years. Even as rural incomes declined in real terms and the cities swelled with migrants from the countryside, the Philippines experienced a boom in imported luxury cars for the rich and appliances for the middle class. By 1990, the economic slide had begun. For 1991, the growth rate is officially estimated at only 2.5–3 per cent.[11]

Similar to the pre-martial law set-up, this economic order was sustained by oligarchs who used their power through the control of the Congress and other state apparatuses to achieve their economic goals. This is best illustrated by the recurring issue of land reform. According to Coronel, land reform legislation during the Aquino presidency was ineffective. It left important decisions like the "timetable for land redistribution and the limits of land retention" to be determined by the landlord-dominated Congress. It also exempted corporations that gave stocks to its farmers. The legislative eventually passed a bill that effectively exempted 70 per cent of the country's agricultural land from redistribution. Many oligarchs were able to hang on to their land. For example, Hacienda Luisita, the 7,000-hectare sugar cane plantation owned by President Aquino's family, remained largely intact after Aquino's land reform efforts.[12] It was not surprising for the Congress to act this way given its elite composition alluded to earlier.

At the level of human rights, it initially seemed like Aquino would push for genuine change to the system. In her first week in office, she freed all Marcos-era political prisoners, including top cadres of the Communist Party of the Philippines (CPP). She also appointed Jose W. Diokno, a former Senator and a prominent human rights crusader, to a commission to investigate military abuses.[13] However, increasing threats from the military, which culminated in many coup attempts against the government, forced Aquino to pander to the military as well, making her more lenient towards human rights abuses. Members of the RAM, mostly from the notorious batch 1971 of the Philippine Military Academy, launched nine abortive coups against her administration. As resistance from the military grew, Aquino became more willing to cooperate with it.[14] After coup attempts in November 1986 and August 1987, for instance, Aquino dismissed several Cabinet members whom the military deemed "leftist".[15]

Aquino's conciliatory approach to the military reinforced the sense of impunity that was fostered during martial law, which allowed for human rights abuses to continue unabated. Amidst coup plots against her regime, it became increasingly difficult for Aquino to discipline the military. For example, according to a *Manila Times* report in May 1986, the Kilusan ng Magbubukid sa Pilipinas (Movement of Farmers in the Philippines) claimed that military operations in the area of one of their regional chapters resulted in nineteen massacres and 500 executions.[16] Similarly, in January 1987, government soldiers fired on farmers demanding land reform in front of the presidential palace. Eighteen died.[17]

Aquino also continued the Marcos policy of using vigilantes in counter-insurgency efforts. She formed Civilian Volunteer Self-Defense Organizations or "vigilantes" as a form of "people power" to defeat the communist rebels. These efforts were encouraged by the U.S. government, which, under Reagan, promoted a "low intensity" strategy to counter-insurgency. Towards the end of 1987 there were over 200 vigilante groups, with an average group size of 150 members. Amnesty International reported in 1988 that there was strong evidence of these groups committing human rights violations with acquiescence from the military. The report added that the vigilantes were the most serious human rights problem in the country. After the Philippine Committee on Human Rights (PCHR) recommended that the government abolish the vigilante groups, Aquino abolished the body. Its members believed that the decision to abolish the committee was triggered by this recommendation.[18] Because the military considered the vigilantes an integral part of their counter-insurgency programme, it was difficult for Aquino to shut down these groups.

These cases indicate fairly clearly the continuities, rather than breaks, of the Aquino regime from previous eras, both martial law and pre–martial law years. As an analytic trope, continuity in fact has a long tradition in the examination of Philippine politics.[19] Observers have noted that the Philippines is remarkable for historical continuity such that the title of a book, *Philippines: A Changeless Land*, may not be entirely hyperbolic.[20] Timberman, the author of this book, wonders: "How could a nation that had gone through so many changes actually [have] changed so little?" As he notes:

> There is sad constancy to the poverty, inequity, and injustice that characterize Philippine society, particularly in the countryside. There is a long history of society and politics and economic affairs being dominated by relatively small and surprisingly durable groups of conservative families. Consequently, there is also a history of successive governments — both democratic and authoritarian — being unwilling or unable to enact much needed socio-economic reform such as land reform. There is timelessness to the highly personalistic nature of politics as well as to the rituals and rhetoric of political discourse. There is a predictable repetitiveness to the charges of election fraud, corruption, nepotism and incompetence.[21]

This seems to have been partly broken during the martial law years as books published during this period tended to bewail the unfortunate break that martial law brought to the otherwise unmolested evolution of Philippine democracy to its "purer" form. Beth Day's book, *The Philippines: Shattered Showcase of Democracy in Asia*,[22] which was published in 1974, eloquently represents this pervasive sentiment from the time.[23]

The immediate post-EDSA period has seen a return to prominence of the theme of continuity, apparently in a much forceful or vigorous form.[24] Owing perhaps to the frustrations over the failure of the Aquino administration to carry out adequate reforms, and sharpened by high expectations tied to the euphoria over EDSA, scholars poured out their disappointments by underscoring the theme of the return to the good old days in Philippine politics. Anderson's article "Cacique Democracy and the Philippines" which appeared in 1988 is exemplary in this regard. Seeing that old oligarchs and familiar political practices that characterized the pre-Marcos and Marcos years were back with a vengeance right after EDSA, he opines that what Marcos did from 1972 to 1986 was merely to push the logic of elite democracy that pervades the Philippine political landscape before and after EDSA.[25]

Francisco Nemenzo's article "From Autocracy to Elite Democracy" is also notable. Writing in 1987, he introduced the article by describing the scene at Corazon Aquino's oath taking on 25 February 1986. He noted that rather than doing it in an open public place where millions of the common people could share the joy of the moment, the oath took place at the exclusive Club Filipino and the guests were a select group of politicians, business tycoons, landlords and their "perfumed ladies". It clearly bespoke, as Nemenzo evocatively put it with a tinge of bitterness, of the "social complexion of the new government".[26]

Given the preponderance of views held by keen observers on the restorationist and/or continuous character of post-EDSA politics, one might wonder why EDSA People Power continues to hold such a strong grip on many observers' imaginations as a critical turning point. The reasons for this are certainly complex and this subject thus entails a separate, thorough treatment. To note briefly, however, part of the reason lies in the vibrant democratization discourse on the global scale, nurtured by the post–Cold War and post-9/11 atmosphere. This atmosphere has bestowed on EDSA the iconic status it holds as an exemplar of peaceful change ushered in through the power of the people. The imagery conjured up by more than a million people rising peacefully to challenge a dictator is a very powerful driving metaphor in the age of global democratization.

Another reason stems from the existing power structure in the Philippines. Notwithstanding the sharper or more virulent rivalries among the oligarchs, as noted above, they are held together by the dogged determination not to be sidelined or dominated again by one man or one group. Martial law was simply a traumatic event for the elites. Their experience of it has made them assert a stance of "never again!" to authoritarian rule. To maintain vigilance, and to rally the common people behind them, a large part of the dominant elites appropriate EDSA and its memories as a foil to counter any attempt to strengthen the state or the presidency, which for reasons right or wrong easily brings the vision of the nightmare that the Marcos years was supposed to be. The recurrent showing of documentaries about the martial law years; the building of monuments such as the EDSA shrine and Bantayog ng mga Bayani (Monument of Heroes);[27] the constant deployment of anti-Marcos rhetoric, signs and symbols in the media and other ideological apparatuses; the erasure of nuances in the writing of the history of the Marcos years, reducing it to one long night of terror and plunder, and erasing whatever policies and projects that worked well and that benefitted the people during that period; the often exaggerated reaction to efforts by the president to strengthen institutions; all these should be understood as part of the "never again!" template. Thus, it may be said that EDSA easily appears as a turning point because it was in fact the case for the life and wellbeing of the elite (and the elite-wannabes), who also happen to have access to the mechanisms that shape political and historical discourses.

In addition, highlighting EDSA as a watershed serves as a smokescreen that hides the fact that the Filipino oligarchy, which includes the Marcoses and their cronies, has, as far as one can remember, regardless of the regime and periods in history, consistently exploited the weaknesses of political institutions to serve its interests at the expense of the majority of the people. By underscoring EDSA, on the one hand, and Marcos' "evilness", on the other, the rest of the oligarchy wish to elude accountability for the continued impoverishment of the nation.[28] By accentuating the evilness of Marcos, they effectively distance themselves from one of their own and thus save the Philippine oligarchy as a collective from the responsibility for the sorry state of the nation. The impression prevails, thus, that the fault lies with Marcos and his gang alone, and not in the deeply entrenched system that he well represented.

The meaning of EDSA, however, cannot be reduced to the expectations of the dominant ideology thesis. Like many other modern societies, the Philippines is so complex that among the eighty million who may be categorized as "common people" one can easily expect that different meanings of EDSA are held for various and perhaps competing reasons. It cannot be safely assumed, as some observers do,[29] that the lack of improvement in their lives precludes a meaningful appropriation of EDSA by at least segments of the "common people". Perhaps it makes sense to hypothesize that it is precisely this lack of improvement in their lives that allows for them to read EDSA as symbolic of their unfulfilled hopes. While the dominant elites find it convenient to utilize EDSA for their purposes, its potentially subversive meanings simmer beneath the surface of Philippine politics. Importantly, because such potential is suppressed by dominant discourses, they can be triggered at certain critical moments. Evidence of this is the EDSA III revolution that almost toppled the Arroyo administration in 2001.[30]

In other words, the effects of EDSA cannot simply be determined by looking at highly visible changes immediately after EDSA — both constituting breaks and continuities from the previous periods as noted above. Thompson argues that the compromises Aquino made to the elite and the military were necessary because the weak post-authoritarian state needed support from influential and powerful forces. He argues that while Aquino's policies "adversely affected the quality of the democracy being restored in the Philippines" in the short-run, "it gave her the breathing space needed to seek democratic consolidation" in the future — one that would manifest in the freer elections that began in the Aquino period.[31] The new state Aquino was trying to build would have collapsed had she not compromised with elements of the military at a time when her government was being threatened by various coup attempts.[32]

As such, the effects of the restoration of democracy in EDSA must be examined based on its more long-term impacts. Although we do not necessarily agree that all these impacts of EDSA point to a deepening of democracy, we suggest that EDSA nonetheless fostered a number of lasting changes that allow us to consider it a historical juncture.

NUANCING BREAKS AND CONTINUITIES

Notwithstanding the preponderance of views pointing to continuity as shown above, a different picture might emerge if one adjusts analytic lenses. For observers like Coronel, Muego, Nemenzo and Anderson who may have nurtured high hopes for visible and substantive, if not truly fundamental, changes at the national level, the failure of the Aquino regime to deliver in these areas highlights its similarity with the previous regimes. If seen from the local viewpoint, as what Kerkvliet's and Mojares's edited volume does,[33] alternative imaginings become possible.

Michael Pinches, who happened to be undertaking fieldwork in the urban poor community of Tatalon in Manila in early 1986, argues that while EDSA "was mainly bourgeois in practice and conception ... many of the working class and poor in places like Tatalon were significant participants and were attracted by the movement's populist character".[34] Prior to 1986, he notes, there was a marked silence instilled through intimidation in areas like Tatalon, with residents claiming, "We are just silent, there is nothing we can do."[35] During the snap elections, however, the new opposition provided leadership and safety for the residents of Tatalon who had grievances against the government.[36] They were also attracted to the figure of Corazon Aquino who represented "both suffering and collective strength".[37]

What we may glimpse from this was the shift in the perception of the people[38] about themselves away from being politically inconsequential or powerless towards the rediscovery of their ability to make a difference, something that is encapsulated in and reinforced by the very notion of People Power. During martial law and the pre–martial law years, people's action or people empowerment was often the preserve of leftist/left-leaning organizations and state-sponsored associations. One thing, among many others, that EDSA did, was to trigger among at least segments of the "common people" the awareness of their power as political agents, of what they can do and achieve as a collective. According to Kerkvliet and Mojares, because it "demonstrated that the social and moral resources" needed for reform are present and because it "enlarged the moral and symbolic capital for the struggle to create a better society", EDSA has inspired Filipino "people for generations to come". The positive change after EDSA "no matter what turn history takes now, is not inconsequential".[39]

In other words, a larger segment than was initially assumed of the Filipinos may have been politicized, directly or indirectly, by the experience that accompanied the increasingly broad-based struggle to depose Marcos. The highly populist politics that characterizes the post-EDSA period, as evident for instance in EDSA III, as well as in the election of popular media and showbiz personalities (of which Erap Estrada was an exemplar), may be an extension of this process of politicization of the masses (lower and middle classes), accompanied by the "massification" of politics, in the course of the anti-Marcos struggle that climaxed in EDSA.

For feminist cultural critic Nefeti Tadiar, People Power was an eruption of revolutionary desires — desires that can be uncovered through "an interpretation of the subjective dynamics of the revolt of the people".[40] While acknowledging that the history of the revolt was eventually written by the economic/political elite, she contends that "the wayward movements of desiring-action coursing through this event continue to insist and might again exert such force (beyond People Power 2) so as to bring about more lasting fruitful socio-political changes".[41] It is in this light that she interprets the role and impact of Corazon Aquino as the most resonant oppositional figure to the repressive law represented by Ferdinand Marcos. Marcos, "the dictator-ally of the US, embodied the blockage of Philippine development and democracy, preventing the Philippines from being all that it could be".[42] In the 1980s, Tadiar further notes, the hypermasculine militarist president suffered from a severe kidney ailment. His declining health, therefore, represented the declining stability of the Philippine socio-political and economic order. Aquino's femininity, manifested in "her political inexperience and girlish demeanor", was the "embodiment of transgression"[43] in light of Marcos using his vast political experience to plunder the state and silence dissent. Similar to Ileto, thus, Tadiar argues that these impulses emanated from the "underside" of Philippine politics.

The reference to the "underside" of Philippine politics foregrounds the fictional oneness of the notion of democracy. This point is analytically significant in that the conjunctural character of EDSA cannot be assessed apart from by the yardstick of democratization. Contested democratic frames necessarily suggest a range of possibilities, including the opposite, that EDSA may not be a conjuncture after all.

To note, more radical scholars have argued that given the sharply iniquitous social structure that characterized the Philippines since the Spanish period, and maintained and even exacerbated during the American period, there never was in fact real democracy in the Philippines. According to this view, what martial law amounted to was, as the subtitle of a book clearly states, *The End of an Illusion* — a long-standing illusion that the Philippines was ever a democracy.[44] While it is undeniable that it is an ideologically driven perspective and one held by a minority, it nonetheless cannot be dismissed as analytically inconsequential. The reason is twofold: the persistent and gross social inequality in the Philippines is a historical fact; and it challenges us to rethink the fundamental basis of the widely held notion of EDSA as a historical conjuncture by driving home the question of what really constitutes a democracy.

Quimpo's clear-cut differentiation between the meaning of elite democracy and democracy from below is instructive. For the elites, so he claims, democracy mainly refers to the maintenance of formal political structures that ensures freedom to exercise electoral politics, something that they can easily influence or manipulate. For the common people, however, this refers to genuine and "greater participation in decision making", which they hope could translate into "social and economic equality".[45]

The notion of "democracy from below" puts in sharp relief the fact that a key event or set of events that happen may carry variable meanings to different sectors in a society. For the majority of Filipinos who have lived in varying levels of poverty, from the Spanish period to the present, the failure of different colonial and postcolonial regimes to provide them better lives sets the platform for rejecting both the Marcos years and EDSA People Power as historical conjunctures. As far as they are concerned these events may be non-events, as their lives hardly changed one generation to another.

Conversely, for the political and economic elites and other groups such as the leftists and Muslim separatists who were sidelined, emasculated, oppressed or terrorized by the Marcos regime, the highly negative impact of this period on them ensured that it would be regarded as a sharp break from the past, as one long, dark night of terror that should "never happen again".

The "massification" of politics mentioned earlier has been paralleled by the fragmentation of the oligarchy as more and more new entrants vie for better position in the scramble for the booty. The result appears to be the intensification of intra-elite rivalries as multiple centres of power, representing tenuous coalitions of families, have emerged. Intra-elite rivalries are certainly not new. It is an outstanding feature of Philippine political history since as early as the Revolution of 1896 and the Malolos Republic. What seems to be different in the post-EDSA period is the multiplicity of centres of power of more or less equal strength. Whereas Marcos and his cronies constituted an exemplary centre of power, practically unchallenged until the 1980s, the post-EDSA period saw no one particularly dominant group. It may have been a result of twin processes that saw Marcos systematically emasculating the traditional oligarchy, from which group could emanate someone who could have filled the vacuum left by him, on the one hand, and cultivating a new set of oligarchs, on the other. As Doherty claims, several families who were not members of the elite circle in the pre-martial law years made it to the list primarily due to favours from the Marcos regime.[46] Included in these new elites are Chinese businessmen, like Philippine Airlines owner Lucio Tan, who were cultivated by Marcos as political allies and who now hold significant influence in post-authoritarian Philippines.[47] The multi-cornered rivalry among the oligarchs is clearly seen in the several presidential candidates (five or more) since the 1992 election. The one just held in 2010 shaped up to be no different.

The fragmentation of the ruling oligarchy is also reflected in the increased fluidity or weakness of the party system in the post-EDSA period. Whereas party-switching, defections and personalistic leadership have always been a prominent feature of electoral politics in the Philippines, this situation intensified in the post-EDSA period where political parties come and go and are revived or become operative only in the lead-up to elections. According to Kasuya, the single-term presidency imposed by the 1987 Constitution may have a role to play in such weakness or instability.[48]

The Philippine state persists to be described as weak,[49] still unable to make its effective presence felt in all corners of its territory and to protect itself adequately from the predatory interests of the oligarchy and other interest groups. In the case of the Arroyo administration, however, we see a regime that Nathan Quimpo characterizes as strong, and he echoes the alarms fairly common in Philippine political discourse against allegedly creeping forms of authoritarianism. The "never again!" subtext is palpable in his article[50] and, while it echoes the concerns of the vocal segment of Philippine society, it is possible that among the silent majority there are not an insignificant number of people who really wish that the presidency, the regime or the state be made really strong to enable it to carry out programmes that will get the Philippines out of its economic doldrums.

Another possibly conjunctural legacy of the martial law–EDSA tandem is the intensification of the moralization of politics at the expense of more secular, critical and analytic explanations. This is not to say that before the Marcos period morality did not play an important role in defining political fault lines. It has always been there. What is quite new is the synergy between the gravity of the sins of one leader (in this case Marcos), on the one hand, and the dramatic manner by which events including the assassination of Ninoy Aquino unfolded leading to EDSA, on the other. This synergy may have made it so much easier to project Manichaean images of politics as a fight between good and evil. The important role played by the Catholic Church and other religious organizations in the struggle against Marcos, accompanied by the frequent mobilization and deployment of religious images and metaphors, ensured that politics unfurled as a morality play.

The moralization of politics that occurred after EDSA emboldened two groups that have since increasingly seen themselves as moral forces in Philippine politics: the Church and the military. The Catholic Church, largely apolitical before the revolt, found itself in the middle of a large political upheaval during EDSA. Shortly after it would argue that the revolution was divinely ordained. This perspective is aptly summarized by Bishop Soc Villegas, aide to Cardinal Sin in 1986:

> There was no way that social scientists, political scientists, could explain what really happened at EDSA. The only fitting conclusion was that it was an intervention by God. To think that military tanks manned by soldiers trained to kill stopped when people waved their rosaries and gave them flowers and gave them food.... The only way to explain it is the grace of God at work in human hearts.[51]

The Philippine Church's notion that God's will is discernible in certain political events, which was strengthened and for them validated by EDSA, encouraged or justified its greater involvement in national politics. EDSA II, for example, witnessed a return of the Church to the centre of national politics, with Cardinal Sin directly opposing a Vatican order not to intervene in the protests against Estrada.[52]

Similarly, elements of the military also became more politicized after EDSA. After the revolt, many of RAM's own members, for instance, felt that the focus of the organization needed to shift from reforms within the military to more political issues.[53] Moreover, the military realized that it could use populist rhetoric to justify its political interventions. The coup attempts against Aquino were largely justified on nationalist grounds, with RAM styling itself as a protector of the people.[54] Even more recent military attempts at destabilizing the Arroyo administration largely mirror the rhetoric developed by RAM post-EDSA. The discourse of the nationalist solider, notwithstanding the differences in their orientations, has also been used as a platform for coup plotters to launch successful political careers. RAM leader Gregorio Honasan and Antonio Trillanes — head of the Magdalo military faction that launched mutinies against Arroyo — have both become senators of the republic.

Beyond the Church and the military, however, other groups, particularly citizens groups, began to see themselves as moral forces after EDSA. This moralization is manifested in the discourse of popular empowerment that various grass-roots NGOs promote.[55] The end of authoritarianism through EDSA also spelled the end of the political poles of martial law, which, we argue, allowed for the surfacing of these new political actors.

During martial law, two versions of "democracy" from different ends of the political spectrum were being put forward. On the one hand was Marcos' democratic revolution from the centre, which saw the state taking on increased powers for the building of a "New Society" through martial rule.[56] On the other hand was the "National Democratic" (ND) revolution of the CPP and its founding chairman Jose Maria Sison/Amado Guerrero, which targeted American imperialism and local reactionaries.[57] The rise of leftists as significant players in national politics owes significantly to the condition brought about by Marcos' authoritarian rule. Marcos, as the communists themselves claim, proved to be their most effective recruiter. From a few dozen armed combatants in 1969, the New People's Army (NPA) grew to an estimated 24,000-strong combatants with mass-base support of a few million by the mid-1980s.[58] Not only did the Left, along with Muslim separatists in Mindanao, constitute powerful military resistance to the dictatorship, its mass organizations also became venues for large-scale political socialization. For example, the 1970s saw student activism peak in the Philippines. The grammar of this activism, which targeted the "U.S.-Marcos dictatorship" and various class inequities in Philippine society, was a product of various youth and student organizations being a part of the ND movement.[59] The Left also made a significant impact on Church, peasant, and labour movements. People Power would not have been possible without the political organization and socialization that occurred in previous years.[60]

Despite its vast contributions to the anti-Marcos struggle, the CPP was excluded from EDSA. In what many critics and Party members consider a major tactical blunder, the CPP and its mass organizations decided to boycott Aquino's campaign for the presidency, labelling the election as nothing more than a contest between a dictator and bourgeois reformists.[61] The boycott stance prevented Party members engaged in united front efforts from building an alliance with Aquino, even though the latter had attempted to woo the Left during the early phase of the campaign. During EDSA, the CPP attempted to play a role in the revolt, but the Aquino camp, which already enjoyed popular support, excluded it from the events.[62]

The CPP's exclusion from EDSA meant that it would also be excluded from the post-authoritarian government of Aquino. More broadly, the success of a peaceful urban insurrection cast doubt on the viability of the

CPP's underground armed struggle from the countryside. Since EDSA, the CPP and its National Democratic movement's strength and influence have declined sharply.[63] Moreover, because of the strategic and theoretical debates sparked by the Left's exclusion from EDSA, the Party split in 1992, resulting in a mass exodus of cadres, soldiers, and Political Officers from the CPP.[64] Thus, EDSA not only ended the Marcos regime but facilitated the decline of the organized Left.

In place of the old Left, various above-ground people's organizations, NGOs, and reformist political parties have emerged. For Quimpo, these new "Left" formations maintain the mass character of the CPP, but unlike it, have come "to appreciate the positive aspects of the country's democracy" despite its inadequacies.[65] Groups like the progressive party Akbayan have recognized "the intrinsic value of formal democratic institutions and procedures" — an approach that has allowed them to participate in the sphere of electoral politics, which had once been the exclusive territory of the elite.[66]

This reconfiguration of politics from below is largely a legacy of the EDSA revolution. Unlike the period of martial law, which pitted two "democratic revolutions" against each other, Philippine politics is now more plural with various groups from below influencing and contesting the formal political sphere. This would not have been possible if not for the democratic space opened up by the revolution. Moreover, we contend that "People Power" was a truly empowering moral discourse that allowed citizens and groups to see the ability of collective action to influence formal political structures.

CONCLUSION

To assess EDSA as a historical conjuncture, one must not treat it as simple change in the type of political regime or system. Not only is this inadequate, it may, at times, prove untenable since various similarities between the politics of immediate post-war, martial law–era, and post-EDSA Philippines reveal the tenacity of many political practices, ideas, structures and institutions. In this chapter, we have attempted to show that broader analytic lenses — ones that consider discursive resonances, that de-centre analysis from central state institutions, and that consider long-term changes in political culture — must be deployed in order to uncover the changes brought about by the revolution. Such an approach may be more speculative than an analysis of institutions, but we contend that the complexity of the event merits such multidimensionality. If, as we have argued, readings of EDSA are based on the way the "evils" of martial rule are interpreted as well as historical representations from the present, it is imperative to delve into the broad social matrices in which these interpretations are occurring.

The EDSA revolution not only ended authoritarian rule, which allowed for the beginning of a democratic transition — however slow and incomplete this transition might have been; it also altered the grammar of politics from below and above. The "moralization" of politics which we point to, for instance, cannot be grasped unless, first, the locus of analysis is shifted away from the state and focused instead on groups like the military, the Church, and people's organizations, and second, unless the discursive resonance of EDSA as a moral uprising is paid due consideration.

Therefore, while we think there is a need to recognize the restorationist critics' analysis of continuing social inequity in the Philippines, our approach has led us to conclude that EDSA cannot simply be assessed in terms of its immediate effects on formal economic and political structures. To reduce the revolution to this discounts the various resonances of the event to various groups. While it is difficult to argue that EDSA allowed for a fundamental alteration of the nature of Philippine politics, it is nonetheless important to see the spaces it opened and the political energies it strengthened. It is in this sense that EDSA can be considered a conjunctural event in Philippine political history.

Notes

1. Mark Thompson, *The Anti-Marcos Struggle: Personalistic Rule and Democratic Transition in the Philippines* (New Haven: Yale University Press, 1995), p. 1.
2. Recent headlines include the following: Frinston Lim, "Cheering Crowds Greet Noynoy, Mar in Tagum", INQUIRER.net, 26 September 2009 <http://newsinfo. inquirer.net/inquirerheadlines/nation/view/20090926-226946/Cheering-crowds-greet-Noynoy-Mar-in-Tagum>; Michael Lim Ubac, "Sentiment for Noynoy also up in Senate, says Kiko", INQUIRER.net, 26 September 2009 <http://newsinfo.inquirer.net/inquirerheadlines/nation/view/20090926-226955/Sentiment-for-Noynoy-also-up-in-Senate-says-Kiko>.
3. Documentary and film projects on Ninoy's life have proliferated recently. These include "The Last Journey of Ninoy" and "Ninoy Aquino & the Rise of People Power" by Tom Coffman. There is also a plan for a biographical film that, according to Kris Aquino, is envisioned to be like the film on Gandhi.

It may be co-produced by Star Cinema with a Hollywood company. Angela Casauay, "Kris Reveals Details on Cory-Ninoy Movie", Sun.Star Network Online, 8 November 2009 <http://www.sunstar.com.ph/manila/kris-reveals-details-cory-ninoy-movie>.

4. See for example Paul D. Hutchcroft, "Review: Oligarchs and Cronies in the Philippine State: The Politics of Patrimonial Plunder", *World Politics* 43, no. 3 (April 1991): 414–50; Benjamin N. Muego, *Spectator Society: The Philippines Under Martial Rule*, Monographs in international studies no. 77 (Athens, OH: Ohio University Center for International Studies, 1988); Francisco Nemenzo, "From Autocracy to Elite Democracy", in *Dictatorship and Revolution: Roots of People's Power* (Metro Manila: Conspectus, 1987), pp. 221–68; Alfred W. McCoy, *The Yellow Revolution* (Bedford Park, South Australia: Flinders University, 1986); Francisco Nemenzo and Ron May, eds., *Philippines After Marcos* (New York: St. Martin's, 1985); David Timberman, *A Changeless Land: Continuity and Change in Philippine Politics* (Armonk, NY: Sharpe; Singapore: Institute of Southeast Asian Studies, 1991); Benedict Anderson, "Cacique Democracy and the Philippines: Origins and Dreams", *New Left Review*, no. 1969 (1988): 3–31.

5. For a chronology of the events that led to EDSA, see Alfred W. McCoy, *Closer Than Brothers: Manhood at the Philippine Military Academy* (New Haven: Yale University Press, 1999), pp. 237–38.

6. One may say that there is nothing ingenious about cutting yellow confetti from phone directories.

7. "The Well-Heeled Go to an Aquino Rally…", *Mr. and Ms.*, 23 September 1983, p. 19. For an analysis of the meanings associated with particular places of protest like Makati, see Eva-Lotta Hedman, "The Dialectics of 'EDSA Dos' ": Urban Space, Collective Memory, and the Spectacle of Compromise", in *Southeast Asia over Three Generations: Essays Presented to Benedict R. O'G. Anderson*, edited by James Siegel and Audrey Kahin (Ithaca, NY: Cornell Southeast Asia Program, 2003), pp. 283–301.

8. "Peaceful Manila Rallies", *Mr. and Ms.*, 7 October 1983.

9. Resil Mojares, "The Dream Goes On and On: Three Generations of the Osmeñas, 1906–1990", in *An Anarchy of Families: State and Family in the Philippines*, edited by Alfred W. McCoy (Quezon City: Ateneo De Manila University Press, 1994); Benedict Kerkvliet and Resil Mojares, "Themes in the Transition from Marcos to Aquino", in *From Marcos to Aquino: Local Perspectives on Political Transition in the Philippines* (Quezon City: Ateneo de Manila University Press).

10. Muego, *Spectator Society*, p. 11.

11. Sheila S. Coronel, "Dateline Philippines: The Lost Revolution", *Foreign Policy*, no. 84 (Autumn 1991): 168.

12. Ibid., p. 169.

13. Coronel, "Dateline Philippines", p. 170.

14. See McCoy, "Closer than Brothers".

15. Mark R. Thompson, "Off the Endangered List: Philippine Democratization in Comparative Perspective", *Comparative Politics* 28, no. 2 (1996): 189.

16. Quoted in Renato Constantino, *Renato Constantino and the Aquino Watch* (Quezon City: Karrel, 1987), p. 56.

17. Coronel, "Dateline Philippines", p. 168. For a first-hand account of this event, known as the "Mendiola Massacre" (the protestors were shot in Mendiola Street), see Jo-Ann Q. Maglipon, *A Smouldering Land* (Quezon City: National Council of Churches in the Philippines and the Forum for Rural Concerns, 1987).

18. David Kowalewski, "Vigilante Counterinsurgency and Human Rights in the Philippines: A Statistical Analysis", *Human Rights Quarterly* 12, no. 2 (1990): 248.

19. See David Wurfel, *Filipino Politics: Development and Decay, Politics and International Relations of Southeast Asia* (Ithaca, NY: Cornell University Press, 1988); David Steinberg, "Tradition and Response", in *Crisis in the Philippines* (Princeton, NJ: Princeton University Press, 1986); Dante C. Simbulan, *The Modern Principalia: The Historical Evolution of the Philippine Ruling Oligarchy* (Quezon City: University of the Philippines Press, 2005); Lewis Gleeck, *President Marcos and the Philippine Political Culture* (Manila: Gleeck, 1987).

20. Timberman, *A Changeless Land: Continuity and Change in Philippine Politics*.

21. Ibid., p. xii.

22. Beth Day, *The Philippines: Shattered Showcase of Democracy in Asia* (New York: Evans, 1974).

23. See also William Butler and International Commission of Jurists (1952–), *The Decline of Democracy in the Philippines: A Report of Missions* (Geneva: International Commission of Jurists, 1977); David Rosenberg, ed., *Marcos and Martial Law in the Philippines* (Ithaca, NY: Cornell University Press, 1979).

24. Muego, *Spectator Society*; Nemenzo and May, *Philippines After Marcos*; Temario C. Rivera, *Landlords and Capitalists: Class, Family, and State in Philippine Manufacturing* (Quezon City: University of the Philippines Press, 1994); Paul D. Hutchcroft, *Booty Capitalism: The Politics of Banking in the Philippines* (Ithaca, NY: Cornell University Press, 1998); Eva-Lotta Hedman, *Philippine Politics and Society in the Twentieth Century: Colonial Legacies, Post-colonial Trajectories* (London: Routledge, 2000); John Bresnan, *Crisis in the Philippines: The Marcos Era and Beyond* (Princeton, NJ: Princeton University Press, 1986). *Oligarchic Politics: Elections and the Party-List System in the Philippines* (CenPEG Books, 2007).

25. Anderson, "Cacique Democracy and the Philippines: Origins and Dreams".

26. Nemenzo, "From Autocracy to Elite Democracy", p. 221. Despite this criticism,

Nemenzo continued to support Aquino amidst the coup attempts against her administration. See Francisco Nemenzo, "A Season of Coups", *Kasarinlan* 2, no. 4 (1987): 17–35.

27. The Bantayog ng mga Bayani is a memorial centre dedicated to remembering the heroes of the Marcos period. See Lisandro E. Claudio, "Memories of the Anti-Marcos Movement: The Left and the Mnemonic Dynamics of Post-Authoritarian Philippines", *Southeast Asia Research* 18, no. 1 (2010): 33–66.

28. For example, in the biography of Salvador "Doy" Laurel, Vice President to Aquino and a member of the oligarchic political elite, written by his wife, martial rule is represented as a period of "darkness". Celia Diaz-Laurel, *Doy Laurel* (Celia Diaz-Laurel, 2005), pp. 102–23.

29. See for example Hedman, *Philippine Politics and Society in the Twentieth Century: Colonial Legacies, Post-colonial Trajectories.*

30. Interpretations of EDSA III in popular media are varied and reflect the contested nature of People Power. Some refer to it as a genuine outpouring of mass support for populist leader Joseph Estrada. Others view it more cynically — a case of a corrupt deposed president exploiting the desperation of the urban poor in order to incite urban violence.

31. Thompson, "Off the Endangered List", p. 189.

32. Ibid.

33. Benedict Kerkvliet and Resil Mojares, eds., *From Marcos to Aquino: Local Perspectives on Political Transition in the Philippines* (Quezon City: Ateneo de Manila University Press, 1991).

34. Michael Pinches, "People Power and the Urban Poor: The Politics of Unity and Division in Manila After Marcos", in *The Philippines Under Aquino*, edited by Peter Krinks (Canberra: Australian Development Studies Network, 1987), pp. 85–102.

35. Ibid., p. 85.

36. Ibid., p. 94.

37. Ibid., p. 97.

38. This refers to people who are outside the ambit of the organized Left.

39. Kerkvliet and Mojares, "Themes in the Transition from Marcos to Aquino", pp. 5, 12.

40. Neferti Xina M. Tadiar, *Fantasy Production: Sexual Economies and Other Philippine Consequences for the New World Order* (Hong Kong: Hong Kong University Press, 2004), p. 187.

41. Ibid., p. 186.

42. Ibid., p. 193.

43. Ibid., p. 194.

44. *The Philippines: The End of an Illusion* (Association for Radical East Asian Studies and Journal of Contemporary Asia, 1973).

45. Nathan Quimpo, *Contested Democracy and the Left in the Philippines After Marcos* (New Haven, CT: Yale University Southeast Asia Studies, 2008), p. 23.

46. John Doherty, *Who Controls the Philippine Economy: Some Need Not Try as Hard as Others* (Manoa: University of Hawai'i Press, 1982).

47. Abinales and Amoroso, *State and Society in the Philippines*, pp. 253–55.

48. Yuko Kasuya, *Presidential Bandwagon: Parties and Party Systems in the Philippines* (Pasig City, Philippines: Anvil, 2009).

49. Patricio N. Abinales, "The Philippines: Weak State, Resilient President", *Southeast Asian Affairs 2008* (Singapore: Institute of Southeast Asian Studies, 2008): 293–312.

50. Nathan Gilbert Quimpo, "The Philippines: Predatory Regime, Growing Authoritarian Features", *Pacific Review* 22, no. 3 (2009): 335–53.

51. Bishop Socrates Villegas, interview by Lisandro E. Claudio, 24 August 2009. Indeed, the resonance of People Power within religious communities has allowed for theological essays to be written about the revolution. See Douglas J. Elwood, ed., *Toward a Theology of People Power: Reflections on the Philippine February Phenomenon* (Quezon City: New Day, 1988).

52. Juliet Labog-Villanueva, "Sin Opposed Vatican Order, Pushed EDSA: Cardinal Threatened to Quit as Archbishop", *Philippine Daily Inquirer*, 21 January 2008 <http://newsinfo.inquirer.net/inquirerheadlines/nation/view/20080121-113651/Sin_opposed_Vatican_order,_pushed_Edsa_II>.

53. Salvador Guerrero, "The Reform the Armed Forces Movement (RAM): A Creation of Historical Experience", *Kasarinlan: Philippine Journal of Third World Studies* 3, no. 3 (1988): 57.

54. This nationalist rhetoric would peak in 1990 when RAM changed its name from Reform the Armed Forces Movement to Rebolusynaryong Alyansang Makabayan (Revolutionary Nationalist Alliance).

55. Quimpo, *Contested Democracy*, p. 52.

56. See Ferdinand E. Marcos, *The Democratic Revolution in the Philippines* (Manila: Dept. of Tourism, 1977).

57. Amado Guerrero, *Philippine Society and Revolution*, 4th ed. (Oakland, CA: International Association of Filipino Patriots, 1980). For an analysis of these two competing "revolutions", see Reynaldo Clemena Ileto, "The 'Unfinished Revolution' in Political Discourse", in *Filipinos and their Revolution*, pp. 177–202.

58. The New People's army grew at an exponential rate during the Marcos years such that, according to Weekly, it was a significant threat to the government in the 80s. By 1985 its troops numbered around 24,000. Kathleen Weekley, *The Communist Party of the Philippines, 1968–1993: A Story of Its Theory and Practice* (Quezon City: University of the Philippines Press, 2001), p. 104.

59. The resonance of these discourses is discussed by Reynaldo Ileto in "The 'Unfinished Revolution' in Political Discourse", in *Filipinos and their Revolution*, pp. 177–202.
60. For an analysis of the implications of the exclusion of the Left on the remembrance of People Power and the Marcos period, see Lisandro E. Claudio, "Memories of the Anti-Marcos Movement".
61. "Memorandum on the Snap Elections", Executive Committee of the Communist Party of the Philippines, 23 December 1985, translated by A.R. Magno in "CPP: Rethinking the Revolutionary Process", *Diliman Review* 34, no. 4 (1986): 17.
62. Dominique Caouette, "Preserving Revolutionaries: Armed Struggle in the 21st Century, Exploring the Revolution of the Communist Party of the Philippines" (PhD dissertation, Cornell University, 2004), pp. 431–32.
63. According to Rutten, NPA membership dropped to 10,300 in 1993, while the latest government estimate published in the *Philippine Daily Inquirer* pegs membership at 5,700. Rosanne Rutten, "Popular Support for the Revolutionary Movement CPP-NPA: Experiences in a Hacienda in Negros Occidental, 1978–1995", in *The Revolution Falters: The Left in Philippine Politics After 1986*, edited by P.N Abinales (Ithaca, NY: Cornell Southeast Asia Program, 1996), p. 116; Joel Guinto, "Teodoro: Troops on Guard vs 'Desperate' Communist Rebels", *Philippine Daily Inquirer*, 31 March <http://newsinfo.inquirer.net/breakingnews/nation/view/20080331-127453/Teodoro-Troops-on-guard-vs-desperate-communist-rebels> (accessed 29 September 2009).
64. For an account of the split, see Joel Rocamora, *Breaking Through: The Struggle Within the Communist Party of the Philippines* (Anvil, 1994).
65. Quimpo, *Contested Democracy*, p. 90.
66. Ibid., pp. 90–91.

References

Abinales, Patricio N., ed. *The Revolution Falters: The Left in Philippine Politics After 1986*. Southeast Asia Program, Cornell University, 1996.
———. "The Philippines: Weak State, Resilient President". *Southeast Asian Affairs 2008*. Singapore: Institute of Southeast Asian Studies, 2008.
Abinales, Patricio N. and Donna J. Amoroso. *State and Society in the Philippines*. Pasig City: Anvil, 2005.
Abueva, Jose. "Ideology and Practice in the 'New Society'". In *Marcos and Martial Law in the Philippines*, edited by David Rosenberg. Ithaca, NY: Cornell University Press, 1979.
Anderson, Benedict. "Cacique Democracy and the Philippines: Origins and Dreams". *New Left Review* (1969): 3–31.

Bello, Walden F. and Severina Rivera. *The Logistics of Repression and Other Essays: The Role of U.S. Assistance in Consolidating the Martial Law Regime in the Philippines.* Washington: Friends of the Filipino People, 1977.

Bonner, Raymond. *Waltzing with a Dictator: The Marcoses and the Making of American Policy.* New York: Times Books, 1987.

Bresnan, John. *Crisis in the Philippines: The Marcos Era and Beyond.* Princeton, NJ: Princeton University Press, 1986.

Butler, William and International Commission of Jurists. *The Decline of Democracy in the Philippines: A Report of Missions.* Geneva: International Commission of Jurists, 1977.

Caouette, Dominique. "Preserving Revolutionaries: Armed Struggle in the 21st Century, Exploring the Revolution of the Communist Party of the Philippines". PhD dissertation, Cornell University, 2004.

Casauay, Angela. "Kris Reveals Details on Cory-Ninoy Movie". Sun.Star Network Online, 8 November 2009 <http://www.sunstar.com.ph/manila/kris-reveals-details-cory-ninoy-movie>.

Celoza, Albert. *Ferdinand Marcos and the Philippines: The Political Economy of Authoritarianism.* Westport, CT: Praeger, 1997.

Claudio, Lisandro E. "Memories of the Anti-Marcos Movement: The Left and the Mnemonic Dynamics of Post-Authoritarian Philippines". *Southeast Asia Research* 18, no. 1 (2010): 33–66.

Constantino, Renato. *Renato Constantino and the Aquino Watch.* Quezon City: Karrel, 1987.

Coronel, Sheila S. "Dateline Philippines: The Lost Revolution". *Foreign Policy*, no. 84 (Autumn, 1991): 166–85.

Day, Beth. *The Philippines: Shattered Showcase of Democracy in Asia.* New York: Evans, 1974.

de Dios, Emmanuel. "The Erosion of Dictatorship". In *Dictatorship and Revolution: Roots of People's Power*, edited by Javate-de Dios, Petronilo Daroy and Lorna Kalaw-Tirol. Manila: Conspectus, 1988.

Diaz-Laurel, Celia. *Doy Laurel.* Celia Diaz-Laurel, 2005.

Doherty, John. *Who Controls the Philippine Economy: Some Need Not Try as Hard as Others.* Manoa: University of Hawai'i Press, 1982.

Doronila, Amando. "The Transformation of Patron-Client Relations and its Political Consequences in Postwar Philippines". *Journal of Southeast Asian Studies* 16, no. 1 (1985): 99–116.

———. *The State, Economic Transformation, and Political Change in the Philippines, 1946–1972.* Singapore: Oxford University Press, 1992.

Elwood, Douglas J. ed. *Toward a Theology of People Power: Reflections on the Philippine February Phenomenon.* Quezon City: New Day, 1988.

Executive Committee of the Communist Party of the Philippines. "Memorandum on Snap Elections". In "CPP: Rethinking the Revolutionary Process", translated by A.R. Magno. *Diliman Review* 34, no. 4 (1986): 17.

Gleeck, Lewis. *President Marcos and the Philippine Political Culture*. Manila: L.E. Gleeck, 1987.

Guerrero, Amado. *Philippine Society and Revolution*, 4th ed. Oakland, CA: International Association of Filipino Patriots, 1980.

Guerrero, Salvador. "The Reform the Armed Forces Movement (RAM): A Creation of Historical Experience". *Kasarinlan: Philippine Journal of Third World Studies* 3, no. 3 (1988): 51–58.

Guinto, Joel. "Teodoro: Troops on Guard vs 'Desperate' Communist Rebels". *Philippine Daily Inquirer*, 31 March 2008 <http://newsinfo.inquirer.net/breakingnews/nation/view/20080331>.

Hamilton-Paterson, James. *America's Boy: A Century of Colonialism in the Philippines*. Holt, 1998.

Hedman, Eva-Lotta. *Philippine Politics and Society in the Twentieth Century: Colonial Legacies, Post-colonial Trajectories*. London: Routledge, 2000.

———. "The Dialectics of 'EDSA Dos'": Urban Space, Collective Memory, and the Spectacle of Compromise". In *Southeast Asia over Three Generations: Essays Presented to Benedict R. O'G. Anderson*, edited by James Siegel and Audrey Kahin. Ithaca, NY: Cornell Southeast Asia Program, 2003.

Hutchcroft, Paul D. *Booty Capitalism: The Politics of Banking in the Philippines*. Ithaca, NY: Cornell University Press, 1998.

———. "Review: Oligarchs and Cronies in the Philippine State: The Politics of Patrimonial Plunder". *World Politics* 43, no. 3 (1991): 414–50.

Ileto, Reynaldo Clemeña. *Filipinos and their Revolution: Event, Discourse, and Historiography*. Quezon City: Ateneo de Manila University Press, 1998.

Kasuya, Yuko. *Presidential Bandwagon: Parties and Party Systems in the Philippines*. Pasig City: Anvil, 2009.

Kerkvliet, Benedict and Resil Mojares, eds. *From Marcos to Aquino: Local Perspectives on Political Transition in the Philippines*. Quezon City: Ateneo de Manila University Press, 1991.

———. "Themes in the Transition from Marcos to Aquino". In *From Marcos to Aquino: Local Perspectives on Political Transition in the Philippines*. Quezon City: Ateneo de Manila University Press, 1991.

Kowalewski, David. "Vigilante Counterinsurgency and Human Rights in the Philippines: A Statistical Analysis". *Human Rights Quarterly* 12, no. 2 (1990): 246–64.

Labog-Villanueva, Juliet. "Sin Opposed Vatican Order, Pushed EDSA: Cardinal Threatened to Quit as Archbishop." *Philippine Daily Inquirer*, 21 January 2008 <http://newsinfo.inquirer.net/inquirerheadlines/nation/view/20080121-113651/Sin_opposed_Vatican_order,_pushed_Edsa_II>.

Lande, Carl Herman. *Leaders, Factions, and Parties: The Structure of Philippine Politics*. New Haven: Southeast Asia Studies, Yale University, 1965.

Lim, Frinston. "Cheering Crowds Greet Noynoy, Mar in Tagum". INQUIRER.net, 26 September 2009 <http://newsinfo.inquirer.net/inquirerheadlines/nation/ view/20090926-226946/Cheering-crowds-greet-Noynoy-Mar-in-Tagum>.

Maglipon, Jo-Ann Q. *A Smouldering Land*. Quezon City: National Council of Churches in the Philippines and the Forum for Rural Concerns, 1987.

Marcos, Ferdinand E. *The Democratic Revolution in the Philippines*. Manila: Dept. of Tourism, 1977.

McCoy, Alfred W. *The Yellow Revolution*. Bedford Park, South Australia: Flinders University, 1986.

———. *Closer than Brothers: Manhood at Philippine Military Academy*. New Haven: Yale University Press, 1999.

McHale, Thomas. "An Econecological Approach to Economic Development". PhD dissertation, Harvard University, 1958.

Mojares, Resil. "The Dream Goes On and On: Three Generations of the Osmeñas, 1906–1990". In *An Anarchy of Families: State and Family in the Philippines*, edited by Alfred W. McCoy. Quezon City: Ateneo De Manila University Press, 1994.

Muego, Benjamin N. *Spectator Society: The Philippines Under Martial Rule*. Monographs in international studies no. 77. Athens: Ohio University Center for International Studies, 1988.

Nemenzo, Francisco. "A Season of Coups". *Kasarinlan* 2, no. 4 (1987): 17–35.

———. "From Autocracy to Elite Democracy". In *Dictatorship and Revolution: Roots of People's Power*. Metro Manila: Conspectus, 1987.

Nemenzo, Francisco and Ron May, eds. *Philippines After Marcos*. New York: St. Martin's Press, 1985.

Oligarchic Politics: Elections and the Party-List System in the Philippines. CenPEG Books, 2007.

"Peaceful Manila Rallies". *Mr. and Ms.*, 7 October 1983.

"The Philippines: The End of an Illusion". Association for Radical East Asian Studies and Journal of Contemporary Asia, 1973.

Quimpo, Nathan. *Contested Democracy and the Left in the Philippines After Marcos*. New Haven, CT: Yale University Southeast Asia Studies, 2008.

———. "The Philippines: Predatory Regime, Growing Authoritarian Features". *Pacific Review* 22, no. 3 (2009): 335–53.

Pinches, Michael. "People Power and the Urban Poor: The Politics of Unity and Division in Manila After Marcos". In *The Philippines Under Aquino*, edited by Peter Krinks. Canberra: Australian Development Studies Network, 1987.

Rivera, Temario C. *Landlords and Capitalists: Class, Family, and State in Philippine Manufacturing*. Quezon City: University of the Philippines Press, 1994.

Rocamora, Joel. *Breaking Through: The Struggle Within the Communist Party of the Philippines*. Anvil, 1994.

Rosenberg, David, ed. *Marcos and Martial Law in the Philippines*. Ithaca, NY: Cornell University Press, 1979.

Rutten, Rosanne. "Popular Support for the Revolutionary Movement CPP-NPA: Experiences in a Hacienda in Negros Occidental, 1978–1995". In *The Revolution Falters: The Left in Philippine Politics after 1986*, edited by P.N Abinales. Ithaca, NY: Cornell Southeast Asia Program, 1996.

Simbulan, Dante C. *The Modern Principalia: The Historical Evolution of the Philippine Ruling Oligarchy*. Quezon City: University of the Philippines Press, 2005.

Steinberg, David. "Tradition and Response". In *Crisis in the Philippines*. Princeton, NJ: Princeton University Press, 1986.

Tadiar, Neferti Xina M. *Fantasy Production: Sexual Economies and Other Philippine Consequences for the New World Order*. Hong Kong: Hong Kong University Press, 2004.

Thompson, Mark. *The Anti-Marcos Struggle: Personalistic Rule and Democratic Transition in the Philippines*. New Haven: Yale University Press, 1995.

———. "Off the Endangered List: Philippine Democratization in Comparative Perspective". *Comparative Politics* 28, no. 2 (1996): 179–205.

Timberman, David. *A Changeless Land: Continuity and Change in Philippine Politics*. Armonk, NY: Sharpe; Singapore: Institute of Southeast Asian Studies, 1991.

Ubac, Michael Lim. "Sentiment for Noynoy also up in Senate, says Kiko, INQUIRER. net, 26 September 2009 <http://newsinfo.inquirer.net/inquirerheadlines/nation/view/20090926-226955/Sentiment-for-Noynoy-also-up-in-Senate-says-Kiko>.

Weekley, Kathleen. *The Communist Party of the Philippines, 1968–1993: A Story of Its Theory and Practice*. Quezon City: University of the Philippines Press, 2001.

Wurfel, David. *Filipino Politics: Development and Decay. Politics and International Relations of Southeast Asia*. Ithaca, NY: Cornell University Press, 1988.

3

THE ROAD TO *DOI MOI* IN 1986
Domestic Dimensions

Ta Minh Tuan

In modern Vietnam one could argue that there were a number of turning points that made history. The proclamation of the independence of Vietnam in September 1945 and the subsequent birth of the Democratic Republic of Vietnam certainly constituted a milestone, which put an end to more than eighty years of French colonial rule. The French returned with an intention to re-capture power leading to the outbreak of the First Indochina War. The Paris Conference in 1954 following Vietnam's victory over the French in Dien Bien Phu marked the complete departure of the French from the North of Vietnam and the partition of the country at the 17th parallel. The United States replaced France to support the government of the Republic of South Vietnam and to scrap the Paris Accord on the holding of a general election to unify Vietnam in 1956. The Second Indochina War (better known as the Vietnam War) followed as a result and lasted for almost twenty years. The unification of Vietnam in 1975 led to American disengagement, ushering in a whole new period for a united Vietnam for the first time in more than one hundred years. However, these thirty years were the time when Vietnam had to fight for independence and national liberation, which was conducive to the shared common feature of constant war and armed struggle both in the North and in the South.

The reconstruction of a war-torn Vietnam only started after the political and institutional reunification of the country in 1976. Hanoi implemented a Soviet-type command economic policy with great hopes of success. Nevertheless, the expansion of the socialist economic sector had not brought about the expected outcomes. In the North of Vietnam, acceleration of implementing co-operatives and enlargement of their size were apparently successful. In substance, agricultural co-operatives had further deteriorated. The size of the co-operatives had gone well beyond the management capacity of the local management boards. Co-operative members were indifferent to their work since they did not enjoy the benefits of increased productivity. In the South of Vietnam, Hanoi's hasty attempt to collectivize agriculture and abolish capitalist business and develop large-scale co-operatives had encountered strong resistance from peasants. They left their land fallow. In the 1978–79 winter-spring crop there was nearly 200,000 hectares of paddy-growing land left uncultivated in the Mekong Delta alone. Many co-operatives were dissolved at the time they were initiated. The objective to basically accomplish agricultural collectivization by 1980 failed.[1] Furthermore, agriculture was heavily hit by natural disasters in 1977 and 1978. As a result, Vietnam had to import a record amount of 1.5 million tons of food in 1979.[2] In Ho Chi Minh City (formerly Saigon), the process of nationalizing private-owned business establishments forced thousands of merchants, big and small, out of their jobs. Industrial and commercial sectors became stagnant. Tens of thousands of people had to move away from the city to earn their living, many of whom were Hoa (ethnic Chinese).

The implementation of all 15 major planned economic targets for the Second Five-Year Plan (1976–80) fell short. The government's official statistics showed that only six targets had achieved 50–80 per cent of projected output while the other nine targets accounted for only 25–48 per cent. Average annual national income growth rate in 1976–80 was merely 0.4 per cent, meaning a sharp decline in *per capita* terms, while population growth rate stood at 2.24 per cent,[3] contributing to increasing difficulties in people's lives. This bad economic situation prevented Vietnam from demilitarizing its large standing army after the horrible war. But feeding millions of men in uniform, including the cost of Vietnam's intervention in Cambodia in 1979, was also a burden on the economy.

To solve the economic problems on their own, co-operatives subcontracted tasks to the households, and factories became engaged in "fence-breaking" (*phá rào*), swapping or selling on the free market to raise cash to buy materials or pay bonuses to workers and making deals with other factories or with agricultural co-operatives to supply materials. "Fence-breaking" began in Ho Chi Minh City, strongly supported by Vo Van Kiet, the city's Party Chief, and later spread to other Southern provinces such as An Giang and Long An. In September 1979, the Sixth Plenum of the Central Committee (Fourth Tenure) of the VCP endorsed these activities, recognizing the need for a more liberal economy consisting of state, collective, joint state-private, private (small business), and individual sectors.

In 1981, the Secretariat issued the Directive 100 CT/TU to make the product contract (*khoán sản phẩm*) a national policy, under which peasant households signed contracts to farm collective land, especially in the areas of transplanting, weeding, and harvesting. Ploughing, irrigation, and pest control usually remained the prerogative of the co-operative, using collective labour. Each household fulfilled its contract by turning over an agreed amount of produce to the co-operative. If it failed to deliver, the deficit would be made up the following year. Any surplus could be retained for internal consumption, sold on the free market, or sold to the state at negotiated prices. In fact, the product contract was the reincarnation of a similar form of an unauthorized contract (*khoán chui*) initiated more than ten years previously by Kim Ngoc, the Party Chief of Vinh Phuc province. The output contract shared many similarities to the Chinese household system, which was introduced in China in December 1981 and was completed in late 1983.

The Government issued Decree 25-CP in January 1981 setting a new "Three-Plan System" (*kế hoạch ba*) that sanctioned the co-existence of planning and market forces in the industrial sector. The decree required a state factory to develop a single plan with three parts. Under Part A, the factory used inputs supplied by the state and gave the resulting output at low prices to the state. Under Part B, it freely disposed of products that it had been established to produce, but only to acquire additional inputs. Under Part C, it could attempt to diversify its products free from outside control, although priority was to be given to state trading organs when the unit disposed of these products. Both the product contract and the "Three-Plan System" remained within the central planning framework; they were aimed simply at improving the internal efficiency of the production units.[4] These piecemeal reform measures were welcomed, injecting a new work spirit in factories and bringing about some additional economic benefit to workers, helping ease their daily living difficulties. However, critics feared that the measures would spur inflation and encourage "negative phenomena" such as speculation, smuggling and corruption, although the changes did trigger a fairly rapid economic recovery.

In an effort to decentralize the economic management and as a part of the 1981–1985 Third Five-Year Plan, Le Duan, the VCP General Secretary confirmed in mid-1984 the plan to build the district into a viable economic structure that would combine industry, agriculture, forestry, and fishery on the one hand with small-scale industry and handicrafts on the other. Provinces were instructed to transfer to districts the control of agricultural support stations and agencies dealing with tractor operations, irrigation, veterinary services, vegetable production, seed and animal species stations, farm implement factories, and transport enterprises. They were also asked to hand over province-operated forestlands and some state-owned enterprises to the districts.[5]

The party leadership perceived the district as the solution to the problems of low productivity, state revenue, and accumulation for local development. It hoped that the district would bring together production forces from the co-operatives, perform a new division of labour, make good use of land, create jobs, and link cultivation and animal husbandry to the processing of agricultural products. The province, in its opinion, was too remote administratively to exert control over basic production units, and it was administratively easier to deal with the district rather than individual co-operatives.[6]

Another step towards improving the economic performance was a resolution on "pricing-salaries-money" (giá-lương-tiền) approved by the Central Committee of the VCP on 17 June 1985. The main content of this measure was aimed at abolishing the subsidies and the bureaucratic centralism by increasing the price of certain commodities, which had been earlier fixed by the government, to approximately their real value on the market. Nonetheless, the simultaneous augmentation of prices, salaries and money supply speeded up the inflation rate. To make things worse, the government ordered a conversion of the Vietnamese currency, by a ratio of ten old Vietnamese dongs for one new dong, in the same year. Policymakers hoped that this would help to slow down inflation and perhaps stop it in the end. They expected that this "antidote" would restrain the demand for consumer goods, thus restoring the fiscal and monetary balance in the economy. In fact, this measure succeeded only in reducing the cash of state-owned enterprises (SOEs) that was kept in reserve and outside their accounting books; while among the population and within the private sector the results were very limited, for the majority of their assets was in the form of gold and U.S. dollars. After the currency conversion, the cash available in the SOEs was almost exhausted, leading to a serious lack of cash. Under these circumstances, the government had to issue money in order to maintain the operation of the SOEs, hence aggravating the inflation even more.

Though there were signs of economic growth during the Third Five-Year Plan, for instance, the average annual growth rate of gross social product was 7.3 per cent, national income 6.4 per cent, total value of industrial production 9.5 per cent, agriculture 4.9 per cent, export volume 15.6 per cent, in general Vietnam again failed to fulfil its overall target for the period from 1981 to 1985.[7] It indicated that the initial steps towards reform produced some positive outcomes, but they were not robust enough to prompt significant transformations in the system. The economic perception of top leaders remained unchanged; as a result, the economy still functioned on the traditional model that had existed since the mid-1950s. Besides, the soaring inflation had nullified all the modest economic gains and social welfare produced by the earlier efforts.

The cost of the war with Cambodia and China added more problems to Vietnam's ailing economy. From 1977 to 1978 Khmer Rouge border raids had badly interrupted agricultural production in the border provinces. Conflict with China in 1978 led to the total cancellation of Chinese aid that could have upgraded Vietnam's transport and light industry sector. A massive exodus of Hoa people from Vietnam dealt a heavy blow to coal mining, fishing, ceramic and textile industries as well as port operations because a high percentage of workers were of Hoa background. The February 1979 Chinese invasion of Vietnam's border region not only resulted in the destruction of many cities, power stations, railway lines and bridges, but also of a major apatite mine that was an important source of fertilizer.[8]

The 150,000 Vietnamese troops that were stationed in Cambodia forced Vietnam to shoulder more economic burdens. Food, clothes, salary and other military needs such as fuel for these troops were provided by Hanoi. Although some analysts argued that all military hardware and ammunition for the Cambodian campaign had been supplied by Moscow for free, it is improbable. Vietnam had, at least partially, to finance this intervention. Until now, Hanoi has not published any figures indicating the economic expenses of its operations in Cambodia. Although Vietnam's counter-attack on Pol Pot's invasion of its Southwest border was obviously justified on the grounds of self-defence, Vietnam's long military presence in Cambodia at the request of the Heng Samrin government left it bogged down there. Consequently, Vietnam suffered heavy casualties,[9] draining Vietnam's manpower which could otherwise have been used to support the country's economic development. An outcome of Vietnam's involvement in Cambodia was probably Hanoi's loss of hundreds of millions of dollars in foreign aid. This was a serious loss for the country that was already critically short of funds. Had this money been available, agricultural production would perhaps have increased somewhat and the consumer industry would have functioned at a higher capacity.

The crisis had grave repercussions on the society as a whole. People's lives became very hard. Wage earners saw their living standards sharply decline over the years. Struggling for daily survival became common. Each individual received less than fifteen kilograms of rice per month. Consumer goods such as clothes, soap, medicines and other household goods were far short of people's needs and, because of the high price, only in the reach of a small urban minority, mostly government and party officials. A great deal of people, mostly in the South, had to obtain the supply of these basic commodities from the parcels sent to them by their relatives abroad, mainly in the West, or from smuggling sources from Thailand. On the other hand, many government officials took advantage of the troubled situation to benefit themselves by means of corruption, embezzlement of public funds, stealing government property and accepting bribes. As a result of such actions, people began to lose their faith in the leadership of the ruling Communist Party and in the economic management of the government.

Social discontent started to pile pressure on the political system. There was an outcry for change. The government did reshuffle some portfolios in February 1980 and 1982 with some personnel changes in which several old and conservative leaders were removed from their positions and younger, less orthodox leaders took over responsibilities for different economic ministries. However, there was no essential change of policy in Vietnam at that time because the economic failure did not provoke a real political crisis. Vietnamese political theorists often remarked that their people's ability to bear sufferings was immense, and they had no other economic and political choice if they wanted to remain independent. The Vietnamese authorities sometimes attributed the socio-economic crisis to the American economic embargo.

However, towards the end of 1984 and early 1985, the situation had worsened rapidly and Vietnam's socio-economic crisis reached its peak in 1986 as inflation jumped up to 774.7 per cent. The people could not keep up with their daily lives anymore and all means of social security were, in practice, wiped out. The question facing the Vietnamese leadership at the moment was whether they would carry out a comprehensive economic reform immediately, or they would be confronted with rising socio-political instability that might threaten their power, given that the people's forbearance had approached its limit.

On the eve of the Sixth Party Congress in December 1986, some scholars even doubted if reforms would take place at all. They argued that the only growth model available for Vietnam if it abandoned the Soviet-type economic development was heavily biased towards Western-styled market-based capitalism. And this model carried two sets of serious dangers for governments trying to survive the transition from a planned to market economy. *First*, it required the almost complete dismantling, as fast as possible, of the system in place. This system did provide the population with a basic livelihood and therefore some basic security. Its removal and the accompanying "shock therapy" which was necessary to quell inflation and bring about macroeconomic stability could impart a profound sense of insecurity and quickly polarize society in which privilege and poverty alike were previously the preserve of very small minorities. *Second*, the introduction of the free market, which enshrines the concept of informed choice, could not but open to question, if not directly undermine, the legitimacy of the Communist Party not accustomed to having to earn the right to rule by being held to account. It was commonplace in the communist countries, and Vietnam was no exception, that the infiltration of the market almost inevitably brought with it the danger of "peaceful evolution" (*diễn biến hòa bình*), an insidious process by which the West, especially the United States, succeeds in spreading a desire for political pluralism alongside status symbol consumer goods.[10] This Western-style path to economic development would definitely undermine the Marxist concept of socialist economy. Other opinion makers argued that under such circumstances, China's economic model may be more appealing and relevant to Vietnam, but no one really ventured to suggest that Vietnam should seriously emulate such a model.

These then were the antecedent conditions and the background against which the state adopted a policy of economic reconstruction. This process set in motion changes to the country's political economy that could neither be controlled afterwards nor reversed. In this regard the introduction of economic renovation constituted a major break from the past and a significant conjuncture in the country's domestic political economy.

The reality of the situation eventually proved that Hanoi was determined to adopt reforms that were similar to China's open-door policy. Nevertheless, most Vietnamese scholars concurred that *doi moi* was a bottom-up process whereby the Communist Party of Vietnam (CPV) learnt the experiences from experimental reforms in various cities and provinces, which were the results of the people's innovation. No specific model of development, China and the Soviet Union included, seemed to appeal entirely to the CPV. To make *doi moi* possible, a pragmatic leader, Nguyen Van Linh, was restored to the Politburo in July 1985. Linh was a pro-reform leader from the South who had been dropped from the Politburo and the Secretariat at the Fifth Party Congress in 1982. He was then elected General Secretary of the VCP at the Sixth Congress.[11] It is possible to identify Linh as one of the engineers of *doi moi*.[12] He openly attacked the "old thinking" of the Party and government officials in his series of articles in *Nhân Dân* (People's Daily — the Party's newspaper). He urged the Party and people at large to exercise what he called the "emancipation of mind" (*đổi mới tư duy*), particularly in the economic sphere. His role in the course of reform in Vietnam has been widely acknowledged. In fact, Linh was very impressed by Gorbachev's "new thinking". He often took Gorbachev as a bright example for party cadres and government officials to learn from. A campaign to put "new thinking" into action was launched in Vietnam after the 1986 Congress in the spirit propagated by Truong Chinh: "look straight at the truth, accurately evaluate the truth and spell out the truth".

According to Dao Duy Tung, a leading political theoretician of the VCP, the emancipation of mind is not only a change in the way of thinking, but also a change of perception. It should be done not only in a certain domain, but also in all scopes of activity of the Party and state. It should not negate everything, but should observe the principle of "continuity" (*kế thừa*) and "development" (*phát triển*). For instance, in order to tackle economic problems, the Party and the government had to rectify their mistakes and shortcomings committed earlier, rearrange production structures, largely readjust investment priorities, unequivocally re-engineer the national economy with an appropriate structure, in which agriculture must be truly given priority, and successfully achieve the three objectives of the programme on food and foodstuffs, consumer goods and products for export. Economic management mechanisms had to be renovated; the bureaucratic centralism and the system of subsidies had to be rooted out; the laws of commodity production that exist objectively during the transitional period had to be recognized and correctly applied; and prejudice against other economic sectors (non-state sectors) had to be removed.[13]

Doi moi in 1986 became a turning point in Vietnam's modern history (or conjuncture as termed by foreign scholars) in many ways. First, the Sixth Party Congress broke, to a large extent, from the previous policies in a wide range of issues, in which the path to economic development was most significant. The Congress presented a *volte-face* on Vietnam's economic policy. It approved "a multi-sectoral economy with a socialist orientation under the State management", and put the different sectors on an equal footing, in which, for the first time, the private economic sector was officially recognized and small businesses were encouraged. A series of policies that undermined the old state structure, culminating in the abolition of the central planning system (or a command economy) and the building of elements necessary for the development of a market economy in the 1990s were formulated. Of these economic policy reforms, five key areas were prioritized:

1. reorientation of production and investment policies to emphasize food staples, consumer goods and exports;
2. promotion of a multi-sectoral economy, giving greater scope to private sector initiative in agriculture, industry and services;
3. fiscal and monetary reform to improve the revenue base, control public expenditures and reduce the rate of inflation;
4. reform of public administration and the management of state enterprises;
5. diversification of foreign economic relations away from the countries of the Soviet bloc, and encouragement of foreign direct investment from Asia and other parts of the world.[14]

This shift in economic policy and its initial success facilitated the process of opening Vietnam's economy to the outside world, beginning from 1989, and gave Vietnam's leaders some important ideas of how a market economy works and the benefits economic integration could bring to Vietnam. Although economic reforms made a breakthrough after the Seventh Party Congress in 1991, it is generally agreed among Vietnamese scholars that the economic policy of the Sixth Party Congress served as the foundation and the catalyst for real economic change in Vietnam.

Second, the Sixth Party Congress thoroughly reviewed the mistakes the Party committed and charted out some political reforms as well. Do Muoi, the Vietnamese Prime Minister at that time, summarized in 1990 *doi moi* as a process of identifying and resolving timely and rightly conflicts emerging in social life in order to guarantee harmonious and even development between economics, society and politics, and between democracy and the rule of law. The relationship between economic reform and political ones needs to be correctly addressed he argued. *Doi moi* in Vietnam should first start with economic activities. Only through economic reform can the people's living standards be improved step by step, and consequently the trust in *doi moi* by the people will be developed. Effective economic reform will then make possible the renewal of the political system. But, this does not mean that Vietnam has to wait for economic reform to be completed before beginning to renew the political system. On the contrary, Vietnam should gradually renovate its political system so as to boost economic reform.[15] In principle, the Party retained its strong leadership over all aspects of Vietnam's society, but in reality the Party gradually loosened its control and transferred part of its power to the Cabinet (the Council of Ministers) and the National Assembly. This was significant political progress as it began to shape Vietnam's future reform of its political system in order to meet the challenges posed by the collapse of the Soviet Union only five years later.

Third, Vietnam's society changed almost entirely after 1986. People were free to pursue their economic choices. Farmers decided what to grow in their fields. Urban dwellers could choose between staying in their jobs in the state sector or moving out to work for the private sector, or opening their own businesses. People thought and cared more about their own lives and their family's well-being than before. They did not hesitate too much to try out new opportunities. One could feel the whole society had been reborn with a new spirit and dynamism. The media began to promote vigorously the emancipation of the mind, calling for bold reform and the acceptance of "good ideas" imported from abroad hitherto banned in the past but becoming applicable and suitable to the changing circumstances in Vietnam. Fresh ideas and indigenous innovation were welcome, first and foremost from within the Party apparatus and then in society. In just a few years, Vietnamese people saw their living standards improve and their daily lives become easier. They started to talk about more luxurious commodities such as motorcycles, refrigerators, and colour television sets that they were now able to afford. People became more confident and developed a new way of thinking and doing things so long as it helped them get rid of poverty. There was a new confidence within the country and the enthusiasm with which the reforms were adopted was palpable. Things were never going to return to the previous state of affairs and a true revolution had occurred.

All policy and social changes would have failed if there was no major shift in Vietnam's international relations. Vietnam was isolated in the world following its intervention in Cambodia in 1979. It maintained its foreign relationships mainly with the Socialist block and sided with the Soviet Union against the United States, China and the Association of Southeast Asian Nations (ASEAN). Notwithstanding the situation, the Sixth Party Congress did not entirely break from the previous "one-sided tilt" (*nhất biên đảo*) policy; it did open the possibility of change in foreign policy and was directly instrumental in the formation of Vietnam's shift in international affairs with Politburo Resolution no. 13 in May 1988. The emancipation of mind helped shape Vietnam's foreign relations perceptions and worldview which acknowledged that the closed-door policy did not serve the country's interests. A policy of multilateralization and diversification of foreign relations was adopted, leading to a series of concrete actions that gradually broke its isolation and opened the country to the outside world, such as Vietnam's withdrawal of its troops from Cambodia in 1989. The foreign policy debate at the top level of the Party in the following three years resulted in the official approval of the guidelines set forth by Politburo Resolution no. 13 at the Seventh Party Congress in 1991.

An important element that constituted the conjuncture in 1986 was the continued existence of the system, although with modifications and improvements to cope with the changing domestic and international setting. Although a market-oriented economic concept was introduced, it did not, however, change the nature of Vietnam's economy immediately and altogether. There were also some important continuities that existed alongside the changes. The government retained its strong control over the economy through state-owned enterprises and could intervene in the market if it found such action necessary. The political structure basically remained unchanged with the monopoly of the Communist Party as the country's only leading force. They all combined to facilitate Vietnam's smoother transition to the last decade of the twentieth century without social, economic and political disruption as had happened in some Eastern European countries in the late 1980s when the Communist governments fell.

As such, from the outset *doi moi* was initiated and driven by the negative impacts of the economic policy failures, which later triggered an acute socio-economic crisis. Political debates at the top level made it possible for pro-reform leaders to convince and then win over conservative ones. The decision to adopt *doi moi* did not put an end to a long process of policy experiments and gradual reforms in Vietnam; rather, it proved reforms were right and necessary, and should be done as the only way to repair the existing errors of the system and save Vietnam from dragging itself deeper into crisis. Vietnam began to undergo real and multifaceted transformations and *doi moi* opened up an entirely new phase of development for Vietnam in the decades to come.

Needless to say, at the time when *doi moi* was implemented, the situation was a contingent one. Party officials could simply have allowed the existing situation to continue that in all likelihood would have undermined the credibility of the Communist Party. With foreign assistance from previous allies like China and the Soviet Union not forthcoming, there was a sense of siege. Yet, at the time when the new policy was implemented, it was by no means certain that the reformists in the Party could have trumped the more conservative faction to bring about robust change. Whereas the luxury of hindsight makes the situation appear inevitable, it was certainly not the case when the crisis was unfolding. There is little doubt that were it not for the introduction of the new economic policy in 1986, the situation in Vietnam would have unfolded differently. It would then indeed be a sorry state of affairs to have won the wars and then lost the peace that followed.

Notes

1. Tran Hoang Kim, *Vietnam's Economy: The Period 1945–1995 and Its Perspective by the Year 2020* (Hanoi: Statistical Publishing House), 1996, p. 202.

2. Unofficial estimates of Vietnamese food imports in 1979 went up 2.5 million tons.

3. Kim, *Vietnam's Economy*, p. 203.

4. Thaveeporn Vasavakul, "Vietnam: Sectors, Classes, and the Transformation of a Leninist State", in *Driven by Growth: Political Change in the Asia-Pacific Region*, edited by James W. Morley (New York: Sharpe, 1999), p. 69.

5. Le Duan's detailed discussion on the district can be traced back to his assessments of the achievements and shortcomings of the Party's leadship in the agricultural activities. For instance, see Lê Duẩn, *Cách Mạng Xã Hội Chủ Nghĩa Ở Việt Nam: Tác Phẩm Chọn Lọc, vol. 3* [Socialist revolution in Vietnam: Selected works] (Hanoi: Su That Publishers, 1980), pp. 466–69.

6. Vasavakul, "Vietnam: Sectors, Classes", p. 70.

7. Communist Party of Vietnam, *Văn Kiện Đại Hội Đại Biểu Toàn Quốc Lần thứ VI* [Sixth National Congress: Documents] (Hà Nội: Nhà Xuất Bản Sự Thật, 1987), p. 19.

8. Nayan Chanda, "Vietnam's Battle of the Home Front", *Far Eastern Economic Review (FEER)*, 2 November 1979.

9. An estimated figure puts the Vietnamese casualties from mid-1977 to December 1988 at 55,000 dead and 60,000 wounded, with thousands more afflicted with malaria (see Gary Klintworth, *The Vietnamese Achievement in Cambodia*, Working Paper no. 181, Strategic and Defence Studies Centre, Australian National University, Canberra, May 1989). Vietnamese casualties have also been said to have exceeded the casualties of the resistance war against the French. Some sources even put the figure up to one million.

10. Adam Fforde and Anthony Goldstone, *Vietnam to 2005: Advancing on All Fronts* (London: Economist Intelligence Unit), 1995, p. 4.

11. Vasavakul, "Vietnam: Sectors, Classes", p. 71.

12. In recent years, more information has emerged to indicate that Trường Chinh, the then General Secretary of the CPV, played a vital role in pushing *doi moi* ahead. He served as a middle-man in the Poliburo to harmonize all the different views and was courageous enough to step down, giving way to Nguyễn Văn Linh. He was the one who reviewed the documents to be presented to the Sixth Congress and he personally left his marks on those documents.

13. Đào Duy Tùng, "Mấy Vấn Đề Về Đổi Mới Tư Duy" [Some issues about emancipation of mind], *Tạp Chí Cộng Sản*, no. 2 (1987): 9–10.

14. Anne Booth, "An Economic Overview of Southeast Asia", in *Southeast Asian Affairs 1992*, edited by Daljit Singh (Singapore: Institute of Southeast Asian Studies), 1992, pp. 35–36.

15. Đỗ Mười, "Diễn Văn Tại Lễ Kỷ Niệm Lần Thứ 45 Quốc Khánh 2-9" [Speech at the ceremony commemorating the 45th National Day on 2 September], *Tạp Chí Cộng Sản*, no. 9 (1990): 8.

References

Booth, Anne. "An Economic Overview of Southeast Asia". In *Southeast Asian Affairs 1992*, edited by Daljit Singh. Singapore: Institute of Southeast Asian Studies, 1992.

Communist Party of Vietnam. *Văn Kiện Đại Hội Đại Biểu Toàn Quốc Lần thứ VI* [Sixth National Congress: Documents], Hà Nội: Nhà Xuất Bản Sự Thật, 1987.

Chanda, Nayan. "Vietnam's Battle of the Home Front". *Far Eastern Economic Review (FEER)*, 2 November 1979.

Duẩn, Lê. *Cách Mạng Xã Hội Chủ Nghĩa Ở Việt Nam: Tác Phẩm Chọn Lọc, vol. 3* [Socialist revolution in Vietnam: Selected works]. Hanoi: Su That, 1980.

Fforde, Adam and Goldstone, Anthony. *Vietnam to 2005: Advancing on All Fronts*. London: Economist Intelligence Unit, 1995.

Kim, Tran Hoang. *Vietnam's Economy: The Period 1945–1995 and Its Perspective by the Year 2020*. Hanoi: Statistical Publishing House, 1996.

Klintworth, Gary. *The Vietnamese Achievement in Cambodia*, Working Paper no. 181. Strategic and Defence Studies Centre, Australian National University, Canberra, 1989.

Mười, Đỗ. "Diễn Văn Tại Lễ Kỷ Niệm Lần Thứ 45 Quốc Khánh 2–9" [Speech at the ceremony commemorating the 45th National Day on 2 September]. *Tạp Chí Cộng Sản*, no. 9, 1990.

Tùng, Đào Duy. "Mấy Vấn Đề Về Đổi Mới Tư Duy" [Some issues about emancipation of mind]. *Tạp Chí Cộng Sản*, no. 2, 1987.

Vasavakul, Thaveeporn. "Vietnam: Sectors, Classes, and the Transformation of a Leninist State". In *Driven by Growth: Political Change in the Asia-Pacific Region*, rev ed., edited by James W. Morley, pp. 59–82. New York: M.E Sharpe, 1999.

4

THE 1988 UPRISING IN MYANMAR
Historical Conjuncture or Praetorian Redux?

Tin Maung Maung Than

The 1988 popular uprising that ended the Socialist era of political governance and state building in Myanmar had all the makings of a significant historical conjuncture[1] that not only transformed the country's political and economic systems as well as the nature of ethnic insurgencies but also brought Myanmar's contentious domestic issues to the attention of the international community. It coincided with the emergence of the triumphant outlook of Western democracies capitalizing on the apparent democratic turn following the collapse of Leninist regimes in Europe and brought about the internationalization of Myanmar's security, political and economic issues, premised upon liberal norms of human rights and democracy. The resulting polarized discourse on the country's political and economic reform agenda became part of the contested legacy of the aborted "Four Eights Movement"[2] representing the crest of the revolutionary tide seen by the counter elites as a harbinger of a new political order. However, the democratic aspirations were not realized and the movement's momentum was quickly dissipated as the Tatmadaw (literally meaning royal force), or Myanmar armed forces, re-emerged as the principal steward of Myanmar's destiny.[3] Differing interpretations of that legacy by the military regime and its domestic and foreign detractors have led to divergent attempts of reproduction that have yet to be resolved. On the other hand, a more paranoid, autocratic and powerful regime than the deposed BSPP (Burma Socialist Programme Party) regime emerged in the aftermath of the 1988 uprising, premised on the perpetuation of the Tatmadaw control over political and economic spaces. However, the new constitutional order that took some two decades to become institutionalized through the 2008 Constitution has given some hope for an irreversible change in the political system. This chapter will attempt to identify antecedent conditions preceding the conjuncture and trace the bankruptcy of the BSPP state leading to the rupture in 1988. It will be shown that the apparent lessons learnt by the Tatmadaw leaders are at odds with the democratic aspirations of the new counter-elites that emerged from the conjuncture. Continuities are also found in agencies and structures dominating the political landscape and the political economy of post-1988 Myanmar. Even the domestic security dynamics that apparently took on a different paradigm with unprecedented ceasefire arrangements seems to be reverting back to the pre-1988 mode as tensions over old issues of autonomy and self-determination flared up recently after two decades of accommodation between the government and the ethnic armed groups.[4]

The chapter is divided into three parts. To appreciate the changes and continuities that manifested after the 1988 uprising (as highlighted in Table 4.1) the first part summarizes the development of Myanmar's political ideology and structures and identifies the important players in the political process in the period "before" the conjuncture. The second part deals with the 1988 uprising itself, while the third part delineates the political structures and processes that evolved "after" the 1988 uprising together with specific examples of change and continuity. This approach is aimed at illustrating the changes in the political and economic system, civil society participation as well as modalities of managing internal security challenges and foreign policy implementation that followed the rupture of the state-society relationship in Myanmar brought about by the historical conjuncture of 1988. Some of these changes occurred fairly quickly while others took some two decades to evolve, while the dominating role of the military in politics continues.

Table 4.1
Myanmar: Changes and Continuities

	Pre-1988 upheaval (Burma)	Post-1988 upheaval (Myanmar)*
Political system and Government (break)	Per 1974 Constitution (Const.74) Single party (BSPP) rule; unicameral parliament; voting to accept or reject BSPP nominee; ex-military BSPP personnel dominated executive, judiciary & legislature; Council of State (President) oversaw Cabinet (Prime Minister)	Per 2008 Constitution (Const.08) Multi-party competition; bicameral parliament; voters' choice; ex-military personnel dominate the executive at central & provincial governments; executive Presidency (selection through electoral college of parliamentarians)
Administrative structure (change)	Four-tier elected hierarchy: central, provincial, township, village/ward; capital city: Rangoon (per Const.74)	Three tier elected: central & two provincial levels; civil administration at district & township; capital city: Naypyitaw (per Const.08)
Military (continuity; more power)	Under BSPP control but dual role for all practical purposes; military personnel were party members; given positions in state agencies & civil service; counter-insurgency (COIN) posture	High autonomy; Commander-in-Chief with unprecedented powers; reserved Cabinet portfolios & 25% parliamentary seats for military (per Const.08); positions in state agencies & civil service; mixed COIN & conventional war-fighting posture
Insurgency (change)	Effected all major ethnic groups; controlled some territory; military solution sought unsuccessfully	Greatly reduced in numbers & territory; all co-opted armed ethnic groups required to be placed under Tatmadaw control but exceptions given; military pressure continues
Society (change)	Virtually no NGOs; BSPP controlled class & mass organizations only; depoliticized public; state-owned media with very limited private print media under tight censorship; some tension between polity and military.	Significant numbers of "national" NGOs; many local or community based CSOs; politicized public; state-owned media with expanded private media (print, radio, TV) under selective censorship; tension between polity and military

continued on next page

Table 4.1 — *cont'd*

	Pre-1988 upheaval (Burma)	Post-1988 upheaval (Myanmar)
Economic system (break)	Inward-looking, command oriented; state monopoly in services, trade & industry with very little room for private sector; ODA dependent; private agriculture under state control; FDI not welcome	Market & export oriented; state ownership largely reduced with increased space for the private sector through privatization & relaxing of state monopolies; no ODA from the West & MLAs; private agriculture mainly free from state control; promote FDI; private oligopolies & rent-seeking
Foreign relations (change)	Strictly neutral & practically reactive; avoided regional organizations; emphasis on personal diplomacy	Neutral & both proactive & reactive; joined regional organizations; sanctioned & criticized by the U.S., EU & Western countries; rely on Chinese & Indian support

Note: BSPP = Burma Socialist Programme Party; CSO = civil society organization; EU = European Union; FDI = foreign direct investment; MLA = multilateral lending agency; NGO = non-governmental organization; ODA = official development assistance.
*The period under military rule before the 2010 elections.

ANTECEDENTS TO THE 1988 UPRISING

A constellation of cherished ideas, notions and themes could be identified as shaping state-building, political power and state-society relations in Myanmar for decades after the country gained independence from Britain in January 1948. Socialism was the core national ideology and national unity, as defined by the ruling elite in relation to the founding myth of Panglong,[5] formed an ideational backdrop to state building, while self-reliance became a preferred strategy of successive regimes. Taken together they foreclosed alternative arrangements, limited policy options and inhibited political and economic change.[6] Religion and the traditional intervention of Buddhist monks (collectively known as the Sangha) in mundane affairs was also a significant factor affecting state-society relations in the otherwise secular state.[7] Strict neutralism and aversion to regional groupings had been the hallmark of Myanmar's foreign policy operating under the long shadow of the Kuomintang intrusion in the decade of the 1950s and the spectre of foreign interference in the country's internal affairs.[8] Some of them lost their exalted status or relevance while others were re-interpreted or underwent significant changes in their character and yet some others continued to persist or linger on in the aftermath of the military coup that truncated the Four Eights Movement. Nevertheless, all of them had influenced the ruling elites in their choice of means and goals and propelled newly independent Myanmar along the path towards a self-reliant socialist state whose eventual failure led to the 1988 uprising that resulted in a new economic paradigm and a unique political system called "discipline flourishing economy". In the following section, socialism as an influential ideational factor is elaborated to better understand the context in which the Myanmar state evolved prior to 1988.

The Socialist Legacy

The socialist legacy of the nationalists' struggle for independence was the most influential ideational anchor in Myanmar politics and political economy until the collapse of the socialist order in 1988. There had "been a widespread acceptance of socialism as the political and economic goal of the Burmese independence movement and of each successive government of Burma since independence".[9] It was also conflated with the legacy of the national hero Bogyoke Aung San who was accorded the legendary role as the father of the Tatmadaw and the architect of independent Myanmar then known as Burma.[10] Consequently,

> [a]lthough socialism was variously interpreted (and implemented) by the leaderships of both the parliamentary and military regimes, its acceptance — as a declarative goal as well as a practical means of solving the country's acute problems — provides the connecting link between Aung San and post-independence Burma's leaders.[11]

Ideas and notions on socialism and its corollaries of economic independence and planning turned out to be remarkably enduring in the post-independence era.[12] Reformulated and reinterpreted by political elites according to their predispositions and experiences, they have inspired recurring visions of creating a just and prosperous society.

For forty years, all Myanmar governments that came to power since the country attained independence in January 1948 claimed to be socialist, professing a preference for equity over growth. The culmination of the socialist legacy was the one-party BSPP state that fell apart under popular revolt in the autumn of 1988.

On the other hand, one needs to trace the evolution of Myanmar's political system and examine the nature of the concomitant stakeholders to situate the 1988 uprising in a historical context. The following sections describe the political setting prior to 1988 and the roles of the military and civil society in the unfolding political process under socialist rule.

Structure of the One Party Socialist State

After a dozen years of parliamentary democracy interrupted by some eighteen months of military caretaker government, a military coup in March 1962 ended constitutional rule and multi-party politics.[13] Thereafter, the military junta that took power abolished all democratic institutions, depoliticized the polity, formed the BSPP as its proxy party and orchestrated the formulation of a new constitution to legitimate its control over the country. The resulting constitution came into force in 1974 instituting a unitary one-party socialist state led by the BSPP.[14] Electoral representation was based on a four-tier hierarchy consisting of three regional people's councils (ward/village, township, and state/division) and the Pyithu Hluttaw (parliament), held on a quadrennial basis. However, given the BSPP's prerogative of nominating "official" candidates, elections implied confirmation rather than competition.[15]

The separation of powers between the executive, judicial and legislative bodies were more nominal than substantive and the BSPP-dominated unicameral Pyithu Hluttaw was supportive of the executive branch as a whole.[16] There were regional and local administrative, judicial, auditing and legal bodies under the central organs of state power.[17] In the administrative hierarchy, executive bodies (people's councils) at different levels were under the supervision of a parallel party hierarchy.[18] The new political order was predicated upon the BSPP exercising centralized authority and pervasive social control through its class and mass organizations over a depoliticized polity.

The resulting political structure was a centralized entity predicated upon a symbiotic relationship among a trinity of institutions, viz., the Party, the state and the military.

Party, State and the Military

Though not assigned a formal political role, the military's influence in Myanmar's governing authority remained undiminished during the BSPP era. In fact, the political leadership was provided by the Party's military formateurs led by (retired) General Ne Win. Although formally subscribing to the BSPP's leading role, the Party organization within the armed forces was structured to ensure that the chain of command was not compromised. The latter reflected the command hierarchy with commanders invariably elected to top Party posts at all levels. Moreover, the military served as a reservoir of human resources for the Party and the state apparatus.[19]

The Party and the government managing Myanmar shared a common ethos in their military heritage. As such, politics resembled a "triangle of accommodation" in which the Party assumed the pre-eminent position relying on the military for support in realizing its goals through the state apparatus.[20] However, tensions between the military and BSPP surfaced from time to time during the fourteen years of one-party rule.[21]

On the other hand, due to economic constraints, a strictly neutral foreign policy and Party control over the distribution of meagre resources, the Myanmar armed forces were professionally weak and poorly equipped. Continuously fighting against multiple ethnic and ideological insurgencies for four decades, by the end of the 1980s, it was facing seventeen major insurgent groups on a self-reliant basis with a force of around two-and-a-half times the combined enemy strength. It was commanded by less than a score of general officers and had very limited conventional fighting capacity.[22]

Civil Society Organizations

Civil society may be described as a "web of all privately-organised interests and groups, above the family level but below the state".[23] Civil society organizations (CSOs) could also be classified as "nonstate, nonmarket groups that take collective action in the pursuit of the public good".[24] It could be argued that in the parliamentary era (1948–62) there was a semblance of civil society comprising trade and student unions as well as religious, social welfare, community, and fraternal associations (based on common native place), as both political and non-political organizations could be formed freely. Most of the trade and student unions were affiliated with political parties. Moreover, the existence of powerful local strongmen patronized by the political elite also led to weakened central authority and repressed societal formations.[25] The civil war, apathy amongst indigenous races towards one another's problems, and political instability in the second half of the 1950s were not conducive towards the emergence of viable CSOs in the formal sense.

After the military takeover in 1962, the junta obliterated all existing societal institutions and suppressed the disparate elements that survived. The formal closing of political space came with the National Solidarity Act of 1964 outlawing all political organizations and forbidding the formation of new political associations without government permission. Only class and mass organizations (such as for youth, labour, peasants, artistes) and GONGO (government organized non-governmental organizations, such as the Red Cross) affiliated to the BSPP were allowed to operate, under Party guidance and control.[26] In this context the marginalization of civil society continued under BSPP rule (1974–88) and there was no room for legitimate CSOs that mobilized social groups that "are separate from but address the state".[27] Therefore, one could conclude that civil society in Myanmar was effectively defunct despite the presence of fraternity associations, orthodox religious societies, and philanthropic groups. It is, however, worth noting that there were a number of informal student and monk groups that resembled politically conscious organizations in democratic countries, some of them influenced or penetrated by cadres of the BCP (Burma Communist Party). These organized clandestine elements came out into the open and morphed into social movement organizations that initiated and sustained the 1988 uprising.[28]

FAILURES OF THE ONE-PARTY STATE

The Myanmar state under BSPP supervision maintained a command and control regime that encouraged the growth of a patronage system. The BSPP monopoly of power led to increasing bureaucratization and a privileged class akin to the Soviet *nomenklatura*.[29] Though "inner-party democracy" and "democratic centralism" were the professed guidelines for the modus operandi of the BSPP, "centralism" appeared to have prevailed over "democracy" in practice.[30] This led to authoritarian practices and structural rigidities as the Party became oblivious to socio-political and economic trends within the polity. The result was the ossification of the *nomenklatura* and the widening of the gulf between the centre and the grass roots leading to systemic weaknesses associated with one-party dominance in an authoritarian setting.[31] Though the top political leadership was aware of problems associated with organizational slack, corruption, and poor policy implementation, the root of such shortcoming was attributed to weaknesses of individuals. The Party Chairman's adage of preferring "goodness" (read loyalty) to "ability" became the Party's maxim, inhibiting critical analyses of policy failures and systemic problems.[32] As an established one-party system operating with impunity, the BSPP failed to discern the erosion of its superstructure and the signs of sclerosis through apathy, confusion, complacency, and corruption.[33] Thus, the BSPP leadership was caught off guard by the explosion of suppressed discontent that engulfed Myanmar in 1988.

Meanwhile, the economy faltered after 1985 due to self-inflicted shortcomings in policies on trade, production and investment.[34] Rising inflation and shortages of consumer goods brought economic hardship to the populace, while the *nomenklatura* enjoyed access to scarce commodities and special services.[35] By 1987 the economy was in dire straits. The state's responses, such as securing the LDC (least developed country) status from the United Nations and demonetizing bank notes, were damaging to the pride and well-being of the polity and did little to arrest the deteriorating economic situation.[36]

The Party's overall response to the economic hardships and political discontent among the masses was more of a hortatory and bureaucratic nature with the Party leadership remaining ambivalent towards much-needed reforms even when faced with sporadic outbreaks of public disorder in the first half of 1988.[37] Failing to establish "performance legitimacy" the political regime of the one-party socialist state collapsed under the weight of economic failures and subsequent mass uprising in reaction to the harsh suppression of dissent and demonstrations.

THE UPRISING OF 1988

By 1987 Myanmar's urban masses suffered under the burden of escalating costs of living and hardship brought about by the failing economy. Public grievances against the government were heightened by the government's inability to resolve economic problems, resulting in an almost bankrupt state.[38] Dissident students and other political activists together with existing underground groups coalesced to form groups that tried to organize anti-government activities in some cities and towns. Following a minor off-campus brawl between some engineering students and some outsiders that broke out near the Rangoon Institute of Technology (RIT) in the middle of March 1988, student protests escalated into a violent riot due to mishandling by local authorities. In the course of its suppression, a student was fatally shot, infuriating students of RIT and other tertiary institutions in Yangon. Instigation by emerging student leaders led to anti-government rallies at the university campuses.[39] This was the beginning of the historic conjuncture that set into motion a runaway sequence of actions and reactions between the regime and the masses that led to the collapse of the socialist order.

When the government closed the universities, students, infiltrated by BCP underground cadres and inspired by leftist revolutionary ideals, decided to expand the target of their mobilization to the entire nation by calling for nationwide protests. The BSPP government initially reacted by forcefully cracking down on the demonstrations. A vicious cycle of demonstrations, repression and respite (which attracted unprecedented external media attention) ensued.[40] Amidst uncertainty and apprehension brought about by the sour mood of the public over what was perceived as unduly harsh repression of demonstrations over genuine grievances, an extraordinary session of the BSPP Congress was convened in July 1988. There, on 23 July, BSPP Chairman U Ne Win mooted the idea of considering a multiparty system, thereby whetting the appetite of the protesters and dissidents for political change towards a multiparty system. He surprised the Party representatives in the audience by stating provocatively:

> I submit to this Congress to seek a decision through a nationwide vote [referendum] which the majority of the people choose from the two, a one-party system or a multiparty system.... whichever of the two the people support ... I shall leave the political arena and turn away from politics.[41]

According to Dr Maung Maung (then Chairman of the Council of People's Attorneys and akin to the Attorney General), his biographer and a legal expert, the Party Chairman "sounded a stern note of warning", to the "people in all the country" that "when mobs resort to anarchy" and the "army" needed to be "turned out, soldiers are trained to shoot straight on order, not overhead into the air".[42] Unfortunately, the Party apparatchiks did not rise to the occasion and make bold decisions that resonated with the restive masses, thereby losing the last chance to redeem the Party.

They dithered and hesitated while waiting for cues from the top that never came. The die was cast when they rejected the referendum proposal of the Party Congress, in essence denied "what mattered most to the people of Myanmar", and all other measures aimed at reforming the economy and replacing the top Party leadership came to naught in the "gathering storm".[43] In fact, the already fragile situation rapidly deteriorated with the election of U Sein Lwin as Party Chairman and state President on 26 and 27 July respectively. The new president's speech to the central organs of state power on 2 August, revealing that wide-ranging economic reforms would "soon" be introduced, failed to impress the protestors; nor did his promise to redress "malpractices" within the Party and the state agencies.[44] When the new leadership deployed army troops to fire upon the demonstrators, the dissidents together with underground elements and veteran politicians reacted by mobilizing the public into a pro-democracy movement for regime change that intensified in August 1988. The movement came to be known as the Four Eights Movement, in view of the bloody confrontation on 8 August 1988 that ignited the fire to push for revolutionary change and set off the action-reaction sequence down the path of confrontation that culminated in the displacement of the BSPP regime by a military junta. Thereafter, the "Four Eights" became the rallying cry for the demonstrators and remains a symbol of resistance for successive generations of dissidents. Violent confrontations between security forces and mobs of protestors as well as clashes among the people themselves ensued and many neighbourhood vigilante groups emerged as concerns for local and communal security heightened. When U Sein Lwin resigned from the Party and state leadership positions on 12 August apparently relenting to popular pressure, the regime's opponents became more confident of ultimate victory; especially when they found an iconic champion in Daw Aung San Suu Kyi (DASSK; married to a British academic and based in the United Kingdom), the only daughter of Myanmar's martyred independence hero General Aung San, who was in town since April to nurse her ailing mother. She entered the fray by writing a letter, entitled "The Formation of a People's Consultative Committee", on 15 August (signed together with a veteran political activist U Htwe Myint) addressed to the Secretary of the State Council.[45]

In a last ditch attempt to calm the public down, the BSPP leadership turned to the civilian Dr Maung Maung to lead the country as Party Chairman and President (from 19 August). By then, the protests had spread to every corner of the country mimicking a "people's power" movement. After Dr Maung Maung, on 24 August, revoked the order for military administration and emergency proclamation and promised to hold a referendum to choose between a single party and a multiparty system, there was a short respite in the tide of demonstrations.[46] On 26 August Daw Aung San Suu Kyi made a historic speech near the place where her father once addressed the people. This propelled her to the centre stage of Myanmar politics as democracy icon and charismatic leader of the disparate mass movement for regime change.[47] In the following weeks, the BSPP virtually stopped functioning as grass-roots cadres melted away while civil servants abandoned their posts and took to the streets joining hundreds of thousands of demonstrating students, workers, monks and even peasants in dozens of cities and towns. The government was paralyzed. Many unions and associations representing a wide range of professions, vocations and interests sprung up, ostensibly to spearhead the mass protests, and strike committees were proliferating. On 9 September, veteran politician U Nu (former Prime Minister deposed by the coup of 1962) unilaterally declared the formation of a parallel government; a gambit that quickly fell through due to lack of support from other popular leaders of the protest movement. Following an extraordinary BSPP congress resolution on 10 September, the extraordinary Pyithu Hluttaw session on 11 September agreed to hold a multiparty election and an election commission was subsequently formed.[48] He also requested the people to call off the demonstrations so that the government could make the necessary arrangements for holding multiparty elections. The commander-in-chief of the Tatmadaw even made an impassioned appeal, on 12 September, to the public urging the people to help restore peace and tranquillity and promising to support the promised free and fair elections in which the Tatmadaw would remain impartial.[49] Unfortunately, the regime's reactions to escalating demands of the emboldened opposition movement were, all along, constrained by its legalistic and formal approach premised upon upholding the state Constitution and BSPP charter. They were perceived as too little too late and failed to bridge the considerable gap in confidence and trust between the government and opposition. Refusing to accept the president's promises and reassurances, demands for an interim government were stepped up and protestors returned to the streets.[50] Meanwhile, the country saw the rise of radical elements that thrived on anarchy. There were also instances of defection by some soldiers and the opposition egged on the soldiers to prove their mettle as "patriotic soldiers" by joining the "revolution" a la the Philippines. The military leaders became increasingly alarmed by the vitriolic abuse hurled at the army by some in the crowds and rumours of Western intervention[51] as well as disinformation and insinuations about fissures and cleavages within the Tatmadaw. The protestors even mobbed the Defence Ministry headquarters on 16 September, hurling vulgarities and daring the soldiers to shoot them.[52] Meanwhile, some groups armed themselves with homemade weapons and even seized the weapons of a heavily armed army platoon trapped by the mob in downtown Yangon.[53] At this stage, the popular leaders of the Four Eights movement remained far from unified and seemed to have no clear "end game" strategy to reach a peaceful resolution involving the military as a stakeholder instead of an adversary.[54] Myanmar's military leaders became increasingly perturbed by the twin spectres of a divided military and an armed uprising under BCP manipulation and on 18 September the then Commander in Chief General Saw Maung stepped in to take over state power from the already "defunct" government.[55] After the coup, the military crushed the opposition movement by sheer force of arms, breaking up demonstrations, smashing protestors' strongholds (popularly known as strike or boycott camps) and arresting many of the protestors. The military junta known as the State Law and Order Restoration Council (SLORC), later reconstituted as the State Peace and Development Council (SPDC) in November 1997, had effectively cut short the Four Eights movement and imposed martial law while retaining the deposed regime's promise of holding free and fair elections in due course.[56] The military leadership of the day interpreted the tumultuous events of 1988 as precipitated by economic deprivation unleashing anarchic societal impulses in the absence of a strong and decisive government whose woes were further aggravated by foreign interference as well as instigation by communist and other agent provocateurs.[57]

THE LEGACIES OF 1988

Though the Four Eights Movement failed to achieve change from a bureaucratic authoritarian regime to liberal democracy as envisaged by its leaders, the historical conjuncture identified with the 1988 uprising did introduce many significant changes in Myanmar.[58] Its legacy includes transformations in the socio-political makeup of Myanmar, the state-society relationship and the long-standing ethnic insurgency problem. Even the country's name was changed from Burma to Myanmar which is nearer to the vernacular name, symbolizing a break from the colonial past and signifying a new nationalist era under military tutelage. A self-contained new national capital, named Naypyitaw (literally meaning Royal Abode), was built from scratch in central Myanmar away from potential protesters and providing strategic depth against foreign invasion.[59] Perhaps the most significant legacy is the total abandonment of socialism as a guiding principle for both politics and economics. Apart from creating a class of nouveau riche,[60] this led to the opening up of the economy to foreign investments, expansion of natural resource exports, marketization of trade and commerce, and deregulation of agriculture (mainstay of the economy), while at the same time increasing opportunities for widespread rent-seeking. As a result, the financial and material resources of the government have increased by leaps and bounds compared to the socialist era. This change, in turn, has allowed the junta to expand its capacity for dealing with subsequent challenges to its authority and legitimacy from home and abroad and rapidly modernize as well as expand the Tatmadaw.

Institutional Change: A New Constitution

The military rulers were cognizant of the people's desire for democracy and spared no effort to formulate a political order that would legitimately ensure their continued dominance of the political arena and the military as an autonomous institution. After two decades of twists and turns during which SLORC oversaw an abrogated election (in May 1990) in which the professed opposition party, the National League for Democracy (NLD) won some 80 per cent of the seats, the junta seems to have got what it wanted in the 2008 Constitution that was arrived at through carefully managed National Convention (NC) proceedings lasting fourteen years. This is part of a seven-step "road map" towards "discipline flourishing democracy" revealed on 30 August 2003 by the (then) Prime Minister General Khin Nyunt. It entailed the reconvening of the NC (suspended since 1996 and reconvened in 2004); a gradual implementation of the NC's deliberative process; drafting a new Constitution according to the basic principles and details endorsed by the NC; holding a national referendum to adopt the Constitution (successfully adopted with over 92 per cent affirmative votes and promulgated on 29 May 2008); holding of free and fair elections (in November 2010) for a hierarchy (national and regional) of legislative bodies or *pyithu hluttaws* (people's assemblies); convening of the national assembly; and finally ushering in a "a modern, developed and democratic nation" governed by leaders elected in accordance with the new Constitution.[61]

The new unitary state with shades of quasi-federalist elements distinctive in its emphasis on the military's direct and indirect roles in governance (reserved portfolios in the Cabinet) and legislative functions (military nominees for one quarter of seats in central and regional parliaments) right down to the regional level.[62] It also ensures complete autonomy for the military in both budgetary and internal matters. In fact, with the support of the National Defence and Security Council (military majority in membership), the military chief could virtually take over state power constitutionally in emergency situations. On the other hand, the constitutional criteria for the executive presidency ensure that the powerful head of state is divorced from party politics, someone with a military background and acceptable to the military.[63]

Emergence of Counter Elites

The Four Eights Movement spawned counter elites in the form of student leaders and democracy activists who have carried on their struggle despite intense repression. The most prominent group is the so-called 88-Generation, student leaders who were arrested for their roles in the Four Eights Movement and released from incarceration in the last couple of years and gained prominence for their renewed activism over human rights, justice and economic hardship issues. They were re-arrested in August 2007 for involvement in public dissent and protest over fuel price hikes and sentenced to long prison sentences, yet remain defiant.[64] They have inspired second-echelon leaders and political activists from among students and youth, many of whom were too young to be part of the Four Eights Movement.[65]

Activists advocating for human rights have also emerged to represent disadvantaged sections of the polity on issues such as HIV/AIDS, forced labour, dispossessed farmers, local injustice and labour rights. They persist despite being harassed and persecuted.[66]

The singular exemplar of counter elites is Daw Aung San Suu Kyi, who won the Nobel Peace Prize in 1991 and many more international prizes and honours for her personal sacrifices and steadfast stand on human rights and democracy in Myanmar, the charismatic leader of the NLD. Internationally acclaimed, but often vilified by the junta as a stooge of

Western neo-imperialism, she stands as a beacon of hope to the supporters of the Four Eights Movement. Despite overwhelming odds she pits her idealism and moral authority against the junta's attempt to fashion a new political order to their advantage.[67]

NGOs and CSOs on the Rise

Immediately upon seizing power, the military government followed its predecessor's example and sought to restrict the organizations that could challenge its rule. In addition, the junta created several new organizations that may be classified as GONGOs, such as the Union of Myanmar Federation of Chambers of Commerce and Industry (UMFCCI), the Myanmar War Veterans Association, the Myanmar Fisheries Federation, the Myanmar Maternal and Child Welfare Association, Myanmar Anti-Narcotics Association, Myanmar National Committee for Women Affairs, and the Union Solidarity and Development Association (USDA). The junta has controlled the way these organizations function by appointing or influencing the choice of their leaders and utilizing them for regime support and social control. For instance, the USDA — an association of some twenty-four million members led by senior government ministers — had been used to mobilize rallies either in support of the regime's goals and actions as well as to monitor and suppress the activities of the opposition movement.[68] The junta also tried to control and co-opt the pre-existing organizations such as the Red Cross, auxiliary fire brigade and professional and vocational associations (e.g., artistes, writers and journalists, musicians, doctors), often by replacing their leadership with people it trusted.

Although the military government restricted political associations, it allowed non-political civil society organizations to operate. A large number of local groups and sociocultural organizations remained and in fact continued to function. In addition, many new development-oriented organizations, working in areas like the environment, health, education, and social welfare, emerged in various parts of the country.

Since the government's expansion of legal associational space in the mid-1990s, both international and domestic NGOs have been allowed to work on social development programmes. Dozens of international NGOs and scores of local CSOs have been actively engaged in activities that include, *inter alia*, poverty alleviation, micro-credit, community capacity building and self-help, HIV/AIDS issues, environmental conservation, agriculture extension, food security, and early childhood care.[69]

Parallel to all these formal associations are also informal groups that are not registered with government agencies but are tolerated by local authorities. Such organizations operate within a grey area; for though the government is aware of their existence, they are not bothered as long as they do not challenge the government. As such, the number of civil society organizations increased quite significantly between 1988 and 2007.

When tropical Cyclone Nargis hit Myanmar in May 2008, leaving over 130,000 dead and missing and affecting some 2.4 million people in the Ayeyarwady Delta, the local CSOs sprung into action and did an exemplary job of relief and rehabilitation, co-operating with INGOs and foreign relief agencies and oftentimes on their own. New CSOs were also formed out of necessity and it remains to be seen whether they can survive in the long run.[70] Nevertheless the scope and acceptance of CSOs has considerably expanded in the post-1988 era partly due to changing political circumstances and partly to the rise in the ethos of unity and self-help triggered by the experience of the chaotic situation during the uprising and a sense of depravation thereafter.

State-society Relationship

After 1988 the military regime, which identified itself with the state, found itself at odds with much of the polity and the state-society relationship had been strained all along. Despite harsh repression small protests and defiant gestures by dissidents punctuated by bombings remained unabated.[71] Large-scale protests by the revered sangha, in 1990 and in September 2007, had to be suppressed by force of arms.[72] Tens of thousands of dissidents have been jailed over the years yet many remain unrepentant. Students have always been difficult to handle though the junta had managed to disperse tertiary students by relocating campuses in major cities to fringe areas far from populated areas and building more colleges and institutes throughout the country. The potential for civil servants joining future protests and the likelihood of demonstrators paralyzing the government is now negligible as the entire government and all its agencies were moved to a new capital called Naypyitaw situated in an isolated area hundreds of kilometres north of Yangon. The new constitutional government that will inherit this SPDC may find the effort to rebuild the trust and gain legitimacy an uphill task.[73]

Ceasefires and Insurgency

The insurgency that plagued Myanmar for more than four decades was drastically transformed when the military junta managed to arrange ceasefires with seventeen major armed groups by exploiting their weaknesses and the changing regional and international situation, especially with the ending of the Cold War. Using a carrot and stick approach and discarding the traditional insistence on total surrender of arms, the former adversaries were allowed to maintain their force structure, bear arms, keep most of the territory, run a quasi-autonomous administration and operate businesses under relaxed rules. Extending direct financial support and developmental assistance, building infrastructure and providing lucrative natural resource extraction franchises sweetened the deals that did not involve written agreement in all but one case (with the Kachins). It was hoped that in time they could be weaned away from illegal practices and be reintegrated within the Myanmar state and eventually disarmed and demobilized. So far, this has not materialized and tensions have arisen as the new Constitution forbids armed groups other than the Tatmadaw. The most powerful among sizeable ceasefire groups had refused to be transformed into a border guard force under military control, threatening the integrity of the 2008 Constitution which stipulates that all "armed forces in the Union shall be under the command of the Defence Services" (Article 338) and whose ratification in the referendum was endorsed by a huge majority in those territories under these intransigent ceasefire groups. This defiance by the Wa, Kachins, Mons and Shan ceasefire groups could well be the most problematic legacy issue in the post-1988 political trajectory carved out by the junta. If unresolved, it would compound the military security problem with a human security dilemma and carries the danger of reverting back to military confrontation after nearly two decades of uneasy peace in the borderlands of Myanmar.[74]

Tatmadaw Redux?

The post-1988 military has become the most powerful and cohesive institution in Myanmar. It has survived the unravelling of the socialist state to become the arbiter as well as the guardian of the Myanmar state.

The Tatmadaw leaders seem to believe that the three principal "national causes", defined as "non-disintegration of the Union, non-disintegration of national [i.e., multiracial] solidarity, and perpetuation of national sovereignty", require fashioning a new political order in line with their own interpretation of Myanmar's historical experiences in nation building. As such, a political configuration that would institutionalize the military's role in "national politics" as a solution to the problem of dysfunctional "party politics" was sought.[75]

It has transformed itself from a resource-poor counter-insurgency oriented force to a relatively modern military, equipped and structured to fight a conventional war. The number of general officers has grown nearly ten times; infantry manpower more than doubled and boasts a largely expanded navy and air force. Modern weaponry and equipment such as armoured personnel carriers, heavy tanks, long-range artillery, multiple rocket launchers, anti-aircraft and short-range missiles, supersonic fighters and attack aircraft, helicopter gunships and advanced communications and electronic warfare suites were acquired from, *inter alia*, China, Russia, Pakistan, Eastern Europe, Israel, and Singapore to the tune of over US$2 billion. This had resulted in a formidable force with upgraded and expanded facilities for armaments production, training, logistics and medical support.[76]

The Tatmadaw has secured a pivotal role in the Myanmar state not only through constitutional arrangements but also by placing military personnel in key roles in the civil service and running its own monopolistic economic enterprises that control lucrative foreign trade deals and profitable industries. The corporate interests of the military have been well looked after.[77]

Externally Oriented Foreign Policy

Under direct military rule Myanmar's foreign policy was portrayed by the government as "independent" and "active". It proclaimed that, "Myanmar will not align with any bloc on international issues except to consistently stand on the side that is right" while it "actively participates in activities for world peace; opposes war, imperialism and colonialism; and maintains friendly relations with all countries."[78]

Facing diplomatic pressure from the United Nations as well as the United States, European Union (EU) and many Western governments — which had imposed sanctions on Myanmar — for not honouring the

1990 elections, repeated breaches of human rights and political repression (including incarceration of some 2,000 "political prisoners" including Aung San Suu Kyi (freed soon after the November 2010 elections), Myanmar had reached out to the Middle East and Africa as well as regional and sub-regional organizations hitherto shunned by successive governments prior to 1988.[79] It joined the Association of Southeast Asian Nations (ASEAN) in July 1997. It also joined BIMSTEC (Bay of Bengal Initiative for Multi-Sectoral Technical and Economic Cooperation) and sub-regional arrangements such as ACMES (Ayeyawady Chao Phraya Mekong Economic Cooperation Strategy) and the MGC (Mekong Ganga Cooperation) initiative and participated in forums such as the GMS summit and Bao Forum.[80] It even applied for an observer status for SAARC (South Asian Association for Regional Cooperation).[81] Such unprecedented outreach could be interpreted as reflecting the "military regime's perceived 'domestic political-security imperative'", whereby sovereignty and territorial integrity, regime security, and "deepening relations" with friendly "international partners" — whose help is vital for economic development — remain the principal objectives of the current foreign policy.[82]

Moreover, Myanmar's economic and political relations with China and India (the two major Asian powers) have grown in an unprecedented manner over the last fifteen years resulting in a convergence of national interests in the respective dyadic relationship and a sort of competition between China and India over Myanmar's natural resources has developed. In fact, from the beginning of military rule in 1988, China has been increasingly involved in Myanmar's economic and military development. Moreover, China had turned out to be a potent shield against Western punitive measures and a counterpoise to international pressures for political liberalization. Similarly, India had assumed a significant role in supporting the military regime through expansion of trade, investment and development assistance since the mid 1990s.[83]

HISTORICAL BAGGAGE AND SPECTRES FROM THE PAST AMIDST SYSTEMIC CHANGE

Despite the aforementioned legacies of the 1988 uprising it is also true that the current major protagonists in Myanmar's political drama who are in contention over their own visions of democracy and security have been largely influenced by different sets of historical baggage informed by negative experiences dating back to the colonial period and as recent as the 1990 elections. This has been further accentuated by personalized authority structures and leadership styles in the military as well as in the democratic opposition.[84] As such, the military leadership has nothing but disdain and contempt for civilian politicians and their so-called "party politics" and is obsessively determined to deter foreign interference, achieve national unity (on its terms), and maintain conformity and public order (especially to prevent a repeat of the 1988 uprising). The ethnic nationalities are, in the main, aspiring to prevent Bamar (Burman) hegemony and restore autonomy which they claim to have been the norm in the past. The NLD and the democratic opposition are trying to create a democratic system of government informed by liberal values and claiming the right to rule by extending indefinitely the legitimacy accorded by decades-old election results. It even declined to re-register as a legal party for the 2010 elections citing unjust election laws and absence of a level playing field, thereby boycotting the forthcoming elections and practically assuring its dissolution as a legal political party.[85]

Vestiges of structural conditions prevalent during the socialist era could also be seen in the post-1988 economy. The formalized economy is split into two transaction circuits: one a kyat-based exchange regime and the other a US$-denominated regime with the latter influencing the former's supply decisions as well. The informal or parallel component comprises the extensive rural-based quasi-subsistence exchange circuit and the illegal black market sector based mainly on transactions involving gold, precious stones, opium, timber, and other scarce and restricted commodities. They are, of course, interconnected by the cross-flows of money, goods and services with each driven by a different economic logic and operating within different parameters that sometimes overlap. The state is concerned mainly with the formal part and, despite occasional forays by the state to control it, the informal part generally lies beyond the umbra of state authority, undermining the latter's attempts to manage the transition process.

As such, the role of the state in Myanmar may not be confined to just providing "public goods" and the "rule of law" conducive to market interactions, but is expected to be more proactive in defining the parameters of development through industrial, trade, and investment policies. Policy measures thus employed would be expected to be more "market-friendly" than in the past, but one cannot rule out direct interventions reminiscent of dirigisme in areas perceived by the military as essential to maintain control over state and society.[86]

The common threads that ran through the increasing interventionist role of the state in Myanmar from 1948 to 1988 had been the notions of self-reliance, the principle of state ownership of the means of production, and the ideals of planned economic development. As such, the primacy of the state's role in relation to (the almost non-existent) non-state institutions and the society at large was taken for granted by the ruling elite who tended to project themselves as the embodiment of the "state qua state". This statist legacy remains and had made the attempts by SLORC/SPDC to institute a market economy open to private initiatives extremely problematic.[87] In fact, the self-reliance paradigm and penchant for planning continued to remain relevant as underlying principles for the modus operandi of the military government. This was especially true in the context of industrialization. The state still made plans following the same methods used during the Socialist era. External trade was controlled by a maze of licences, rules, regulations, and procedures that kept changing, as the state encountered what it perceived as challenges by domestic and foreign business interests. Prices of "essential commodities" such as rice and cooking oil were still "regulated" and Committees for Reduction of Consumer Prices chaired by senior military commanders endeavoured to suppress price inflation through restrictive administrative measures. Diverging trends in the official and the free market exchange rates were, more often than not, tackled by administrative measures against currency traders.[88] Recent privatization of state assets was seen by some observers as more of an "asset stripping" to the benefit of the cronies and ruling elite than a well thought out divesture.[89] In essence, it may be seen as a continuation of the pre-1988 era albeit with a much larger portion for the private sector in the formal economy.

On the other hand, significant systemic change in the political and economic fronts could also be discerned in the post-1988 era. These created their own path-dependent trajectory for the evolution of new forms of political governance and economic configuration shaped by the SLORC/SPDC regime despite resistance and countermeasures from counter elites and regional as well as international players. The inexorable movement towards elections in 2010 under the military's terms and conditions is illustrative of Myanmar's political trajectory since 1990 when the SLORC refused to accept the election results as the right to rule. In fact, the 1990 election result was formally abrogated by the new election law announced in March 2010. The adoption of a market-oriented economy, despite many shortcomings, was also a measure with important consequences that set it apart from the pre-1988 socialist command economy, launching a practically irreversible process of commodification and marketization.

The matrix depicted as Table 4.1 illustrates significant changes and continuities in Myanmar's economy, politics and society as well as international relations brought about by the 1988 upheaval.

CONCLUSION

One could argue that the 1988 uprising was indeed a historical conjuncture that changed the nature of Myanmar's political system in significant ways either due to new or latent socio-political forces unleashed by the episode or by the reaction of the ruling elite whose self-professed historical legacy and core values were threatened by the event. Examples of the former are the rise of counter elites like the 88 Generation students and the socio-political activists challenging the legitimacy, authority and core values of the military elite; the emergence of Daw Aung San Suu Kyi as the icon for political change emphasizing the need for liberal democracy and respect of universal human rights; the expanded role of CSOs in Myanmar society and the dissonance between state and society brought about by political repression and a sense of disfranchisement together with economic deprivation. As for the latter, the ruling junta's interpretation of the episode and the domestic and international repercussions as constituting an existential threat to regime security and personal safety resulted in the following measures that assured and promoted the Tatmadaw's corporate interests and had a profound impact on the nature of constitutional design and management of state-society relations.

These include abandoning socialism as a guiding ideology in both politics and economics; selectively opening up the economy to take advantage of market forces and the international economic environment yet retaining control thorough chokeholds and patronage; drawing rent from the national economy to accumulate financial resources at its disposal; expanding and modernizing the military and creating more opportunities for the officer corps for career advancement and to secure perks in the state sector; building a new capital from scratch and physically segregating/isolating the (unreliable) civil servants and (troublesome) tertiary students from the society at large; transforming the handling of the insurgency problem from pure military terms to a developmental and status quo–maintenance approach by accepting non-institutionalized ceasefires with major ethnic insurgent groups that emphasized re-integration without demanding immediate demobilization and disarmament; and reaching out to draw diplomatic and material support from rising powers in Asia, leveraging on the country's geostrategic position and newly found natural resources while taking advantage of new and long-standing regional and sub-regional organizations.

Nevertheless, it appears that changes in state-society relations and political structure introduced by the apparent historic conjuncture of 1988, operating within a complex milieu of ideational and ethnic divisions, international pressures and military reassertion, remain unconsolidated and reproduction of the resulting legacy is still contested, contentious and problematic. It remains to be seen whether a definitive conclusion can be drawn about their long-term impact and irreversibility and to view them as a clean break from the past.[90]

Notes

1. Conjunctures are "interaction affects between distinct causal sequences that became joined at particular points in time"; see Paul Pierson and Theda Skocpol, "Historical Institutionalism in Political Science", in *Political Science: The State of the Discipline*, edited by Ira Katznelson and Helen V. Milner (New York: Norton, 2001), p. 702.
2. This term is used by the opposition camp, which calls for regime change and liberal democracy. The word *uprising* was the term used by the last BSPP President Dr Maung Maung in his account of the tumultuous period; see Maung Maung, *The 1988 Uprising in Burma* (New Haven: Yale University Press, 1999).
3. See, e.g., Nawarahta, *Destiny of the Nation* (Yangon: New & Periodicals Enterprise, 1995).
4. See, e.g., Anna Louise Strachan, "Going to the Polls: Opportunity or Setback for Myanmar's Ceasefire Groups", *CSA Security Watch* 11 (February 2010).
5. For the Panglong myth, see M.J. Walton, "Ethnicity, Conflict and History in Burma: The Myths of Panglong", *Asian Survey* 48, no. 6 (2008): 889–910.
6. See, e.g., Margaret Weir, "When Does Politics Create Policy?" in *Rethinking Political Institutions: The Art of the State*, edited by Ian Shapiro, Stephen Skowronek and Daniel Gavin (New York: New York University Press, 2006), p. 172.

7. See, e.g., Donald E. Smith, *Religion and Politics Burma* (Princeton, NJ: Princeton University Press, 1965); and Kyaw Yin Hlaing, "Challenging the Authoritarian State: Buddhist Monks and Peaceful Protests in Burma", *Fletcher Forum of World Affairs* 32 no. 1 (2008): 125–44.

8. Nationalist Chinese (Kuomintang) forces routed by Mao's Chinese Communists entered the Shan States and remained ensconced for more than a decade (with covert U.S. support) despite repeated attempts by the Myanmar government to dislodge them through diplomatic efforts at the United Nations and military operations. The United States had been accused repeatedly of interfering in ethnic minority issues and Thailand apparently pursued for decades a policy of utilizing ethnic insurgencies along the border as a buffer. See, *inter alia*, Maung Maung, *Grim War against KMT* (Rangoon: n.p., 1953); and Robert H. Taylor, *Foreign and Domestic Consequences of the KMT Intervention in Burma*, Cornell University Southeast Asia Program, Data Paper no. 93 (Ithaca, NY: Cornell University Southeast Asia Program, 1973); Leilar Thu Tit Oo [An Observer], *Myanmar-American Hset-hsan Yei Thamaing* [History of Myanmar American Relations] (Yangon: Digest Media Bank, 2007); and Maung Aung Myoe, *Neither Friend nor Foe, Myanmar's Relationship with Thailand Since 1988: A View from Yangon* (Singapore: Institute of Defence and Strategic Studies, 2002).

9. Jan Becka, "Planning for New Burma: Major-General Aung San's Views of Economic Development", *Archiv Orientalni* 56 (1988): 12.

10. See, e.g., "Socialism … was an early choice for the freedom movement in Burma … It was the policy of Burma's architect of independence, Bogyoke Aung San", (*Working People's Daily* [hereafter *WPD*], 4 January 1966.

11. Becka, "Planning for New Burma", p. 13.

12. They were received from abroad in the 1930s mainly in the form of "leftist" literature. Incidentally, in articulating concepts like socialism it was found to be necessary to introduce a new terminology in the vernacular. See Robert H. Taylor, "Burmese Concepts of Revolution", in *Context, Meaning and Power in Southeast Asia*, edited by Mark Hobart and Robert H. Taylor (Ithaca, NY: Cornell University Southeast Asia Program, 1986), pp. 80–81.

13. The military coup, staged on the early morning of 2 March 1962, could also be seen as a historical conjuncture because it replaced ruling politicians with military elites, banned free press, abolished unions and depoliticized the polity, nationalized the economy, and left a military-dominated one-party system as its legacy. For details on events leading to the coup, see, e.g., Mya Han and Thein Hlaing, *1958–1962 Myanma Nainganyei* [Myanmar's politics], vol. 4 (Yangon: Universities Press, 1991).

14. See *The Constitution of the Socialist Republic of the Union of Burma* (Rangoon: Ministry of Information, 1974), pp. 2, 4.

15. Voting was confined to either accepting or rejecting the BSPP-approved

candidate. The public, realizing that "elections are not presented as a possible redistribution of power", rarely attempted to nominate an alternative candidate (Theodore H. Friedgut, *Political Participation in the USSR* [Princeton, NJ: Princeton University Press, 1979], p. 72).

16. A BSPP Central Committee meeting was convened before every Pyithu Hluttaw session to determine the agenda and set the stage for the latter.

17. The Council of State, formed with Pyithu Hluttaw representatives, was the highest state authority. The central organs of state power constituted the Council of Ministers (Cabinet), the Council of People's Justices, the Council of People's Attorneys, and the Council of People's Inspectors, whose members were Pyithu Hluttaw representatives selected from a candidature list prepared by the Council of State and approved by the BSPP Central Committee. All central organs of state power were accountable to the Pyithu Hluttaw and, when it was not in session, to the Council of State.

18. The party hierarchy included the Regional Party Committee (RPC; at the state/division level); party unit (township); and party branch, section, and cell (ward/village). Between the quadrennial party congresses the Central Committee was responsible for party affairs but in practice the CEC and the party secretariat were in charge.

19. Although there was no attempt to establish a personality cult, the paramount position of Ne Win in the BSPP (chairman), the state executive (chairman of the Council of State or president), or the military (founding father) was beyond dispute.

20. Senior military officers were Pyithu Hluttaw representatives. Active and retired military personnel maintained an extensive "old boys" network. For party/state development, see, e.g., Robert H. Taylor, *The State in Myanmar* (Singapore: NUS Press, 2009), pp. 316–21.

21. See, e.g., Taylor, *State in Myanmar*, pp. 371–72.

22. See, e.g., Tin Maung Maung Than, "Burma's National Security and Defence Posture", *Contemporary Southeast Asia* 11, no. 1 (1989); and Maung Aung Myoe, *Building the Tatmadaw: Myanmar Armed Forces since 1948* (Singapore: Institute of Southeast Asian Studies, 2009).

23. Adrian Leftwich, "Bringing Politics Back In: Towards a Model of the Developmental State", *Journal of Development Studies* 31, no. 3 (1995): 415.

24. Muthiah Alagappa, "Civil Society and Political Change: An Analytical Framework", in *Civil Society and Political Change in Asia*, edited by Muthiah Alagappa (Stanford, CA: Stanford University Press, 2004), p. 32.

25. See Taylor, *State in Myanmar*, pp. 269–70.

26. For details, see Mya Han et al., *Myanma Nainnganyei Sanitpyaung Karla (1962–1974)* [Myanmar's politics in the period of systemic change], vol. 1 (Yangon: Universities Press, 1993), pp. 51–56, 138–280.

27. Naomi Chazan, "Engaging the State: Associational Life in Sub-Saharan Africa", in *State Power and Social Forces: Domination and Transformation in the Third World*, edited by Joel S. Migdal, Atul Kohli and Vivienne Shue (Cambridge: Cambridge University Press, 1994), p. 278. For a case study on civil society in Myanmar, see David I. Steinberg, "A Void in Myanmar: Civil Society in Burma", in *Strengthening Civil Society in Burma: Possibilities and Dilemmas for International NGOs*, edited by Tom Kramer and Pietje Vervest (Chiangmai: Silkworm Books, 1999), pp. 1–14.

28. See, e.g., Kyaw Yin Hlaing, "Burma: Civil Society Skirting Regime Rules", in Alagappa, "Civil Society", pp. 392–98; and Aung Zaw, "Secrets of Commune 4828", *Irrawaddy* (August 2008), pp. 30–33.

29. Like the Soviet system it encompassed not only key positions determined by party nominations or requiring the latter's consent but also the functionaries who served in them (see, for example, Michael Voslensky, *Nomenklatura: Anatomy of the Soviet Ruling Class*, translated by Eric Mosbacher [London: Bodley Head, 1984], p. 2).

30. For an elaboration of democratic centralism see *[1973 Khu Hnit] Dutiya Akyein Parti Nyilargun Parti Baho Kommiti Okahta Gyi Ei Maintgun Myar Hnint Parti Baho Kommiti Ei Nainganyei Asiyinkhanzar* [Second Party Congress 1973: Speeches of the Central Committee Chairman and the Political Report of the Party Central Committee] (Yangon: Burma Socialist Programme Party, 1974), pp. 235–37.

31. For systemic shortcomings of one-party systems, see, Samuel P. Huntington, "Social and Institutional Dynamics of One-Party Systems", in *Authoritarian Politics in Modern Society: The Dynamics of Established One-Party Systems*, edited by Samuel P. Huntington and Clement H. Moore (New York: Basic Books, 1970), pp. 40–44.

32. See the Chairman's address at the sixth-day session of the Fourth Party Congress, in "The Supplement", *WPD*, 9 August 1981.

33. According to the last BSPP-sanctioned president, Dr Maung Maung, the pathology became more acute after U Ne Win relinquished state duties in 1981 (Maung Maung, *1990 Uprising*, pp. 259, 261–63). See also the comment by a former CEC member, quoted in David I. Steinberg, *Crisis in Burma: Stasis and Change in a Political Economy in Turmoil*, ISIS Paper no. 5 (Bangkok: Institute of Security and International Studies, Chulalongkorn University, 1989), p. 42. For an illuminating Myanmar perspective, see Kyaw Yin Hlaing, "Reconsidering the Failure of the Burma Socialist Programme Party Government to Eradicate Internal Economic Impediments", *South East Asia Research* 11, no. 1 (2003): 5–58.

34. For details, see Tin Maung Maung Than, *State Dominance in Myanmar: The Political Economy of Industrialization* (Singapore: Institute of Southeast Asian Studies, 2007), pp. 193–226.

35. Party, state and military elites were provided with housing, official and family cars as well as access to special shops stocked with imported and restricted consumer goods and were allowed to go abroad for medical treatment.
36. The United Nations announcement in December that according LDC status to Myanmar undermined decades of BSPP's self-congratulatory rhetoric on economic achievements through socialist planning and aroused indignation among proud Myanmars (see Taylor, *State in Myanmar*, pp. 379, 382). The demonetization of currency notes (worth kyats 25 and above) on 12 September 1987 (the second time in two years and the third since May 1964) without any compensation wiped out some 70 per cent of the people's cash holdings leading to student unrest and closure of schools for several weeks (ibid., pp. 380–61).
37. See, e.g., *WPD*, 11 August 1987 as well as 10 October 1987; and Tin Maung Maung Than, "Burma in 1987: Twenty-Five Years after the Revolution", in *Southeast Asian Affairs 1988* (Singapore: Institute of Southeast Asian Studies, 1988), pp. 90–92.
38. See, Taylor, *State in Myanmar*, pp. 376–82 for a summary of the self-inflicted spiraling descent to economic paralysis.
39. See, e.g., Megan Clymer, "Min Ko Naing, 'Conqueror of Kings' Burma's Student Leader", *Journal of Burma Studies* 8 (2003): 33–63 for a personalized account of a student leader's involvement in clandestine activities and the protest movement.
40. Foreign media personnel were not welcome during BSPP rule but some sneaked into the country getting visas under false pretenses. By 1987 the economic malaise attracted more international media attention and Myanmar language radio broadcasts by the BBC and VOA increasingly became influential as alternative and more reliable (than state media) sources of information and foreign journalists were present during many disturbances and protests. See, e.g., Dominic Faulder, "Memories of 8.8.88", *Irrawaddy* (August 2008), pp. 34–37.
41. *WPD*, 24 July 1988.
42. See Maung Maung, *1988 Uprising*, pp. 40–41. In fact according to the English translation the actual statement was "if in future there are mob disturbances, if the army shoots, it hits" (*WPD*, 24 July 1988).
43. See Maung Maung, *1988 Uprising*, p. 53. For a BSPP insider's account of the dramatic events relating to this episode, see ibid., pp. 38–53.
44. *WPD*, 3 August 1988.
45. See, "The First Initiative", in *Aung San Suu Kyi, Freedom from Fear and Other Writings*, edited by Michael Aris (London: Penguin, 1991), pp. 192–97.
46. See *The Guardian*, 28 August 1988.
47. With her entry, notions of liberal democracy combined with Buddhist ethics gained prominence over leftist revolutionary ideals that buttressed the

movement. See, for example, Aris, *Aung San Suu Kyi*, Part Two, for her early views.

48. For details, see Maung Maung, *1988 Uprising*, pp. 187–190; 197–202.

49. Ibid., pp. 228–30.

50. However, the protest leaders could not agree on the formation of an interim government, see Clymer, "Min Ko Naing", p. 52.

51. The one-day visit by Congressman Stephen J. Solarz (Democrat), Chairman of the Subcommittee on Asia and Pacific Affairs of the House Committee on Foreign Affairs, on 4 September during which he mooted the idea of an interim government in his meeting with Dr Maung Maung and also met some opposition leaders raised expectations among the demonstrators and heightened the fear of foreign intervention among the military leadership. See Maung Maung, *1988 Uprising*, pp. 163–66 for Dr Maung Maung's account of the visit.

52. See, e.g., SLORC Chairman General Saw Maung's address to news media on 5 July 1989, reproduced in *General Saw Maung's Addresses and Discussion in Interview* [sic] with *Foreign Correspondents* (Rangoon: Ministry of Information, News & Periodicals Enterprise, 1989), p. 214.

53. This confrontation happened on 17 September at the trade ministry building in which an unruly mob forced a platoon of heavily armed soldiers (from the 6th Light Infantry Regiment of the elite 44th Light infantry Division), who reportedly were under orders to eschew violence, to surrender their weapons that included a mortar, machine guns and automatic rifles (see ibid., pp. 213, 215; and Maung Maung *1988 Uprising*, pp. 224–26).

54. See e.g., "The Price of Disunity" (cover story), *Irrawaddy* (August 2008), pp. 26–29; and Min Zin, "Where's the End Game Strategy", *Irrawaddy* (August 2008), pp. 38–39.

55. See Maung Maung, *1988 Uprising*, p. 242. Dr Maung Maung contended that the "takeover happened ... because of grave provocation ... took place on the 16th and 17th" in Yangon. He was referring to the incident on the 16th at the defence ministry and the disarming of the army unit at the trade ministry on 17th September (ibid., p. 243). For the army's perspective on BCP links to the uprising, see *General Saw Maung's*, pp. 215–16, 222–23, 226–27.

56. For details of the popular uprising, see, *inter alia*, Bertil Lintner, *Outrage: Burma's Struggle for Democracy* (Bangkok: White Lotus, 1990) for a sympathetic account; and for a different perspective in which the popular leaders of the opposition movement were faulted for resorting to extra-legal means to take over state power and unleashing destructive forces beyond their control, see, Maung Maung, *1990 Uprising*.

57. See, e.g., *Burma Communist Party's Conspiracy to Take over State Power* (Rangoon: Ministry of Information, 1989).

58. See, also, Mary Callahan, "Myanmar's Perpetual Junta: Solving the Riddle

of the Tatmadaw's Long Reign", *New Left Review* 60 (November–December 2009): 44–51.

59. See, e.g., Maung Aung Myoe, *The Road to Naypyitaw: Making Sense of the Myanmar Government's Decision to Move its Capital*, Asia Research Institute Working Paper No. 79, Singapore (November 2006).

60. This constitutes the small number (less than a score) of tycoons (derided as cronies by the regime's detractors) linked with military patronage and a larger but relatively less wealthy circle comprising immediate and extended families of the military elite. The former came into prominence within a decade of military rule by establishing oligopolies in timber, gems, motor vehicle trade, real estate, construction, telecommunications and banking as well as import-export business in general. The latter mainly profited from rents and concessions in resource extraction, telecomunications, real estate and foreign trade licences. See, e.g., Callahan, "Political Authority", p. 49; Aung Zaw, "Tycoon Turf", *Irrawaddy*, September 2005, pp. 20–31; idem., "A Different Breed", *Irrawaddy* (September 2008), pp. 28–29; and Aung Zaw et al., "Tracking the Tycoons", *Irrawaddy* (September 2008): 30–35.

61. *New Light of Myanmar*, 31 August 2003.

62. There will be a bicameral legislature at the central or national level and fourteen unicameral regional legislatures together with six quasi-autonomous governing bodies for ethnic minority zones.

63. The president, who would be elected by a parliamentary electoral caucus, has the constitutional authority to appoint the Cabinet and heads of regional governments as well as heads of judiciary and other organs of state power. For details, see *The Constitution of the Union of Myanmar (2008)* (Naypyitaw: n.p., 2008); for a summary of important points in the Constitution, see Taylor, *The State in Myanmar*, pp. 496–503.

64. See, e.g., Callahan, "Myanmar's Perpetual Junta", p. 52; and Richard Horsey, "The Dramatic Events of 2007 in Myanmar: Domestic and International Implications", in *Dictatorship, Disorder and Decline in Myanmar*, edited by Monique Skidmore and Trevor Wilson (Canberra: ANU E Press, 2008), p. 17.

65. See, e.g., "In Burma, Carefully Sowing Resistance; Fragile Oppposition Wary of Confrontation", *Washington Post*, 10 August 2009.

66. The more prominent groups have names like "Generation Wave", "Guiding Star", "Human Rights Defenders and Protectors", "Myanmar Development Organization", while others are relatively obscure and localized. Most remain independent of political parties and work among the grass roots.

67. See, e.g., Zaw Oo, "Aung San Suu Kyi: Gandhian Dissident Democrat", in *Dissident Democrats: The Challenge of Democratic Leadership in Asia*, edited by John Kane, Haig Patapan and Benjamin Wong (Basingstoke: Palgrave Mcmillan, 2008), pp. 241–70.

68. The SPDC chairman was the patron of the USDA and regional chapters were led by trusted ministers. See, e.g., the website of the USDA at <http://www.usda.org.mm/eng/index.php>.

69. See, e.g., <http://www.ngoinmyanmar.org/index.php>.

70. See, e.g., AP, "Local Heroes Emerge to Help Cyclone Victims", *Irrawaddy* online, 16 May 2008 <http://www.irrawaddy.org/article.php?art_id=12071>; Min Lwin, "Meet the 'Handy Youths' of the Irrawaddy Delta", in *Irrawaddy* online, 6 June 2008 <http://www.irrawaddy.org/article.php?art_id=12545>; and Wai Moe, "Is Cyclone Aftermath Creating a Burmese Civil Society?" in *Irrawaddy* online, 18 June 2008 <http://www.irrawaddy.org/article.php?art_id=12816>.

71. For bombing incidents, see, e.g., Tin Maung Maung Than, "Myanmar in 2008: Weathering the Storm", in *Southeast Asian Affairs 2009*, edited by Daljit Singh (Singapore: Institute of Southeast Asian Affairs, 2009), pp. 207–8.

72. See, e.g., Callahan, "Myanmar's Perpetual Junta", pp. 51–56; and Stephen McCarthy, "Overturning the Alms Bowl: The Price of Survival and the Consequence for Political Legitimacy in Burma", *Australian Journal of International Affairs* 62, no. 1 (2008): 298–314.

73. See, e.g., ibid., p. 314; and International Crisis Group, *Burma/Myanmar: After the Crackdown*, Asia Report No. 144, January 2008.

74. See, e.g., Mary Callahan, *Political Authority in Burma's Ethnic Minority States: Devolution, Occupation, and Coexistence*, East-West Center Policy Studies 31 (Washington, DC: East-West Center, 2007); and Marie Lall, "Ethnic Conflict and the 2010 Elections in Burma", Chatham House Asia Programme Paper ASP PP 2009/04 (November 2009); and for a recent report see Yeni, "A Fragile Peace", in *Irrawaddy* (February 2010), pp. 16–21.

75. See Nawrahta, *Destiny of the Nation*, pp. 106–8, 110, 114–15.

76. See Maung Aung Myoe, *Building the Tatmadaw* for a comprehensive review of all aspects of Myanmar armed forces.

77. The Myanmar Economic Holdings and Myanmar Economic Corporation are two commercial conglomerates established by the military to engage in trade, services and industrial production. See ibid., Chapter 6.

78. See "Foreign Policy of the Union of Myanmar", Myanmar Ministry of Foreign Affairs web page, <http://www.myanmar.com/mofa/foreignpolicy/foreignpolicyview.html>. The new government that assumed power at the end of March 2011 has not come out with any major foreign policy declaration and is expected to maintain the policy formulated by its predecessor.

79. See, e.g., Deutsche Presse-Agentur, "Myanmar Plans Embassy in Kuwait", 9 December 2008.

80. See, e.g., Maung Aung Myoe, "Regionalism in Myanmar's Foreign Policy:

Past, Present and Future", Asia Research Institute Working Paper No. 73, Singapore (September 2006).

81. See, e.g., paragraph 40 in the declaration at the conclusion of the Fifteenth SAARC Summit available at <http://www.saarc-sec.org//data/summit15/summit15declaration.htm> (accessed 17 February 2009).

83. Jurgen Haacke, *Myanmar's Foreign Policy: Domestic Influences and International Implications*, Adelphi Paper 381 (London: International Institute for Strategic Studies, 2006), pp. 9, 100.

83. Tin Maung Maung Than, "Asian Regional Power: Junta's Lifelines but Not Change Agents?" in *Development and Cooperation* 2/2007; K. Yohme, "India-Myanmar Relations (1988–2008): A Decade of Redefining Bilateral Ties", Observer Research Foundation Occasional Papers No. 10. New Delhi, 2009; and Li Chenyang, "Myanmar/Burma's Political Development and China-Myanmar relations in the Aftermath of the 'Saffron Revolution'", in *Myanmar/Burma: Challenges and Perspectives*, edited by Xiaolin Guo. Stockholm: Institute for Security and Development Policy, 2008, pp. 107–28.

84. See, e.g., cover story, "The Rise and Rise of Burma's Military", *Irrawaddy* (March 2006), p. 22; and Claudia Derichs et al., "Gendering Moral Capital: Morality as a Political Asset and Strategy of Top Female Politicians in Asia", *Critical Asian Studies* 38 no. 3 (2006): 245–70.

85. See, Marawaan Macan-Markar. "In Opting for Poll Boycott, NLD Goes for Broke", Inter Press Service, 31 March 2010, in BurmaNet News, 31 March 2010.

86. For a similar view, see Steinberg, "Myanmar: The Roots of Economic Malaise", pp. 107–9.

87. For similar views in the context of a longitudinal survey of Myanmar's "developmental disaster" since independence, see Anne Booth, "The Burma Development Disaster in Comparative Historical Perspective", *SOAS Bulletin of Burma Research* [online e-journal] 1, no. 1 (2003): 1–23.

88. See, e.g., "Burma Said Revoking Money-Dealing Licenses in Bid to Stabilise Currency", AFP report, dated 24 June 2001, posted on the Internet in BurmaNet News (25 June 2001); and *Country Profile 1999–2000, Myanmar (Burma)* (London: EIU, 1999), pp. 34, 39, 40.

89. See, eg., Ba Kaung, "Selling Off the State Silver", *Irrawaddy* (March 2010) at <http://www.irrawaddy.org/article.php?art_id=17928>.

90. The government of President Thein Sein, installed in March 2011 after his military-backed Union Solidarity and Development Party won some 80 per cent of the contested seats, appears to be embarking on unprecedented political and economic reforms (within the ambit of the 2008 Constitution) while reaching out to the iconic opposition leader Aung San Suu Kyi and armed ethnic opposition groups (see, e.g., Jim Della-Giacoma, "The Burma

Spring", *Foreign Policy* online, 13 October 2011 <http://www.foreignpolicy. com/articles/2011/10/13/burma_prioner_release_spring>. If the reforms and the political reconciliation process could be sustained and successfully implemented that would be a real breakthrough for Myanmar. That would be the most positive and lasting legacy of the 1988 uprising further consolidating the changes it had initiated and reinforcing the view that it was a significant historical conjuncture.

References

Alagappa, Muthiah. "Civil Society and Political Change: An Analytical Framework". In *Civil Society and Political Change in Asia*, edited by Muthiah Alagappa. Stanford, CA: Stanford University Press, 2004.

Associated Press. "Local Heroes Emerge to Help Cyclone Victims". *Irrawaddy* online, 16 May 2008 <http://www.irrawaddy.org/article.php?art_id=12071>.

Aung San Suu Kyi. "The First Initiative". In *Freedom from Fear and Other Writings*, edited by Michael Aris. London: Penguin, 1991.

Aung Zaw. "Secrets of Commune 4828". *Irrawaddy* 16, no. 8 (August 2008): 30–33.

———. "Tracking the Tycoons". *Irrawaddy* 16, no. 9 (September 2008): 30–35.

Ba Kaung. "Selling Off the State Silver". *Irrawaddy* 18, no. 3 (March 2010) <http:// www.irrawaddy.org/article.php?art_id=17928>.

Becka, Jan. "Planning for New Burma: Major-General Aung San's Views of Economic Development". *Archiv Orientalni* 56 (1988).

Booth, Anne. "The Burma Development Disaster in Comparative Historical Perspective". *SOAS Bulletin of Burma Research* [online e-journal] 1, no. 1 (2003): 1–23.

Callahan, Mary. *Political Authority in Burma's Ethnic Minority States: Devolution, Occupation, and Coexistence.* East-West Center Policy Studies 31. Washington, DC: East-West Center, 2007.

———. "Myanmar's Perpetual Junta: Solving the Riddle of the Tatmadaw's Long Reign". *New Left Review* 60 (November–December 2009): 44–51.

Chazan, Naomi. "Engaging the State: Associational Life in Sub-Saharan Africa". In *State Power and Social Forces: Domination and Transformation in the Third World*, edited by Joel S. Migdal, Atul Kohli, and Vivienne Shue. Cambridge: Cambridge University Press, 1994.

Clymer, Megan. "Min Ko Naing, 'Conqueror of Kings' Burma's Student Leader". *Journal of Burma Studies* 8 (2003): 33–63.

Derichs, Claudia, Andrea Fleschenberg, and Momoyo Hüstebeck. "Gendering Moral Capital: Morality as a Political Asset and Strategy of Top Female Politicians in Asia". *Critical Asian Studies* 38 no. 3 (2006): 245–70.

Deutsche Presse-Agentur. *Myanmar Plans Embassy in Kuwait*, 9 December 2008.

Faulder, Dominic. "Memories of 8.8.88". *Irrawaddy* 16, no. 8 (August 2008): 34–37.

Friedgut, Theodore H. *Political Participation in the USSR*. Princeton, NJ: Princeton University Press, 1979.

Haacke, Jurgen. *Myanmar's Foreign Policy: Domestic Influences and International Implications*, Adelphi Paper 381. London: International Institute for Strategic Studies, 2006.

Horsey, Richard. "The Dramatic Events of 2007 in Myanmar: Domestic and International Implications". In *Dictatorship, Disorder and Decline in Myanmar*, edited by Monique Skidmore and Trevor Wilson. Canberra: ANU E Press, 2008.

Huntington, Samuel P. "Social and Institutional Dynamics of One-Party Systems". In *Authoritarian Politics in Modern Society: The Dynamics of Established One-Party Systems*, edited by Samuel P. Huntington and Clement H. Moore. New York: Basic Books, 1970.

International Crisis Group. *Burma/Myanmar: After the Crackdown*. Asia Report No. 144 (January 2008).

Kyaw Yin Hlaing. "Reconsidering the Failure of the Burma Socialist Programme Party Government to Eradicate Internal Economic Impediments". *South East Asia Research* 11, no. 1 (2003): 5–58.

———. "Challenging the Authoritarian State: Buddhist Monks and Peaceful Protests in Burma". *Fletcher Forum of World Affairs* 32, no. 1 (2008).

Kyaw Zwa Moe. "The Price of Disunity". *Irrawaddy* 16, no. 8 (August 2008): 26–29.

Lall, Marie. "Ethnic Conflict and the 2010 Elections in Burma". Chatham House Asia Programme Paper ASP PP 2009/04 (November 2009).

Leftwich, Adrian. "Bringing Politics Back In: Towards a Model of the Developmental State". *Journal of Development Studies* 31, no. 3 (1995): 415.

Leilar Thu Tit Oo [An Observer]. *Myanmar-American Hset-hsan Yei Thamaing* [History of Myanmar American relations]. Yangon, Digest Media Bank, 2007.

Li, Chenyang. "Myanmar/Burma's Political Development and China-Myanmar relations in the Aftermath of the 'Saffron Revolution'". In *Myanmar/Burma: Challenges and Perspectives*, edited by Xiaolin Guo. Stockholm: Institute for Security and Development Policy, 2008.

Lintner, Bertil. *Outrage: Burma's Struggle for Democracy*. Bangkok: White Lotus, 1990.

Macan-Markar, Marawaan. "In Opting for Poll Boycott, NLD Goes for Broke". Inter Press Service, BurmaNet News, 31 March 2010.

Maung Aung Myoe. *Neither Friend nor Foe, Myanmar's Relationship with Thailand Since 1988: A View from Yangon*. Singapore: Institute of Defence and Strategic Studies, 2002.

———. "Regionalism in Myanmar's Foreign Policy: Past, Present and Future", Asia Research Institute Working Paper No. 73. Singapore, September 2006.

———. *The Road to Naypyitaw: Making Sense of the Myanmar Government's Decision to Move its Capital*, Asia Research Institute Working Paper No. 79. Singapore, November 2006.

———. *Building the Tatmadaw: Myanmar Armed Forces since 1948*. Singapore: Institute of Southeast Asian Studies, 2009.

Maung Maung. *Grim War against KMT*. Rangoon: n.p., 1953.

———. *The 1988 Uprising in Burma*. New Haven, CT: Yale University Press, 1999.

McCarthy, Stephen. "Overturning the Alms Bowl: The Price of Survival and the Consequence for Political Legitimacy in Burma". *Australian Journal of International Affairs* 62, no. 1 (2008): 298–314.

Min Lwin. "Meet the 'Handy Youths' of the Irrawaddy Delta". *Irrawaddy* online, 6 June 2008 <http://www.irrawaddy.org/article.php?art_id=12545>.

Min Zin. "Where's the End Game Strategy". *Irrawaddy* 16, no. 8 (August 2008): 38–39.

Ministry of Foreign Affairs. *Foreign Policy of the Union of Myanmar* <http://www.myanmar.com/mofa/foreignpolicy/foreignpolicyview.html>.

Ministry of Information. *The Constitution of the Socialist Republic of the Union of Burma*. Rangoon: Ministry of Information, 1974.

———. *Burma Communist Party's Conspiracy to Take over State Power*. Rangoon: Ministry of Information, 1989.

Mya Han et al. *Myanma Nainnganyei Sanitpyaung Karla (1962–1974)* [Myanmar's politics in the period of systemic change], vol. 1. Yangon: Universities Press, 1993.

Mya Han and Thein Hlaing. *1958–1962 Myanma Nainganyei* [Myanmar's politics], vol. 4. Yangon: Universities Press, 1991.

Nawarahta. *Destiny of the Nation*. Yangon: New & Periodicals Enterprise, 1995.

[1973 Khu Hnit] Dutiya Akyein Parti Nyilargun Parti Baho Kommiti Okahta Gyi Ei Maintgun Myar Hnint Parti Baho Kommiti Ei Nainganyei Asiyinkhanzar [Second Party Congress 1973: Speeches of the Central Committee Chairman and the Political Report of the Party Central Committee]. Yangon: Burma Socialist Programme Party, 1974.

Pierson, Paul and Skocpol, Theda. "Historical Institutionalism in Political Science". In *Political Science: The State of the Discipline*, edited by Ira Katznelson and Helen V. Milner. New York: Norton, 2001.

Smith, Donald E. *Religion and Politics Burma*. Princeton, NJ: Princeton University Press, 1965.

South Asian Association for Regional Cooperation. *Colombo Declaration*. SAARC-SEC <http://www.saarc-sec.org/Fifteenth-SAARC-Summit/74/> (accessed 17 February 2009).

Steinberg, David I. *Crisis in Burma: Stasis and Change in a Political Economy in*

Turmoil, ISIS Paper no. 5. Bangkok: Institute of Security and International Studies, Chulalongkorn University, 1989.

———. "A Void in Myanmar: Civil Society in Burma". In *Strengthening Civil Society in Burma: Possibilities and Dilemmas for International NGOs*, edited by Tom Kramer and Pietje Vervest. Chiangmai: Silkworm Books, 1999.

Strachan, Anna Louise. "Going to the Polls: Opportunity or Setback for Myanmar's Ceasefire Groups". *CSA Security Watch* 11 (2010).

Taylor, Robert H. *Foreign and Domestic Consequences of the KMT Intervention in Burma*, Cornell University Southeast Asia Program, Data Paper no. 93. Ithaca, NY: Cornell University Southeast Asia Program, 1973.

———. "Burmese Concepts of Revolution". In *Context, Meaning and Power in Southeast Asia*, edited by Mark Hobart and Robert H. Taylor. Ithaca, NY: Cornell University Southeast Asia Program, 1986.

———. *The State in Myanmar*. Singapore: NUS Press, 2009.

Tin Maung Maung Than. "Burma in 1987: Twenty-Five Years after the Revolution". In *Southeast Asian Affairs 1988*. Singapore: Institute of Southeast Asian Studies, 1988.

———. "Burma's National Security and Defence Posture". *Contemporary Southeast Asia* 11, no. 1 (1989).

———. "Asian Regional Power: Junta's Lifelines but Not Change Agents?" In *Development and Cooperation* 2 (2007).

———. *State Dominance in Myanmar: The Political Economy of Industrialization*. Singapore: Institute of Southeast Asian Studies, 2007.

———. "Myanmar in 2008: Weathering the Storm". In *Southeast Asian Affairs 2009*, edited by Daljit Singh. Singapore: Institute of Southeast Asian Affairs, 2009.

Voslensky, Michael. *Nomenklatura: Anatomy of the Soviet Ruling Class*, translated by Eric Mosbacher. London: Bodley Head, 1984.

Wai Moe. "Is Cyclone Aftermath Creating a Burmese Civil Society?" In *Irrawaddy* online, 18 June 2008 <http://www.irrawaddy.org/article.php?art_id=12816>.

Walton, M.J. "Ethnicity, Conflict and History in Burma: The Myths of Panglong". *Asian Survey* 48, no. 6 (2008): 889–910.

Weir, Margaret. "When Does Politics Create Policy?" In *Rethinking Political Institutions: The Art of the State*, edited by Ian Shapiro, Stephen Skowronek, and Daniel Gavin. New York: New York University Press, 2006.

Yeni. "A Fragile Peace". In *Irrawaddy* 18, no. 2 (February 2010): 16–21.

Yohme, K. "India-Myanmar Relations (1988–2008): A Decade of Redefining Bilateral Ties". Observer Research Foundation Occasional Papers No. 10. New Delhi, January 2009.

Zaw Oo. "Aung San Suu Kyi: Gandhian Dissident Democrat". In *Dissident Democrats: The Challenge of Democratic Leadership in Asia*, edited by John Kane, Haig Patapan, and Benjamin Wong. Basingstoke: Palgrave Mcmillan, 2008.

5

CAMBODIA'S HISTORICAL CONJUNCTURES AND THEIR SIGNIFICANCE

Ramses Amer

The main aim of this chapter is to analyse and assess the impact of historical conjunctures on modern Cambodian society. Important changes in modern Cambodia are assessed with the goal of identifying a selected number of historical conjunctures to be included in the study. The conjunctures that are selected are presented empirically and their impact on Cambodian society is outlined. The study also includes a discussion and assessment of the relative importance of the selected conjunctures.

The study is structured in the following way. First, historical conjunctures for inclusion in the study are selected. Second, the selected historical conjunctures are empirically presented. Third, the impact of the conjunctures on Cambodian society is outlined. Fourth, the relative importance of the conjunctures is discussed and assessed in the concluding section.

THE HISTORICAL CONJUNCTURES

Selecting the Historical Conjunctures for Inclusion in the Study

Cambodia's modern history since it gained formal independence from

France in 1953 displays a number of relevant historical conjunctures.[1] In the context of this study a select number will be studied. Interestingly, the fact that Cambodia gained independence from France in 1953 is in itself a historical conjuncture since it implied that Cambodia was not part of the First Geneva Conference on Indochina held in 1954 and that the anti-French forces — The Khmer Issarak — were not given any area to regroup in within Cambodia contrary to the situation in both Laos and Vietnam. Instead, some of its cadres were relocated to the Democratic Republic of Vietnam (DRV). This would impact not only on the country but also on the perception of Vietnam within the Cambodian communist movement.[2] Notwithstanding the importance of this event it will not be included in the study. Instead, historical conjunctures ranging over a period from 1970 to the early 1990s will be included. They are the overthrow of Prince Norodom Sihanouk in 1970, the fall of Phnom Penh in 1975, the military intervention of Cambodia by Vietnam in 1978–79, and the United Nations' peacekeeping operation in Cambodia in 1992–93. All four conjunctures had profound impact on Cambodian society and the 1970 conjuncture created the conditions for the 1975 conjuncture which would set the stage for developments that led to the Vietnamese intervention. Finally, the situation created by the intervention would only be fully addressed through the peacekeeping operation which established the current political system in Cambodia and also shaped the civil society in the country. The final withdrawal of Vietnamese troops from Cambodia in September 1989 may have been important but it was unilateral and not part of a comprehensive settlement of the so-called Cambodian Conflict and hence it cannot be considered to have been a historical conjuncture in parity with the Vietnamese intervention in the late 1970s or the peacekeeping operation in 1992–93.

Developments in Cambodia after 1993 also deserve to be discussed, in particular two main events. First, the culmination of the power struggle between the then First Prime Minister Prince Norodom Ranariddh and the then Second Prime Minister Hun Sen in 1997 leading to the defeat of the former. The second development is the demise of the Party of Democratic Kampuchea (PDK) (also known as the Khmer Rouge) in 1998 which put an end to the group's military struggle against the central government. The first event was indeed dramatic and was regarded as a de facto coup by the international community, but given that the two parties in the coalition remained in power, i.e., members of the political party of Prince Ranariddh

— Front uni national pour un Cambodge indépendant, neutre, pacifique et coopératif (FUNCINPEC) — opted not to support him, the main impact was to weaken Ranariddh as a politician. It will therefore not be considered as a historical conjuncture of major significance for inclusion in this study. As for the demise of the PDK, it brought an end to the main security threat in rural areas, in particular in the northwest of the country, and it was an event of major symbolic significance given the history of the PDK in particular when it was in power during the second half of the 1970s. However, the PDK had been considerably weakened by internal struggles and defections and as such no longer constituted a major threat to either the Cambodian government or to the country at large. Consequently, the demise of the PDK will not be included in this study.[3]

To sum up, the four historical conjunctures to be examined in the context of this study are the following. First, the overthrow of Prince Norodom Sihanouk in 1970; second, the fall of Phnom Penh in 1975; third, the military intervention by Vietnam in 1978–79; and fourth, the United Nations' peacekeeping operation in 1992–93.

The Overthrow of Prince Norodom Sihanouk in 1970

In early 1970 Prince Sihanouk's grip on power began to erode and this process culminated when he was officially removed from the position as head of state on 18 March, following a vote by the National Assembly. Lon Nol was retained as prime minister with Siriwak Sri Matak as his assistant. This political evolution would have a serious impact on the domestic situation in Cambodia, or the Khmer Republic as the country was renamed, and on its relations with the different Vietnamese actors.[4]

The Fall of Phnom Penh in 1975

The Cambodian government managed to remain in power up to 17 April 1975 when the capital Phnom Penh was captured by the Royal Government of National Union of Cambodia (RGNUC) forces. In fact it was primarily the forces of the Communist Party of Kampuchea (CPK). After the capture of Phnom Penh and the downfall of the Khmer Republic, the CPK took over political power in the country, although officially the RGNUC with Prince Sihanouk as head of state was in power until April 1976. The country was then renamed Democratic Kampuchea (DK). Radical policies were implemented resulting in political violence and a large number of deaths among the Cambodian population.

The Vietnamese Military Intervention in 1978–79

Vietnam launched its decisive military intervention against Cambodia on 25 December 1978 with an estimated 100,000 troops and the capital Phnom Penh was captured on 6 January 1979. The Vietnamese troops were supported by some 20,000 members of the Kampuchean National Front for National Salvation (KNUFNS). Cambodian refugees in Vietnam had created the KNUFNS on 2 December 1978. The overthrown government was not captured and managed to escape to areas along the Thai-Cambodian border.

The United Nations Peacekeeping Operation in 1992–93

On 16 October 1991 the Security Council of the United Nations adopted Resolution 717 in which it was decided to establish the United Nations Advance Mission in Cambodia (UNAMIC) to be sent to Cambodia immediately after the signing of the Paris Agreements on Cambodia.[5] The formal decision to set up the United Nations Transitional Authority in Cambodia (UNTAC) was taken by a unanimous Security Council decision on 28 February 1992.[6] UNTAC was officially established with the arrival in Phnom Penh of Yasushi Akashi, the Personal Representative of the Secretary-General of the United Nations, on 15 March 1992. The withdrawal of UNTAC from Cambodia took place between August and December 1993. On 24 September 1993 Cambodia's new Constitution was promulgated and the Constituent Assembly was transformed into a legislative assembly. This political development formally terminated UNTAC's mandate in Cambodia.

DEVELOPMENTS FOLLOWING THE FOUR CONJUNCTURES

The Overthrow of Prince Norodom Sihanouk in 1970

The removal of Prince Sihanouk took place in the midst of a propaganda campaign against the Vietnamese. In fact the attacks on Sihanouk were primarily centred on his alleged pro-Vietnamese stand. The verbal propaganda against the Vietnamese community soon turned into physical abuse and attacks all over Cambodia. Vietnamese houses, boats, property and religious shrines were attacked. The offices and residences in Phnom Penh of the diplomatic representatives of the DRV and of the Provisional Revolutionary Government, formed in the Republic of Vietnam (ROV) by the National Liberation Front (NLF), were sacked. The violence against the ethnic Vietnamese escalated when elements of the armed forces and the police joined in the attacks and the killings which caused the deaths of thousands of ethnic Vietnamese.[7]

Far from protecting the Vietnamese, the new Cambodian authorities introduced a number of discriminatory measures. The Vietnamese were only allowed to move around between 7 and 11 a.m., making it impossible for them to attend schools and to work. The Vietnamese fishermen had their fishing licences withdrawn. Public and private organizations as well as persons living in state-owned houses were banned from employing Vietnamese staff. Furthermore, the authorities "recommended" that the Vietnamese language should not be used in public.[8]

The ROV authorities intervened officially and a growing awareness, on the part of the Cambodian authorities, of the negative international repercussions of the attacks on the Vietnamese prompted a change of attitude. The authorities called on people to "actively protect" the Vietnamese in the spirit of maintaining cordial links between the Cambodian and Vietnamese people. An agreement was reached between the ROV and the Cambodian government on the issue of the ethnic Vietnamese in Cambodia on 27 May 1970.[9]

Despite the new signals the ethnic Vietnamese continued to flee from their homes and they sought refuge in eighteen camps set up in certain towns, primarily in Phnom Penh, to cope with the flow of internal refugees. By the month of May the number of people in the camps reached its peak at 90,000. From May to August 1970 these refugees were "repatriated" to the ROV. On 13 August the last camp was closed down in Phnom Penh. However, the exodus of ethnic Vietnamese from Cambodia continued and by the end of September 1970 a total of 197,378 Vietnamese had officially left for the ROV. According to the ROV authorities, 28 per cent of the "repatriated" claimed to be Cambodian citizens. In fact, the ROV authorities estimated that 300,000 ethnic Vietnamese living in Cambodia prior to the exodus had Cambodian citizenship. In March 1971 the ROV officially estimated that approximately 250,000 ethnic Vietnamese had been "repatriated" from Cambodia.[10]

The ethnic Vietnamese in Cambodia had been caught in an upsurge of officially sponsored anti-Vietnamese sentiments which linked them to the military presence of DRV and NLF armed forces in Cambodia. Already before Prince Sihanouk was removed from power the transport of arms through Cambodian territory to the DRV-NLF troops had been stopped. The Cambodian authorities tried to force the DRV-NFL troops out of eastern Cambodia but suffered a near total defeat in two military offensives carried out in late 1970 and in 1971. In 1970 Cambodia was firmly dragged into the Vietnam War with American and ROV military incursions. The Cambodian government faced a military challenge of an internal opposition that brought Prince Sihanouk into a coalition with the CPK in the self-proclaimed RGNUC. The Cambodian government survived thanks to American material and military support, such as air strikes against the RGNUC-controlled areas, which were particularly intense during the first half of 1973. The RGNUC could rely on support from the DRV-NLF troops up to the end of 1972 when they withdrew from Cambodia. By then the RGNUC was strong enough to continue their struggle with only material support from its foreign allies, China and the DRV.[11]

The Fall of Phnom Penh in 1975

One of the first measures after the capture of Phnom Penh was to evacuate the population to the countryside. This was only the first step in what became a big social experiment at a very high casualty cost within the population. The new government carried out radical social and economic changes that resulted in a large number of deaths from diseases and malnourishment. Several hundred thousand people were executed by the government. The policies implemented during the DK years 1975–78 led to a death rate in Cambodia of an estimated 750,000 to 1,000,000 deaths above the normal death rate.[12] An estimated 50 per cent of the total ethnic Chinese in the country perished. The Cham minority also suffered a very high death rate. The fate of the ethnic Vietnamese was one of renewed exodus as some 170,000 were expelled from Cambodia in 1975. As the Vietnamese were then estimated at about 200,000 by the mid-1970s only some 30,000 remained in the country and many of them died of starvation, diseases or executions between 1975 and 1978. This meant that the Vietnamese minority had all but completely disappeared from Cambodia.[13]

Developments in Cambodia indicated that beginning in early 1977 policies became even more radicalized and it also signalled a foreign policy shift towards open confrontation with Vietnam. Domestic developments display both purges within the ruling party and conflict within it leading to an open armed confrontation in 1978 when the central government's military defeated the leadership in the Eastern Zone.

On the foreign policy front military clashes occurred along the common border between Cambodia and Vietnam as early as May and June 1975. This situation was settled and remained relatively stable during the second half of 1975 and throughout 1976. In early 1977 Cambodia embarked on a more active course to emphasize its claims on certain border areas that were under Vietnamese control. Cambodia began patrolling such areas and later escalated its military activities to attacks and shelling against Vietnam. Eventually Vietnam responded with attacks into Cambodia and by the end of 1977 the relations between the two countries had reached a state of war. This situation continued to prevail throughout 1978 until Vietnam launched its military intervention on 25 December 1978. The roots of the conflict between the two countries were both ideological and nationalistic.[14]

The Vietnamese Military Intervention in 1978–79

Vietnam's military intervention led to the overthrow of the Cambodian government, i.e., DK, but the ousted leadership was not captured. In early January 1979 Cambodians who had earlier taken refuge in Vietnam formed a new government in Phnom Penh. On 10 January 1979 the country was officially renamed the People's Republic of Kampuchea (PRK).

The new administration — the PRK, with Vietnamese support, gained control of the major populated areas, but the overthrown government remained militarily active in rural areas, particularly along the Thai-Cambodian border. The armed opposition against the PRK was made up of DK, i.e., the overthrown government, also known as the PDK, and two smaller non-communist groups, the Khmer People's National Liberation Front (KPNLF) led by Son Sann, and FUNCINPEC led by Prince Sihanouk. The latter two groups joined the DK to broaden the coalition (Coalition Government of Democratic Kampuchea — CGDK) in order to secure international support which was being reconsidered after evidence of DK atrocities that amounted to genocide against the local population.

The PRK was fairly successful in consolidating itself within the country and in meeting the basic needs of the population after a severe food shortage in the early years of its existence.[15] Internationally the

PRK relied on support from Vietnam, Laos, the Union of Soviet Socialist Republics (USSR), and countries pursuing a pro-Soviet foreign policy, but failed to get international recognition from other countries. It also failed to be recognized by the General Assembly of the United Nations, which continued to allow the overthrown government to represent Cambodia. This implied that the PRK was denied much needed development assistance from the United Nations.[16]

International reactions to the Vietnamese military intervention were generally negative with the only support for Vietnam's action coming from the pro-Soviet countries. The member states of the Association of Southeast Asian Nations (ASEAN)[17] were unanimous in their condemnation for what was regarded a violation of the territorial integrity of a small state and turning Thailand into a "frontline state" facing Vietnamese troops. China, Japan and the United States as well as all member states of the North Atlantic Treaty Organization (NATO) also condemned the action. This broad coalition assured that the General Assembly, with a growing majority from 1979 and throughout the 1980s, condemned the intervention and called for an immediate withdrawal of foreign forces from Cambodia.[18]

During the first half of the 1980s there was a sharp polarization of positions with regard to the situation in Cambodia, both at the regional and at the global level, and no signs of compromise or rapprochement. The military situation in Cambodia was characterized by offensives by the PRK backed by Vietnamese troops during the yearly dry seasons. The most important of these military offensives took place during the dry season 1994–95 when all camps of the CGDK on Cambodian territory were overrun. This implied that the forces of the CGDK had to launch all operations from bases in Thailand.

The second half of the 1980s saw important changes in the interaction among the Cambodian parties, among the regional actors in Southeast Asia and among the major powers. At the regional level the early steps were bilateral discussions between Indonesia and Vietnam. At the national level Prince Sihanouk met with Hun Sen, prime minister of the PRK, in Paris in late 1987. It was the first high-level meeting between representatives of the two Cambodian governments. The regional dialogue brought about an unprecedented meeting in Indonesia in July 1988, known as the first Jakarta Informal Meeting (JIM1), with the participation of the member states of ASEAN, Laos, Vietnam and the four Cambodian parties. JIM2 was held in February 1989 and JIM3 was held in February 1990. At the international level a Paris Conference on Cambodia (PCC) was convened for a month beginning 30 July 1989.[19] However, none of these meetings resulted in any agreement on the appropriate model for resolving the Cambodian conflict. Despite the impasse on the diplomatic front, Vietnam went ahead with the declared intention of withdrawing the last of its troops from Cambodia in late September 1989. This withdrawal was at least partly facilitated by the election of a new government in Thailand in August 1988 that downgraded the Vietnamese security threat and expressed a desire to turn the battlefields of Indochina into market places.

During 1990 the focus of attention shifted from regional initiatives to the work of the five permanent members of the Security Council (Perm Five)[20] aiming at formulating a common stand in regard to the conflict in Cambodia. On 28 August the Perm Five reached an understanding and they presented a document entitled "Framework for a comprehensive political settlement of the Cambodia conflict", which, among other things, included provisions for the creation of UNTAC. The Perm Five also urged the Cambodian parties to create a Supreme National Council (SNC) to act as the legitimate body and source of authority in Cambodia and to represent Cambodia in international organizations.[21]

The Cambodian parties responded positively to the "Framework" and accepted it as a basis for a comprehensive settlement of the Cambodian conflict at a meeting in Jakarta on 9 and 10 September. They also decided to create a Supreme National Council (SNC) that would have twelve members, six from the State of Cambodia (SOC)[22] and two from each of the three parties of the National Government of Cambodia (NGC).[23]

Subsequently, the Security Council unanimously adopted a resolution that endorsed the Framework as a basis for a comprehensive settlement of the Cambodian conflict.[24] The General Assembly also unanimously adopted a resolution that welcomed the Security Council's resolution and the Framework.[25]

Despite these positive developments, the conflict resolution process did not progress further during the closing months of 1990. This was primarily due to two factors. First, the Cambodian parties failed to agree on the role that Prince Sihanouk should play in the SNC since he was not one of the original members. This led to a situation where the SNC could not fulfil its envisaged duties. Second, the Perm Five presented a more detailed blueprint for a comprehensive settlement of the Cambodian conflict on 26 November 1990. When this proposal was formally presented to the members of the SNC, at a meeting in Paris on 21 to 23 December, they failed to agree on all parts of it.[26] Second, it later became evident that the SOC had expressed displeasure about certain provisions in the draft. The main complaints were that the proposal would lead to a de facto dismantling of the SOC administration and that it would facilitate a return to power of the PDK. Furthermore, there were no references to the "genocide" carried out by the PDK while in power. The other three Cambodian parties accepted the November blueprint. The situation remained deadlocked during the first five months of 1991, with the only notable progress being a ceasefire implemented in May, following a call from the Secretary-General of the United Nations to the Cambodian parties.

In an attempt to break the deadlock, a meeting attended by the four Cambodian parties was arranged in Jakarta on 2–4 June 1991. The meeting ended on an inconclusive note mainly due to the fact that the PDK opposed some compromises that were agreeable to the other three parties. However, following this meeting a dramatic change in the relationship between the Cambodian parties took place. At a series of meetings from late June to September the Cambodian parties reached agreements on the major disputed points. First, the SOC and the NGC would be preserved and continue to function in the zones which they controlled, pending the general elections. Second, the SNC would set up its headquarters in Phnom Penh and represent Cambodia at the United Nations. Furthermore, Prince Sihanouk was chosen as chairman of the SNC. Third, the parties agreed to stop receiving foreign military assistance. Fourth, they agreed to cut their military forces by 70 per cent (i.e., to demobilize them) and that the remaining 30 per cent would hand over their weapons to United Nations supervisors and enter cantonments. This would take place when the proposed UNTAC had been established in Cambodia. Finally, the electoral system was to be proportional within each of Cambodia's provinces but not at the national level.

It was also decided that the PCC would be reconvened in late October 1991. During this second session of the PCC held on 23 October 1991 the "Agreement on a comprehensive political settlement of the Cambodia Conflict"[27] and the "Agreement Concerning the Sovereignty, Independence, Territorial Integrity and Inviolability, Neutrality and National Unity of Cambodia"[28] were signed by the following participating states: Australia, Brunei Darussalam, Cambodia,[29] Canada, China, France, India, Indonesia, Japan, Laos, Malaysia, the Philippines, Singapore, Thailand, the USSR, the United Kingdom (UK), the United States, Vietnam, and Yugoslavia.[30]

The signing of these Agreements brought about a formal resolution to the Cambodian conflict.

The United Nations Peacekeeping Operation in 1992–93[31]

UNTAC was officially established with the arrival in Phnom Penh of Yasushi Akashi, the Personal Representative of the Secretary-General of the United Nations, on 15 March 1992. The withdrawal of UNTAC from Cambodia took place between August and December 1993. On 24 September Cambodia's new Constitution was promulgated and the Constituent Assembly was transformed into a legislative assembly. This development formally terminated UNTAC's mandate in Cambodia.

In the administrative field UNTAC was given extensive powers to supervise the existing administrative structures in Cambodia. For example, all bodies acting in the field of foreign affairs, national defence, finance, public security, and information would be under direct UNTAC control. Other units could also come under direct UNTAC control, if deemed necessary. Furthermore, all police would operate under its supervision and control.

In the military field UNTAC's mandate related to three major aspects. First, it was to supervise, monitor and verify the withdrawal of foreign forces and their non-return to Cambodia, as well as the cessation of foreign military assistance to the Cambodian parties. Second, it was to supervise the ceasefire which was to be observed by the Cambodian parties upon the signature of the Paris Agreements in October 1991. Third, during the demobilization and cantonment process of the armed forces of the Cambodian parties, UNTAC should supervise the regrouping and relocating of all forces to cantonment areas, and control and guard their military equipment. In regard to the elections, UNTAC's role was to be fully and exclusively in charge of the organizing and conduct of the general elections to be held in Cambodia during the peacekeeping operation.

In assessing the peacekeeping operation, the major positive feature was the success of the general elections, carried out from 23 to 28 May 1993, both in terms of registration of voters and of the impressive turnout in the elections. In fact 89.56 per cent of the nearly 4.7 million registered voters participated in the elections. Another notable success was the repatriation of some 365,000 Cambodian refugees ahead of the general elections. Despite major efforts to promote respect for human rights and to combat politically motivated violence in the country, the United Nations did not

succeed in creating a truly politically neutral climate for the elections. The
United Nations also failed to adequately address the problem of regularly
occurring armed attacks against the Vietnamese minority in Cambodia. To
a certain extent the actions taken by the United Nations had the effect of
worsening the situation of the ethnic Vietnamese. Another shortcoming
was the decision to pay salaries to the peacekeepers in U.S. dollars, thus
contributing to the dramatic depreciation of the local currency and causing
a sharp increase in the cost of living for the Cambodian population.
However, the most serious shortcoming was in the military field where the
demobilization and cantonment of the military forces had to be abandoned
because the PDK refused to join in the process. As a consequence, the stage
was set for continued civil war in the country following the withdrawal
of UNTAC.

CONCLUDING ANALYSIS

The four historical conjunctures have had major impacts on developments
in Cambodia and they have also had considerable external and foreign
relations implications. All four have to be taken into account to properly
understand the developments shaping modern Cambodia. Today it
may appear as though the fourth conjuncture, i.e., the United Nations'
peacekeeping operation in 1992–93, has had the most profound impact
on Cambodia since its legacy can clearly be seen in Cambodian politics
and in society, in particular through the multiparty system still in place
and through the considerable number of NGOs operating in the country.
Many of these NGOs are foreign funded. However, of the four historical
conjunctures, the last one has had the least dramatic impact in terms of
militarized conflicts affecting the country. In fact the fourth conjuncture
of 1992–93 did not bring about an end to the internal military conflict in
Cambodia as the PDK opted out of the political process and continued to
combat the government until the PDK crumbled in the late 1990s. While
the overthrow of Prince Norodom Sihanouk in 1970 led Cambodia to
be fully dragged into the Second Indochina Conflict and also led to the
exodus of ethnic Vietnamese following government-sponsored attacks
on the minority. The fall of Phnom Penh in 1975 ushered in the policies
of the DK years with its dramatic cost in human life and also a foreign
policy leading to military confrontation with Vietnam. Undoubtedly, the
DK years caused the most profound trauma in Cambodian society. The
Vietnamese military intervention in 1978–79 brought about an end to the

DK policies. The military conflict with groups opposing the Vietnamese presence continued unabated through the 1980s and the Cambodian conflict became a conflict situation with domestic, regional, and global dimensions and ramifications.

The pattern of developments affecting Cambodia suggests that the developments that followed the 1970, the 1975 and the 1978–79 historical conjunctures eventually led to the subsequent conjunctures. The overthrow of Prince Norodom Sihanouk in 1970 led to the political and military developments that made possible the rise to power of the CPK through military victory over the Khmer Republic. The fall of Phnom Penh and the takeover by the CPK led to the introduction of the radical domestic policies during the DK-years resulting in the large number of deaths within the Cambodian population. It also led to the gradual radicalization of the foreign policy conducted by DK with an increasingly anti-Vietnamese foreign policy from early 1997. The foreign policy towards Vietnam also became more assertive leading to a militarized conflict. This conflict would eventually lead to the Vietnamese military intervention in late 1978 and the removal of the PDK from power, symbolized by the capture of Phnom Penh in early January 1979. The Vietnamese military intervention in 1978–79 did bring back some normalcy to Cambodian society, but the overthrown government with other groups resisted militarily and the negative international reaction denied the PRK international recognition. In fact, the Cambodian Conflict had internal, regional and global dimensions. The model for a resolution that was eventually agreed upon — outside the framework of the United Nations but with the active participation of the Perm Five of the Security Council — was one that would not only end the Cambodian Conflict, through the Paris Agreements on Cambodia of October 1992, but also encompassed an ambitious United Nations' peacekeeping operation, in other words historical conjuncture four in 1992–93. Looking back at this process it was indeed a compromise that all, including the Cambodian parties, had to sign-up to. This was most difficult for the PRK/SOC that controlled most of Cambodia and the vast majority of the population living in these areas. However, with the refusal of a broad coalition of countries to recognize it, even after the Vietnamese withdrawal in September 1989, the PRK/SOC had to reluctantly go along to break out of international isolation. That strategy has eventually paid off for the Cambodian People's Party (CPP) — the ruling party within the SOC — but only after a rather disappointing performance in the 1993 general elections and the complicated power-sharing situation of the 1990s.

The four historical conjunctures clearly represent radically different trajectories compared with other possible scenarios. A few examples can be provided. First, if Prince Norodom Sihanouk had not been overthrown in 1970, Cambodian politics and also its foreign relations would not have been altered radically. Second, if Prince Sihanouk had not been overthrown he would not have entered into an alliance with the CPK and consequently the domestic, regional and international developments that contributed to strengthen the CPK would not have taken place and the CPK would not have been in a position to seize power in 1975. Second, if Vietnam had not intervened militarily in Cambodia and not removed the PDK from power in 1979, the PDK would have been able to continue to govern Cambodia and pursue its radical domestic policies. Third, had the PRK/SOC been granted broader international recognition following the intervention, then the so-called Cambodian conflict would have been different and the peacekeeping operation would have been of a different nature or there might possibly not have been any peacekeeping operation in Cambodia. In fact the political system of Cambodia could have been shaped very differently had the PRK/SOC been recognized as Cambodia's legitimate government by the United Nations.

External actors and factors have played important roles in Cambodia and have influenced developments in the country. The Second Indochina conflict affected Cambodia both in the 1960s and during the first half of the 1970s. The conflict situation and the actions of both regional and global powers had considerable impact on developments in Cambodia. Both the 1970 and the 1975 conjunctures were considerably affected by external developments and the policies and actions of external actors. The 1978–79 conjuncture was brought about as a direct result of a foreign military intervention and is thus a direct result of the actions of an external actor, i.e., Vietnam, and of Cambodia's relations with this external actor. In the broader regional context of the so-called Third Indochina Conflict, another external actor was important in the 1978–79 conjuncture, namely China. In the context of the so-called Cambodian conflict from 1979 to 1991, external actors, their actions and their relationships with each other had considerable impact on Cambodia. Given its direct military presence in the country, Vietnam's influence was the most evident. Other regional actors as well as global actors, including the superpowers and also the United Nations, all had considerable impact directly or indirectly during the period of the Cambodian Conflict. The fourth conjuncture, i.e., the United Nations peacekeeping operation in 1992–93, was external in nature and had profound impacts on Cambodian society and politics. With its extensive mandate, UNTAC could directly influence development in the country beyond that of a traditional peacekeeping operation.

From this overview it is evident that the role, influence and impact of external actors have been considerable in the developments connected with the four historical conjunctures affecting Cambodia. However, this does not imply that Cambodia has been a one-sided victim of external events, factors and actors. In fact the actions, behaviour and policies of Cambodian leaders and politicians must also be taken into account, i.e., Cambodia's historical conjunctures and their impact on society cannot be blamed or attributed to foreign interference alone. In this regard, the conjunctures represent a mixture of local and externally sponsored developments. Nonetheless, one striking observation is that in connection with all four conjunctures in Cambodia from 1970 to the early 1990s, one person played a pivotal role for better and for worse, namely Prince Norodom Sihanouk.

Notes

1. For an overview of developments in Cambodia since 1946 see Ben Kiernan, "Introduction: Conflict in Cambodia, 1945–2006", in *Conflict and Change in Cambodia*, edited with an Introduction by Ben Kiernan and Consulting Editor Caroline Hughes (London: Routledge, 2007), pp. vii–xix.
2. For an analysis of this issue and its impact on perception of the DRV see Ramses Amer, "Cambodia and Vietnam: A Troubled Relationship", in *International Relations in Southeast Asia: Between Bilateralism and Multilateralism*, edited by N. Ganesan and Ramses Amer (Singapore: Institute of Southeast Asian Studies, 2010), pp. 92–116.
3. For details on political developments in Cambodia in the 1990s see David Roberts, *Political Transition in Cambodia: Power, Elitism and Democracy* (London: Routledge, 2000); David Roberts, "Democratization, Elite Transition, and Violence in Cambodia, 1991–1999", in Kiernan, *Conflict and Change*, pp. 26–44; and Caroline Hughes, "International Intervention and the People's Will: The Demoralization of Democracy in Cambodia", in Ibid., pp. 45–68.
4. David P. Chandler, *A History of Cambodia*, 2nd ed. (St. Leonards, NSW: Allen & Unwin, 1993), p. 204; and Peter A. Poole, *The Expansion of the Vietnam War into Cambodia: Action and Response by the Governments of North Vietnam, South Vietnam, Cambodia, and the United States*, Papers in International Studies, Southeast Asia Series, 17 (Athens, OH: Southeast Asia Programme, Center for International Studies, Ohio University, 1970), pp. 17–19.
5. United Nations Security Council Resolution 717 (16 October 1991) (S/RES/717 [1991]).

6. United Nations Security Council Resolution 745 (28 February 1992) (S/RES/745 [1992]).

7. Chandler, *A History of Cambodia*, p. 205; Chou Meng Tarr, "The Vietnamese Minority in Cambodia", *Race & Class* 34, no. 2 (1992): 34; Charles Goldblum, "Les relations inter-ethniques au Cambodge dans la presse Phnom-penhoise de langue française (1963–1970)" [The inter-ethnic relations in Cambodia in the French language press of Phnom Penh (1963–1970)], *Asie du Sud-Est et Monde Insulindien* 5, no. 3 (1974): 28–30, 44–51; Poole, *The Expansion of the Vietnam War*, p. 26; and Joseph Pouvatchy, "L'éxode des vietnamiens du Cambodge en 1970" [The exodus of the Vietnamese of Cambodia in 1970], *Mondes Asiatiques*, no. 7 (Automne 1976): 340–42.

8. Ibid., p. 342.

9. Ibid., p. 342 and pp. 348–49; and *Accord relatif au problème des ressortissants vietnamiens au Cambodge* [Agreement relating to the problem of the Vietnamese residents in Cambodia] (Saigon, 27 May 1970).

10. Pouvatchy, "L'éxode des vietnamiens", pp. 342–47. Pouvatchy expresses some reservations regarding the Vietnamese figure of 300,000 ethnic Vietnamese with Cambodian citizenship which he found to be rather on the high side. He also notes that the Cambodian authorities "seemed" to have encouraged Cambodian citizens of Vietnamese ethnicity to leave the country (Ibid., p. 343).

11. Chandler, *A History of Cambodia*, pp. 206–8; and Poole, *The Expansion of the Vietnam War*, pp. 27–29 and 38–56.

12. The most expert study of the years 1975 to 1978 is Michael Vickery, *Cambodia 1975–1982* (Boston: South End Press, 1984).

13. In 1978 Vietnam requested assistance from the United Nations High Commissioner for Refugees (UNHCR) to cope with 341,400 refugees who had arrived from Cambodia since 1975. Among these refugees there were 170,300 ethnic Vietnamese. The figures for the number of refugees in Vietnam in 1978 is taken from *The Boat People: An "Age" Investigation with Bruce Grant* (Harmondsworth, Middlesex: Penguin Books, 1979), p. 98.

14. Information about the relations between Cambodia and Vietnam is derived from Amer, *Cambodia and Vietnam* and from Ramses Amer, *The United Nations and Foreign Military Interventions: A Comparative Study of the Application of the Charter*, 2nd ed., Report 33 (Uppsala: Department of Peace and Conflict Research, Uppsala University, 1994), pp. 38–40. For an overview of the accusations put forward by the two countries against each other see ibid., pp. 195–201.

15. The most extensive studies of the PRK years are Michael Vickery, *Kampuchea: Politics, Economics, and Society* (London: Frances Pinter, 1986); Michael Vickery, "Notes on the Political Economy of the People's Republic of Kampuchea (PRK)", *Journal of Contemporary Asia* 20, no. 4 (1990): 435–65; and Grant Curtis, *Cambodia: A Country Profile* (Stockholm: Swedish International Development

Authority, 1990). For the early years see also Ben Kiernan, "Kampuchea 1979–1981: National Rehabilitation in the Eye of an International Storm", in *Southeast Asian Affairs 1982*, edited by Huynh Kim Khanh (Singapore: Institute of Southeast Asian Studies, 1982), pp. 165–75.

16. For a detailed analysis of the United Nations decisions with regard to Cambodia's representation see Amer, *The United Nations*, pp. 89–108. For an analysis of the implications of these decisions see Ramses Amer, "The United Nations and Kampuchea: The Issue of Representation and its Implications", *Bulletin of Concerned Asian Scholars* 22, no. 3 (1990): 52–60. See also Gareth Porter, *Kampuchea's UN Seat: Cutting the Pol Pot Connection*, Indochina Issues, no. 8 (1980); Michael Leifer, "The International Representation of Kampuchea", in *Southeast Asian Affairs 1982*, pp. 47–59; and Colin Warbrick, "Kampuchea: Representation and Recognition", *International and Comparative Law Quarterly* 30, no. 1 (January 1981): 234–46.

17. In 1979 ASEAN had five member-states — Indonesia, Malaysia, the Philippines, Singapore, and Thailand. Brunei Darussalam joined ASEAN in 1984.

18. For a detailed analysis of the General Assembly resolutions and related voting see Amer, *The United Nations*, pp. 124–46 and 302–6.

19. For more details concerning the 1989 Paris Conference on Cambodia see *Cambodia — The 1989 Paris Peace Conference. Background Analysis and Documents*, compiled and edited by Amitav Acharya, Pierre Lizée and Sorpong Peou (Toronto: Centre for International and Strategic Studies, York University, and Millwood, New York: Kraus International, 1991); and Michael Haas, "The Paris Conference on Cambodia, 1989", *Bulletin of Concerned Asian Scholars* 23, no. 2 (1991): 42–53.

20. The Perm Five in 1990 were China, France, the USSR, the United Kingdom, and the United States.

21. United Nations General Assembly and Security Council Document A/45/472-S/21689 (31 August 1990).

22. The PRK changed its official name to the SOC in April 1989.

23. The CGDK officially changed its name to the NGC in February 1990.

24. United Nations Security Council Resolution 668 (20 September 1990) (S/RES/668 (1990)).

25. United Nations General Assembly Resolution 45/3 (15 October 1990) (A/RES/45/3).

26. United Nations General Assembly and Security Council Document A/46/61-S/22059 (11 January 1991).

27. United Nations General Assembly and Security Council Document A/46/608-S/23177 (30 October 1991).

28. Ibid.

29. Cambodia was represented by the SNC under the leadership of its president — Prince Sihanouk (ibid).

30. Yugoslavia represented the Non-Aligned Movement (ibid).

31. Information derived from Ramses Amer, "United Nations Transitional
    Authority in Cambodia (UNTAC) (1992–1993), in *Southeast Asia: A Historical
    Encyclopedia, From Angkor Wat to East Timor, Vol. III: R-Z*, edited by Ooi Keat
    Gin (Santa Barbara, CA: ABC-CLIO, 2004), pp. 1369–71. See also Amitav
    Acharya, "Cambodia, the United Nations and the Problems of Peace", *Pacific
    Review* 7, no. 3 (1994): 297–308; Ramses Amer, *Peace-keeping in a Peace Process:
    The Case of Cambodia*, Report 40 (Uppsala: Department of Peace and Conflict
    Research, Uppsala University, 1995); Karl Farris, "UN Peacekeeping in
    Cambodia: On Balance, a Success", *Parameters* 24, no. 1 (1994): 38–50; Trevor
    Findlay, *Cambodia: The Legacy and Lessons of UNTAC*, SIPRI Research Report
    no. 9 (Solna: Stockholm International Peace Research Institute [SIPRI] and
    Oxford: Oxford University Press, 1995), and Raoul M. Jennar, "UNTAC:
    'International Triumph' in Cambodia?" *Security Dialogue* 25, no. 2 (1994):
    145–56.

References

United Nations Documents
United Nations General Assembly Documents
Resolution 45/3 (15 October 1990) (A/RES/45/3).

United Nations Security Council Documents
Resolution 668 (20 September 1990) (S/RES/668 [1990])
Resolution 717 (16 October 1991) (S/RES/717 [1991])
Resolution 745 (28 February 1992) (S/RES/745 [1992]).

United Nations General Assembly and Security Council Documents
A/45/472-S/21689 (31 August 1990)
A/46/61-S/22059 (11 January 1991)
A/46/608-S/23177 (30 October 1991).

Other references
Accord relatif au problème des ressortissants vietnamiens au Cambodge [Agreement
    relating to the problem of the Vietnamese residents in Cambodia]. Saigon,
    27 May 1970.
Acharya, Amitav. "Cambodia, the United Nations and the Problems of Peace".
    Pacific Review 7, no. 3 (1994): 297–308.
Amer, Ramses. "The United Nations and Kampuchea: The Issue of Representation
    and its Implications". *Bulletin of Concerned Asian Scholars* 22, no. 3 (1990):
    52–60.
———. *The United Nations and Foreign Military Interventions. A Comparative Study
    of the Application of the Charter*, 2nd ed., Report 33. Uppsala: Department of
    Peace and Conflict Research, Uppsala University, 1994.

————. *Peace-keeping in a Peace Process: The Case of Cambodia*, Report 40. Uppsala: Department of Peace and Conflict Research, Uppsala University, 1995.

————. "United Nations Transitional Authority in Cambodia (UNTAC) (1992–1993). In *Southeast Asia: A Historical Encyclopedia, From Angkor Wat to East Timor, Vol. III: R-Z*, edited by Ooi Keat Gin. Santa Barbara, CA: ABC-CLIO, 2004.

————. "Cambodia and Vietnam: A Troubled Relationship". In *International Relations in Southeast Asia: Between Bilateralism and Multilateralism*, edited by N. Ganesan and Ramses Amer. Singapore: Institute of Southeast Asian Studies, 2010.

Boat People, The: An "Age" Investigation with Bruce Grant. Harmondsworth, Middlesex: Penguin Books, 1979.

Cambodia — The 1989 Paris Peace Conference: Background Analysis and Documents, compiled and edited by Amitav Acharya, Pierre Lizée and Sorpong Peou. Toronto: Centre for International and Strategic Studies, York University, and Millwood, New York: Kraus International, 1991.

Chandler, David P. *A History of Cambodia*, 2nd ed. St. Leonards, NSW: Allen & Unwin, 1993.

Chou Meng Tarr. "The Vietnamese Minority in Cambodia". *Race & Class* 34, no. 2 (1992): 33–47.

Curtis, Grant. *Cambodia: A Country Profile*. Stockholm: Swedish International Development Authority, 1990.

Goldblum, Charles. "Les relations inter-ethniques au Cambodge dans la presse Phnom-penhoise de langue française (1963–1970)" [The inter-ethnic relations in Cambodia in the French language press of Phnom Penh (1963–1970)]. *Asie du Sud-Est et Monde Insulindien* 5, no. 3 (1974): 25–51.

Farris, Karl. "UN Peacekeeping in Cambodia: On Balance, a Success". *Parameters* 24, no. 1 (1994): 38–50.

Findlay, Trevor. *Cambodia: The Legacy and Lessons of UNTAC*, SIPRI Research Report No. 9. Solna: Stockholm International Peace Research Institute (SIPRI) and Oxford: Oxford University Press, 1995.

Haas, Michael. "The Paris Conference on Cambodia, 1989". *Bulletin of Concerned Asian Scholars* 23, no. 2 (1991): 42–53.

Hughes, Caroline. "International Intervention and the People's Will: The Demoralization of Democracy in Cambodia". In *Conflict and Change in Cambodia*, edited with an Introduction by Ben Kiernan and Consulting Editor Caroline Hughes. London: Routledge, 2007.

Jennar, Raoul M. "UNTAC: 'International Triumph' in Cambodia?" *Security Dialogue* 25, no. 2 (1994): 145–56.

Kiernan, Ben. "Kampuchea 1979–1981: National Rehabilitation in the Eye of an International Storm". In *Southeast Asian Affairs 1982*, edited by Huynh Kim Khanh. Singapore: Institute of Southeast Asian Studies, 1982.

————. "Introduction: Conflict in Cambodia, 1945–2006". In *Conflict and Change in Cambodia*, edited with an Introduction by Ben Kiernan and Consulting Editor Caroline Hughes. London and New York: Routledge, 2007.

Leifer, Michael. "The International Representation of Kampuchea". In *Southeast Asian Affairs 1982*, edited by Huynh Kim Khanh. Singapore: Institute of Southeast Asian Studies, 1982.

Poole, Peter A. *The Expansion of the Vietnam War into Cambodia: Action and Response by the Governments of North Vietnam, South Vietnam, Cambodia, and the United States*, Papers in International Studies, Southeast Asia Series, 17. Athens, OH: Southeast Asia Programme, Center for International Studies, Ohio University, 1970.

Porter, Gareth. *Kampuchea's UN Seat: Cutting the Pol Pot Connection*, Indochina Issues, no. 8 (1980).

Pouvatchy Joseph. "L'éxode des vietnamiens du Cambodge en 1970" [The Exodus of the Vietnamese of Cambodia in 1970]. *Mondes Asiatiques*, no. 7 (Autumn 1976): 339–49.

Roberts, David. *Political Transition in Cambodia. Power, Elitism and Democracy*. London and New York: Routledge, 2000.

———. "Democratization, Elite Transition, and Violence in Cambodia, 1991–1999". In *Conflict and Change in Cambodia*, edited with an Introduction by Ben Kiernan and Consulting Editor Caroline Hughes. London and New York: Routledge, 2007.

Vickery, Michael. *Cambodia 1975–1982*. Boston: South End, 1984.

———. *Kampuchea: Politics, Economics, and Society*. London: Frances Pinter, 1986.

———. "Notes on the Political Economy of the People's Republic of Kampuchea (PRK)". *Journal of Contemporary Asia* 20, no. 4 (1990): 435–65.

Warbrick, Colin. "Kampuchea: Representation and Recognition". *International and Comparative Law Quarterly* 30, no. 1 (1981): 234–46.

6

CHANGING THE RULES
Historical Conjuncture and
Transition in Indonesia

Ehito Kimura

In 1998 Indonesia faced the political consequences of economic turmoil and decades of repression. The Asian financial crisis had triggered *reformasi*, but it was arguably the oppression of the New Order regime, thirty-three years of increasingly centralized authoritarian rule, that fuelled the anger and passions of so many Indonesians. By May of the same year, student demonstrators were openly calling for President Soeharto to step down, an act unimaginable a few months prior. There was an increase in ethnic violence and communal riots, not only in Jakarta, but throughout the archipelago. And as if to punctuate matters, forest fires raged on the resource-rich island of Kalimantan, covering much of the region with smog. At the time, observers of Indonesia expressed pessimism about the country's future prospects.

A decade on, Indonesia has experienced a remarkable recovery. It is currently the leading democracy in Southeast Asia, some might say, the *only* democracy in the region. Much of the ethnic and religious conflict that flared up in the waning days of the New Order and the political transition has tapered off. The economy has undergone an impressive revival. To be sure, many problems remain, including corruption, elite entrenchment and the spectre of violent Islamic fundamentalism. But a decade ago, few would have predicted Indonesia would be as politically and economically successful as it is today.

How did such a period of uncertainty and turmoil result in a seemingly stable and successful political regime? One reason for Indonesia's success today may be rooted in the historical moment of political transition sandwiched between these two periods. The resignation of Soeharto and the transition thereafter symbolized a massive rupture in Indonesian political development and began the process of building an entirely different kind of regime. Scholars call moments such as these historical conjunctures or critical junctures. Among the major reforms were democratization and far-reaching decentralization. The decision to implement these reforms and the particular way this was done, I argue, helps to account for the outcomes we see today.

This chapter examines Indonesia's historical conjuncture from two different perspectives, as both input and outcome. In terms of outcome, it argues that scholars of institutional change have tended to look at critical historical junctures as contingent or spontaneous events that cannot be explained on the basis of prior historical conditions. While there are elements of chance embedded in them, I argue that these junctures themselves emerge from a combination of long-term structural changes and short-term triggers. In Indonesia, I argue that structural changes were necessary but not sufficient to explain the emergence of the critical historical juncture in 1999.

I also argue that the historical conjuncture approach helps us to see Indonesia's transition in a new way. Democratization and decentralization were particular choices made in a fluid environment, and were reformist rather than revolutionary. Actors who designed the institutions did so as a way to address the spectre of state collapse, but also their own political survival. This then explains the solid gains in political stability, particularly in holding free and fair elections. But at the same time, it recognizes some of the remaining problems, including the lack of institutionalized political parties, the entrenchment of elites and the persistence of corruption.

The rest of the chapter proceeds in four parts. The first part explores the term, critical historical conjuncture, and argues for its further conceptual refinement. It then places the conjuncture in the context of the Indonesian experience and argues that the period following the fall of Soeharto and the transition to democracy marks the third historical critical juncture in Indonesia's history. The second part examines the sources leading up to the conjuncture, highlighting long-term structural changes as well as short-term triggers. The third part examines the character of the historical conjuncture itself and the key choices adopted by political actors during that period. The fourth part examines current outcomes that can be attributed to the transition, including territorial resilience, electoral democracy and elite entrenchment. The sixth part concludes the article.

HISTORICAL CONJUNCTURES AND THE INDONESIAN EXPERIENCE

Critical historical conjunctures are periods when events begin to lead down a particular path and certain legacies are formed. Often, these moments are identified and analysed in the context of broader arguments about path dependence, the idea that "once a country or region has started down a track, the costs of reversal are very high".[1] Once a path is set, a process of increasing returns drives what scholars refer to alternatively as "lock-in" or "inertia".[2] In this sense, critical junctures are often seen as key moments that "shape the basic contours of social life".[3]

By definition, these junctures are not isolated events that can be identified and analysed independently. They are relational and connected to larger outcomes. As Capoccia notes, "a historical moment that constitutes a critical juncture with respect to one institution may not constitute a critical juncture with respect to another".[4] To be sure, some events, such as Indonesia's transition, affect a broad array of outcomes ranging from politics, the economy and social relations. But a critical historical juncture must be critical to something, or it otherwise has little meaning.

The emphasis on the relational aspect of these moments has meant that historical conjunctures themselves are often simply afterthoughts in an analysis employing path-dependent methodology. These junctures are seen as periods when an "original ordering moment triggered particular patterns, and the activity is continuously reproduced even though the original event no longer occurs".[5] But the juncture itself is often relegated to the beginning or end of an elaborate causal chain of an explanatory historical path.[6]

This chapter adopts a definition of a critical historical conjuncture that goes beyond treating it as a bookend to path-dependent explanations. To borrow from Capoccia, critical junctures can be characterized as periods when particular actors have a wider than normal range of possible options, where the choices they make create a significant impact on subsequent outcomes. They are "a relatively short period of time during which there is a substantially heightened probability that agents' choices will affect the outcome of interest".[7] With this definition in hand, instead of identifying a particular outcome and working backwards to the critical historical conjuncture, this chapter focuses on the historical conjuncture itself, and seeks to analyse the way in which it came about, and how that in turn influenced outcomes.

In Indonesia, the most recent case of a historical critical juncture involves the fall of the Soeharto regime and Indonesia's subsequent political transition. The transition after the fall of the New Order constitutes a critical historical conjuncture because it marked a massive change from previous and more stable periods of Indonesia's political history. But beyond the rupture, the transition also represented a period of institutional fluidity when key actors had more choices available to them to make important decisions. Furthermore, the legacy of those choices arguably had important implications for the future.

During Indonesia's transition, major political actors, including the president, made key choices about Indonesia's political regime. Would Indonesia adopt democracy? If so, what kind? How would accountability be organized? How much power would the central government have? The argument I put forth is that the rules and institutions established on political parties, elections and centre-periphery relations had critical implications for what kind of regime Indonesia would become, and how that regime would fare a decade later.

Exploring a concrete case of a critical juncture raises some compelling questions. For example, how long does a juncture last and how do we know when one has begun or ended? Bertrand argues that Indonesia has experienced three periods of critical historical junctures. The first juncture encompassed the period of Indonesian nationalism and "the decades during which the Indonesian nation was constructed".[8] The second period ran roughly from 1957 to 1968, leading up to and including the fall of Sukarno and the rise of Soeharto. The third and most recent critical juncture, he argues, began in 1998, with the fall of Soeharto with no indication of a conclusion.

Bertrand's periodization raises questions of whether the concept of a critical juncture loses meaning if it can stretch out for so much time. In fact, if we abide by Bertrand's argument, from the 1920s up to 1968, there were only seven years in which Indonesia was not in the midst of a "critical juncture". Given that it has only been ten years since the fall of the New Order, it is worth asking if Indonesia is still in a critical juncture, or whether it has stabilized.

This chapter proceeds from the notion that placing temporal limits on critical junctures is an exercise in futility. While decades may seem a long time, Indonesia's revolutionary period is critical for understanding the broader trajectory of the Indonesian nation-state after independence and, in that regard, such a time frame is acceptable. Furthermore, the revolutionary period was highly fluid and unstable and, in that regard, it does adhere to our definition of a period when a wider range of "feasible options" existed. In this sense, critical junctures should not be defined exclusively by their duration; they are likely to vary according to historical context.

Similarly, when addressing the most recent historical juncture, one way to evaluate whether this period has ended or if it is ongoing is to ask whether Indonesia is still in a period of "institutional fluidity". For the most part, this chapter suggests that the period of fluidity has passed. I argue that the historical critical juncture began with the fall of Soeharto in May 1999 and ends with the election of Susilo Bambang Yudhoyono in 2004. By this time, much of the instability with regard to political institutions, ethnic conflict and terrorism had ended or at least begun to wane.

Critical historical junctures then are important moments within an institution's life that has significant bearing on future outcomes. In Indonesia, the political transition between the fall of Soeharto and the beginning of a stable government found in Susilo Bambang Yudhoyono represents such a period. A full examination of this historical conjuncture means addressing two separate but related questions. First, how did the historical juncture come about in the first place and what were the tangible outcomes of the juncture itself?

ROOTS OF THE HISTORICAL CONJUNCTURE

Where and how do critical historical junctures arise? Two competing explanations address broad structural factors on the one hand and short-term triggers on the other. The relationship between long-term causes and short-term triggers can be tricky. For example, some might argue that short-term events simply hastened the inevitable. I argue below that short-term triggers did much more, by actually shaping the kind of transition that would occur. This is consistent with what evolutionary biologists call "punctuated equilibriums", in which broad long-term slow-moving effects interact with moments of swift disequilibrium brought on by external and contingent events.[9]

Structural Factors: The Long Arc of Development

Among the more prominent theories about political change are structural theories about the relationship between economic development and political change.[10] While less focused on uncovering the roots of critical historical junctures per se, these scholars argue that the roots of political transition involve an increasingly powerful middle class that emerged from economic development.

In looking at Indonesia, scholars have put forth several, often complementary, arguments about the role of economic development and political change. Aspinall, for example, shows how an expanded middle class led to a corresponding growth in a more active and vocal civil society in the form of non-governmental and civil society organizations.[11] This trend mirrored a larger boom internationally, though in Indonesia most such organizations were not outwardly political and worked primarily on issues of labour, poverty and environmentalism. Groups such as Walhi, INFID and the Legal Aid Foundation were prominent, both nationally and internationally, and became what Aspinall calls a "proto-opposition", which formed the basis of an alternative political imaginary to the New Order.[12]

Similarly, scholars have argued that the rise of the middle class also led to a demographic shift in the educational institutions of Indonesia. On university campuses, student activism increased with demands for more campus autonomy and a more responsive government on social issues, such as poverty. The 1990s saw an increase in student gatherings and demonstrations that had been largely absent in the 1980s.[13] Lane argues that part of the reason for the surge in activism in the 1990s was due to the sheer growth of tertiary education and by implication the widening demographic of students that attended university. Instead of being a place for the children of privileged elites, a growing middle class began to fill the ranks of new schools in Jakarta, but, more importantly, across much of the rest of the archipelago.[14] While campuses were not yet the hotbeds of dissent they would become later in the decade, the shift in the late 1980s and early 1990s laid the groundwork to that end.

A third set of arguments focuses on the way political parties began to assert more influence, offering themselves as a broad and popular alternative to the dominant state party, GOLKAR. Much of this emerged from frustrations about corruption and lack of accountability in the regime in the 1980s and 1990s. Throughout much of the New Order, Soeharto sought to render opposition parties impotent by merging them with one another and banning them from organizational activities in rural areas. But in the 1990s one opposition party in particular, the Indonesian Democratic Party, Partai Demokrasi Indonesia or PDI, emerged to challenge the repressive New Order apparatus and flex its own political muscle. While PDI was in many ways a product of the New Order regime's reorganization of the party system, internal rifts in the party and long-running frustrations with the corrupt leadership served as an opening for Megawati Sukarnoputri, daughter of the late President Sukarno. In 1993, with fervent backing of many in her own party, Megawati ascended to the leadership of the Indonesian PDI.[15] With Mega, the party found a symbolically powerful, if cautious leader who became the major face for political reform in the late New Order.[16]

Megawati was not the sole voice of dissent during the 1990s. Hefner also highlights the importance of "Civil Islam" around the same time. Muslim leaders and organizations played a key role voicing opposition to the regime to the extent that they could. Abdurrahman Wahid, Nurcholish Madjid and Amien Rais all represented varying strains of opposition, pushing for liberal democratic institutions, such as free elections, unhampered political parties and a strong legislature in their demands for political reform. Wahid and Rais both led large Muslim political organizations, NU and Mohammadiyah, respectively, and in different ways played key roles in both the *reformasi* movement and the transitional politics in the post-Soeharto era.[17]

To be sure, the support of Megawati and other leaders did not come exclusively from the middle or urban classes. For the most part, leaders refrained from openly criticizing the New Order regime and gained popularity in different parts of the archipelago. But the populist message focusing particularly on constitutionalism did appeal to the middle class, who formed an important part of the opposition coalition later on.

Some scholars disagree on the mechanism but still emphasize the important role of economic classes. Sidel, for example, argues that the independence of the bourgeois, usually ethnic Chinese, in the Philippines, Thailand and Indonesia played a critical role in establishing and consolidating democracy in these countries. In Indonesia, he points to the role capital flight from the Chinese played in bringing down the Soeharto regime.[18] Others such as Bellin have argued the middle classes tend to be "contingent" democrats whose support for political change depends on state dependence and fear.[19]

A final relationship between development and democracy in the Indonesian context involves centre-periphery relations. By the 1980s the oil-boom model on which Indonesia had relied was seen as unsustainable, administrative capacity in the regions was improving, and the centralized system was seen as costly and inefficient.[20] The national budgeting process was also getting more and more complex and regional parliaments became increasingly more assertive about their role in local development.[21] And in the 1980s, manufacturing-led economic growth accelerated urbanization and helped raise Indonesian disposable income. These factors led to an increase in public service demand and a serious backlog in infrastructure investment.[22]

There were other more mundane problems with Indonesia's centralized fiscal policies over the years: delays in loan-financed infrastructure projects; reduction in quality of many projects; poor fiscal accounting at the local level; failure of central agencies taking care of project implementation; and problems of redundant administration. Because of these problems, the Indonesian leadership, concerned about its image domestically and internationally, slowly began to acknowledge the importance of an economic reform programme.[23]

These problems also fed the perception among resource-rich regions about how much of the revenue produced in the regions should go to the central government and be redistributed elsewhere. As economic growth increased, so too did the perceived disparities between Java and the so-called "Outer Islands", which also led to major frustrations with the regime.

All of this is to say that economic growth can pose serious challenges for the leaders of closed, centralized political systems. However, there are also a number of limitations with the argument. For one, while there certainly seems to be some truth to the argument about the relationship between development and democracy, it has trouble predicting the timing of the transition to democracy. Clearly, there needs to be some kind of trigger, and these are more difficult to theorize. Second, there are clear exceptions to this in Southeast Asia, notably Singapore, but also currently Thailand, Malaysia and Vietnam, all of which have had robust economic growth but less than complete democratic reforms.

Furthermore, in Indonesia, much of Soeharto's legitimacy had also been based on the economic prosperity many Indonesians experienced under his rule. In the 1970s much of the economic growth came from petroleum exports and other natural resources. By the 1990s Indonesia and other Southeast Asian economies were dubbed "miracles" because of their ability to attract high levels of foreign direct investment (FDI), attain double digit growth, in turn leading to growth in an upwardly mobile middle class.[24] As long as economic growth persisted, the mass of people were reluctant to challenge the authoritarian tendencies of the regime. This makes the argument of an inevitable shift to democracy difficult to assess. The pressures of middle-class mobility appear to have been cancelled out by the high levels of growth.

The structural conditions for reform arguably laid a foundation for the changes, but only given the appropriate triggers. Development, in other words, was a necessary but not sufficient factor for the political changes that would occur in the late 1990s. But we should not cast the fall of Soeharto as inevitable in any way. Though there was some political opposition to Soeharto, the New Order was able to largely contain that opposition because of its monopoly on the coercive apparatus of the state, and the growth of the economy presented an emerging tension but not necessarily an irreconcilable one.

Short-Term Factors: Triggering Political Change

When the Asian financial crisis of 1997 struck Indonesia, it did not simply hasten an inevitable process of political change in the regime. The trigger itself and the way actors behaved amid the crisis significantly shaped the outcome of the *reformasi* and Indonesia's political transition. It is worth reflecting on what aspects of this short punctuated burst of events can be seen as important in bringing about that change.

The Asian financial crisis triggered economic turmoil across the region and Indonesia experienced widespread capital flight with the rupiah depreciating nearly 10 per cent just in the month of August. Currency speculators also bet against the rupiah, and the Bank of Indonesia was unable to sustain their interventions to keep the currency stable. By January of 1998 the rupiah lost 85 per cent of its value, trading at around 5,000 rupiah to the dollar, and the stock market fell by more than 50 per cent, from 743 to 335.[25] In early 1997 unemployment hovered at around 14 per cent, but by 1998 it had risen to around 40 per cent.

The first and most fundamental result of this economic crisis is that it undercut the most compelling basis of the New Order regime, that of performance legitimacy. With this pillar gone, anger against the regime began to emerge from a number of directions leading to broad popular discontent. It is safe to say: "No Crisis, no *reformasi*."

On the one hand, the crisis produced massive economic displacement in the form of unemployment and inflation. Furthermore, economic reforms initiated by the IMF followed neoliberal policies that cut government spending to balance the budget. In retrospect, this seemed to be the wrong medicine for Indonesia, which had a relatively well-balanced budget. But the result of those cuts produced uncertainty about the cost of basic goods, such as food and petroleum. This in turn led to panic runs in the markets of basic commodity goods and protests against price hikes and the elimination of subsidies.

While the Asian financial crisis certainly laid the groundwork for pressure against Soeharto, the president's own reaction also contributed to his downfall. In the weeks and months after the onset of the crisis, it became evident that Soeharto had little intention of initiating any substantive political or economic reforms. World leaders from the United States, Germany, Singapore, Japan, and the United Kingdom called or sent emissaries to Soeharto urging him to embrace a broader reform, including deregulation of the banking sector and dealing with issues of foreign debt.[26] Soeharto proceeded to initiate some reforms but also protected many of his family businesses, including the notorious national car project headed by his son "Tommy".[27]

The government had always walked a fine line between tolerating levels of corruption to retain bureaucratic support and cracking down periodically to keep some semblance of credibility with the domestic and international public.[28] Soeharto could never credibly launch any anti-corruption campaign of substance without threatening the entire power structure of the country and the way it was ruled. As the level of corruption particularly around Soeharto's family and friends reached dizzying heights, many in Indonesia began to express resentment of Indonesia's First Family.[29] In the waning days of Soeharto's presidency, one of the major themes of the Indonesian *reformasi* movement focused on eliminating KKN, the Indonesian acronym for Corruption, Collusion and Nepotism.

Much of Soeharto's subsequent moves were attempts to shore up political power and surround himself with loyalists. In February and March of 1998, the People's Consultative Assembly convened for its quinquennial deliberations. President Soeharto delivered a speech on the account of government policy of the last five years, painting an optimistic picture of the government's accomplishments over the course of the previous term and then his re-election by acclamation to a seventh term as president. The next day, Habibie's nomination as vice president was accepted by the People's Assembly, a move seen largely as placing a loyalist in the seat of the vice presidency to protect his own position.[30]

Less than two weeks later, Soeharto announced the members of his new Cabinet, which was seen broadly as a consolidation of power, including appointments to close cronies and even his daughter, Siti Hardiyanti Rukmana. Soeharto did not appoint any other political moderates, nor did he appoint any reformist Muslim leaders to his Cabinet. The selection of the Soeharto Cabinet may have been one of the biggest strategic blunders by Soeharto. It is possible that if he had shown some inkling of reform on this occasion then he might not have suffered the same consequences. Instead, he galvanized the entire moderate Muslim opposition against him.[31] This was a key turning point because of the way it alienated potential allies and solidified an otherwise divided opposition against him.

All of this reignited a new wave of protests and disappointed the international community's hopes that Soeharto would press for political and economic reform.[32] Protests mounted in Jakarta through March and April, though mostly confined to college campuses. On 12 May, military sharpshooters shot and killed four student demonstrators at a rally in Trisakti University in Jakarta. Massive riots followed in May, much of them in the northern area of Jakarta's Chinatown. Over 1,000 people were killed, houses and shops were razed, and large-scale gang rapes were reported.[33] Foreign embassies began to evacuate their staff, and many of the ethnic Chinese who could afford to also fled abroad to Singapore and elsewhere. By mid-May, there was intense pressure on Soeharto to step down. Student demonstrators first demonstrating on campuses moved to the parliament building, occupying the People's Congress building.[34]

If Soeharto had lost the confidence of the mass of Indonesians in the midst of economic crisis, the violence in Chinatown and the Trisakti massacre also led to his abandonment by the elite. Elite fragmentation, as scholars have argued, creates regime instability.[35] At this point, most members of the national legislature were also calling on Soeharto to resign. The military representatives and even GOLKAR eventually joined those calls for Soeharto to step down. Finally, on 21 May 1998, Soeharto officially resigned, bringing an end to the New Order regime, and his vice president, Habibie, was immediately sworn in as president.[36]

This section has suggested that the triggering mechanism of the Asian financial crisis played a key role in the fall of Soeharto. It did more than simply hasten an inevitable collapse of the New Order. It clearly shaped the outcomes in significant ways. Furthermore, Soeharto's choices in reaction to the crisis also played a key role, as arguably did choices made in other countries affected by the crisis. In this regard, it is not simply the external shocks that undercut Soeharto's New Order, but also the domestic political mobilization and the regime's response to that mobilization. For this reason, while external factors are important, the domestic factors seem to be the key variable that led to Soeharto's fall.

CHANGING THE RULES IN HISTORICAL CONJUNCTURE

If we define critical junctures as moments when agents have a wide flexibility in choices, then the period of Indonesia's transition after the fall of the New Order qualifies as one such period. Policymakers chose certain kinds of reforms over others and implemented them in very specific ways. On the one hand, Soeharto's hand-picked successor, B.J. Habibie, and the regime more generally needed to separate itself from the New Order regime and offer themselves as a legitimate and forward looking alternative.[37] When seen in this light, early reforms including freeing up political parties, removing restrictions on the media and press, releasing political prisoners, preparing for elections, and allowing a referendum in East Timor make a great deal of sense.[38] Said differently, the reforms of democratization and decentralization instituted during the transition exemplify this paradox of political reform and regime maintenance as well.

At the same time, the way in which these reforms were designed were arguably more reformist and incremental rather than revolutionary. Habibie and other political elites also clearly wanted to retain power and thus worked to make the institutional rules advantageous to themselves. In many instances, they failed, but in others, they succeeded. In this regard, the institutional reforms during the critical historical juncture are not simply reforms demanded from below, nor policies implemented by neutral experts.[39] They were profoundly political with many actors who had their own strategic interests in mind.

Democratization: Electoral and Party Reform

The revival of political parties was one of the first major political reforms in post-Soeharto Indonesia and among the most critical. The reforms were simultaneously liberalizing and constraining. On the one hand, political parties that had been merged and then emasculated during the New Order gained new life. New laws allowed political parties to form with only fifty signatures from citizens twenty-one years of age or older and registration with a court and the Ministry of Justice.[40] As a result, dozens of new political parties emerged in 1999.

At the same time, the new laws did lay out strict rules about which parties could participate in national elections. Specifically, the new rules required parties to have offices established in at least one-third of Indonesia's provinces and at least half of all districts in those provinces as a way to prevent regional or ethnically based parties.[41] The party system has also had enormous influence on the composition of legislative bodies. For example, election laws eliminated the possibility of non-party candidates and gave a high degree of control to the central party leadership over the selection of candidates.[42]

New laws also limited the number of military parliamentarians from 75 to 38 in the 1999 elections, and eventually to zero.[43] During the New Order, one-fifth of the seats in the national legislature were allocated to the military, and senior officers held key posts in the bureaucracy, regional administrative services, governorships, and the Cabinet.[44] Increased professionalism and reform also saw the military disengage from the electoral process other than to ensure minimal violence and disruption, whereas in the past the military had been instrumental in rigging elections in favour of the regime.[45]

The character of a new electoral system also came under considerable discussion in 1999. The government put forth a proposal for a mixed system that would see 76 per cent of seats contested on a district-plurality basis, and 24 per cent contested according to the rules of proportional representation.[46] The system sought to make legislators more accountable to their local geographic communities while still retaining some of the

PR system so smaller parties would not be disadvantaged. However, this proposal was rejected both because it was likely to give the government party, GOLKAR, a broad advantage, and because it weakened the ability of political parties to control their own candidates.[47]

Thus, all parties agreed on a completely proportional electoral system. The question then turned to the size of the electoral districts. Again, the government sought to make electoral districts smaller. This too was seen by opposition parties as distinctly advantageous to GOLKAR which had a much firmer presence at the local level during the New Order. Thus, in 1999 the electoral districts were established at the provincial levels, regardless of population. Seats were allocated proportionately with the average per province being 17 seats, but varying widely depending on population density. West Java, for example, had 82 seats, while Bengkulu and East Timor each had 4 seats.[48]

The election committee also came up with a formula to balance representation between Java and the Outer Islands. If representation mirrored the demographic distribution of the population, then legislative seats would have been divided along a 60–40 ratio between Java and the Outer Islands. Instead, legislative seats were divided nearly evenly, 234 (50.6 per cent) for Java and 228 (49.4 per cent) for the Outer Islands. Seats were distributed to cities with more than 450,000 people first. The remaining seats were redistributed between the provinces based on population.[49]

For this reason, the number of votes needed to secure a seat varied widely depending on the location of the district. In the densely populated province of East Java, one parliamentary seat required 287,199 votes. A seat from Irian Jaya (West Papua) in contrast would only require 63,547 votes.[50] Thus, in the 1999 elections, PDIP won 34 per cent of the votes and received 33 per cent of the seats (153), because many of its votes were concentrated on Java. In contrast, GOLKAR won 22 per cent but received 26 per cent of the seats because they secured many votes from the less densely populated Outer Islands.[51] Other parties faced more or less similar kinds of disparities, gaining or losing advantage depending on where their votes came from.

These early decisions in representation and electoral competition laid the foundations for the next several elections. Although the rules changed, sometimes in significant ways, the overall principle around political parties did not. The political party reforms went a long way towards giving organizational representation to some of the key cleavages in Indonesian society. At the same time, there were simply too many social or cultural groups in Indonesia for all to be represented, particularly along geographic or ethnic lines. In this way, the new electoral rules both liberalized and limited party formation.

Decentralization: Devolving Power Downward

The second pillar of *reformasi* after 1999 was the design and implementation of far-reaching decentralization. Again, it is worth reflecting on why this became such an important reform measure. During *reformasi*, one of the tensions that began to emerge was the articulation of regional frustrations against the central government. Regionalists included a spectrum of groups who agreed broadly about the problems inherent in the over-centralized regime.

At one extreme were ethnic nationalist groups who sought independence, arguing that Indonesia had forcibly integrated them into the nation state without their approval, including East Timor, Aceh and West Papua.[52] But plenty of other groups in the regions expressed frustration with Jakarta, well into the Soeharto era. Those in natural-resource rich regions such as Riau and Kalimantan also resented the centralized policies of Jakarta, arguing that they should be able to keep more of the revenue generated from their region for themselves.

As a response, the Habibie government initiated milestone legislation that passed in 1999 and was implemented under the Wahid administration in 2001. Two laws, Law 22 of 1999 on Regional Administrations and Law 25 of 1999 on Inter-Government Financial Balance, devolved almost all substantive power, except in a few key areas (foreign affairs, international trade, monetary policy, national security and legal systems) to the regency, a sub-provincial level known in Indonesian as the *kabupaten*.[53]

On the one hand, Law 22 on administration devolved a broad range of public service delivery functions to the local level, such as planning, financing, implementing, evaluating and monitoring of such services. More importantly, the new laws devolved significant political powers downward by strengthening the role of the elected local councils, Dewan Perwakilan Rakyat Daerah or DPRD. The local districts were given far-reaching autonomy and accountability that for the most part bypassed the province and was directed to the central government. Thus, new responsibilities included work in the areas of environment, labour, public works and natural resource management.[54] Local legislatures also gained power independent of the local chief executive, with the power to hold the leader accountable.

Law 25 on fiscal balance focused on empowering and raising local economic capabilities. Local government was given the power to tax, charge local fees and collect revenue from local businesses.[55] In the case of any budgetary shortfalls, they would also be allotted regional development or "equalization" funds from the central government.

The justification for the new decentralization laws was based along two principles, efficiency and equality. By devolving power to the local level, proponents argued that government would be "closer to the ground", and thus better able to assess the needs of the local population and be more responsive to their demands.[56] At the same time, proponents also argued that decentralization would give more incentives to local actors to provide better services, based on economic theories that people could move if they were not happy in their particular district.[57]

Decentralization was also seen as a way to alleviate some of the regional tensions in Indonesia that had risen to fever-pitch during the period of political turmoil. On the one hand, devolving power to the local regions alleviated resentment about the way the New Order government had controlled local offices and officials. Similarly, the new fiscal arrangements allowed several regions to retain a larger portion of revenues from natural resources, which was ordinarily sent to Jakarta and redistributed accordingly. Although separate from Laws 22 and 25, the government also gave special autonomy to key regions, and, in the case of East Timor, let it go altogether.[58]

Strategically, districts, not provinces, were chosen as the main level of autonomy in the newly decentralized Indonesia. This was because of the fear that autonomy at the provincial level would exacerbate regional tensions rather than alleviate them. Decentralization as designed in Indonesia actually then weakened provincial power by strengthening the districts. All of this is to say that the 1999 decentralization plan was a compromise reacting to pressures for increased autonomy, increased freedoms, yet deeply concerned about maintaining national unity.

In sum, democratization and decentralization formed the two pillars of political reform during Indonesia's transition. These processes changed significantly over the course of the transition in terms of particular rules, but they never changed fundamentally in their promotion of political competition, accountability and devolution of power. These emerged and took shape in the form they did because of the pressures that had been placed on the New Order state and the demands societal groups had on reform. Ultimately, they created "tracks" that laid the foundation for Indonesia's territorial and political stability.

OUTCOMES (AND NON-OUTCOMES) IN CONTEMPORARY INDONESIA

Not all critical historical junctures produce significant change. Demonstrations in Burma for democracy in 1988, for example, did little to bring about political change and, if anything, entrenched the military junta in power. In the Indonesian context, too, the outcomes for the country as it underwent a massive political transition were largely uncertain. A decade later, we can see that the Indonesian geo-body has survived, and that electoral democracy seems to be largely entrenched. While these may seem ordinary achievements in many states, I define them as "successes", given the expectations at the time. This section outlines some of these outcomes and examines their relationship to the critical juncture itself.

Territorial Resilience

First of all, we know that Indonesia has remained a coherent nation state. While this may appear to be an obvious statement, at the time of the political crisis, there were significant questions about the future of the archipelago. With violence in East Timor, Aceh, Papua, Kalimantan and elsewhere, many wondered whether Indonesia might fragment into several pieces. From a regional comparative perspective, this may not be particularly striking, since no state in Southeast Asia has ever splintered (with the possible exception of Malaysia and Singapore). But Indonesia's territorial resilience has been a major concern for the state practically since its very inception.

As we have seen, both democratization and decentralization reforms were carefully calibrated to prevent Indonesia's fragmentation. Indonesia's party system remains highly centralized and elections operate on a proportional representation system. And only parties with national representation may compete in the electoral process. These rules all prevent the emergence of regional or ethnic parties or issues in national-level politics.

Decentralization was also painstakingly designed to be as far-reaching as possible, yet to minimize the possibilities of state fragmentation by circumventing the province and devolving authority directly to the districts. One way in which this occurred is that decentralized power and local level political competition reframed centre–periphery tensions into periphery–periphery tensions. Among other things, this created a plethora of new districts and provinces throughout Indonesia.[59] Decentralization thus may have been responsible for some ethnic conflict early on, but combined with processes of democratization, it may have actually helped to feed competition into the electoral system and prevent local and ethnic nationalism from emerging.

STABLE DEMOCRACY

A second and related point is that Indonesia's democracy has been remarkably stable over the past decade. With each successive election, Indonesia has solidified its reputation as able to hold free and fair elections. A number of important characteristics about these elections are worth noting. First, they have been largely free from violence and from fraud. Second, results have tended to back secular parties rather than religious parties. And third, they have been successful despite a high level of complexity.

How can we understand these outcomes? First, the decision on the part of the government to both democratize and decentralize likely had an important role here. In dispersing power so widely, and by empowering both the executive and legislative institutions at the local, regional and national level, the rules made electoral competition a central part of the electoral system. This in turn may also have led to an increasing level of certainty that reinforced people's notions in the institutions themselves, instead of engaging in conflict extra-institutionally. Furthermore, while many cited concerns over the ever-changing rules of the Indonesian election system over the past three elections, this flexibility and willingness to adapt also was an important component to electoral stability.

Regarding the reforms themselves, many were concerned at the time of the elections about the complexity of the election laws and the process of selecting parties and candidates.[60] However, this complexity also reflected a thoroughness in the system that raised its level of legitimacy. Said differently, the criticisms that Indonesia was receiving for changing its electoral rules so frequently, and doing so in a complex manner, may have had positive outcomes by providing stability during the elections.

In dispersing power so widely, and by empowering both the executive and legislative institutions at the local, regional and national levels, the rules made competition a central part of the electoral system and institutionalized that competition.

Elite Continuity and Entrenchment

A third key choice during this period of fluidity might be better characterized as a "non-choice", namely the refusal to implement too much reform that could threaten elite interests. This "non-choice" darkens an otherwise sunny picture of the post-*reformasi* period and has led to elite entrenchment. These "non-choices" included a reluctance to engage in extensive military reform, to combat high levels of corruption and institutionalize political parties.

For example, even though the military ultimately exited from political office, military reform faced strong opposition during the Wahid presidency and ultimately failed in significant ways. Most critically, the military was able to hold on to its territorial command structure despite efforts to eliminate it. The territorial command structure, whose design is rooted in the guerrilla tactics used during the Indonesian Revolution, is arguably at the core of the military's power and autonomy. Military presence in the territories was the primary source for off-budget financing and thus gave it a great deal of economic independence. Furthermore, while technically disengaged from politics, their continued presence and activity in the regions may also have been a source of stability.[61]

In addition to the military, similar manifestations of elite entrenchment are evident in the political party system. For one, the dominant party of the New Order, GOLKAR, continues to flex its political muscle. Given that this party was specifically designed to give the New Order a stranglehold on the political system, it is remarkable that it has survived the transition to democracy.

At the same time, political parties also continue to be characterized by strong leaders, many of whom rose to prominence during the New Order, rather than political platforms and ideologies. For example, in the most recent presidential election, three of the most prominent presidential or vice-presidential candidates were former military officers in Soeharto's army, including Susilo Bambang Yudhoyono, Wiranto and Prabowo Subianto. Other candidates included prominent figures such as Megawati Sukarnoputri, daughter of Indonesian national leader Sukarno and leader of PDI-P, and Jusuf Kalla, a business crony during the Suharto regime who entered politics in the late 1980s.[62] Even more indicative of the lack of institutionalization was the way candidates paired up, perhaps the most surprising pair being Megawati Sukarnoputri, known for opposing the New Order, and Prabowo Subianto, a notorious commander who led the special forces Kopassus during the New Order.

Scholars also argue that while Indonesia's democratic reforms have instituted vertical accountability between elected officials and the public, it has actually eroded horizontal accountability and created an "accountability trap".[63] Slater argues that political parties form cartels in which nearly all political parties are included in the ruling coalition, effectively eliminating the existence of an opposition party. This creates a situation where downward accountability becomes largely meaningless because competition between the parties becomes eliminated.

Finally, even through the realm of decentralization, whilst it did offer a new form of empowerment in many local regions and may have headed off territorial fragmentation, it has also spurred a process of local elite capture. Hadiz argues that the conflicts between groups after decentralization are not between predatory interests and neoliberal reforms, but between different kinds of predatory coalitions.[64] He traces the links between predatory groups, such as the *preman* in the North Sumatran underworld and the money politics prevalent in East Java to how such groups make alliances and mobilize with groups at the national level.[65]

In sum, this section argues that Indonesia's historical conjuncture produced real and tangible results, including the stabilization of Indonesia's geo-body and an institutionalized set of rules about competitive elections. At the same time, agents also implemented these reforms in a way that did not fundamentally threaten previous elites and in fact worked to entrench elites under these new institutional rules.

CONCLUSION

This chapter has sought to explore the concept of a critical historical conjuncture in the context of Indonesia's recent political transition. Defining a historical conjuncture as a period when agents have a broader range of choices, and where those choices can lead to significant change, it argued that Indonesia faced such a period between the time that Soeharto resigned from office in 1998 and the stabilization of the country around 2004. Both the factors leading to the historical conjuncture as well as the outcomes from that historical moment were analysed.

In terms of exploring the origins of critical historical conjunctures, the Indonesian case study illuminates the complexity of the phenomenon. For the most part, studies of path dependence have used critical junctures as starting points that are random or unexplained events. An in-depth case study shows us how the interplay of long-term structural factors, such as economic development, and short-term triggers served to bring about Indonesia's critical juncture. Structural factors on their own, I argue, may be necessary but are not sufficient to explain Soeharto's fall and the subsequent changes. Instead, they tended to narrow the scope of decisions and constrain actors, but the outcomes were highly contingent on external factors and the choices of political actors.

When considering the outcomes of historical conjunctures, the Indonesian case has shown how choices adopted in the form of democratization and decentralization led to significant kinds of outcomes. These choices were arguably reformist rather than revolutionary and had simultaneous goals of political reform and political survival. On the one hand, the outcomes of territorial resilience and the implementation of a competitive multiparty electoral system paint an optimistic picture of Indonesia's current political climate. On the other hand, this is tempered and qualified by the continued entrenchment of Indonesia's political elite at both the national and local levels.

While historical conjunctures as input and outcome have been analysed separately, the chapter also shows how the two are intimately related. The historical conjuncture and the decisions adopted by key agents emerged from the pressures in the previous period where the regime was perceived to be uncompetitive and over-centralized. In this sense, the period of the historical conjuncture links the two eras before and after and shapes the trajectory of Indonesia's current political situation.

Finally, Indonesia's experience tells us that critical historical conjunctures do not always lead to change. In fact, continuity may be as important an outcome as big historical change. Indonesia's territorial resilience can be seen as an example of this, where policy choices seem to have reinforced territorial continuity. I have also suggested that critical junctures may be characterized by "non-choices" as much as particular choices. A decision not to enact far-reaching military reform, for example, is in and of itself a "choice" that had important consequences later on. Furthermore, while elements of change and continuity may in fact coexist, the Indonesian case illustrates how these may even depend on one another. Said differently, significant changes in the political system were possible only because they did not immediately threaten the existing political elite.

To be sure, not all outcomes in Indonesia or elsewhere can be attributed solely to the most recent historical conjuncture. In fact, many legacies may persist despite key changes that are implemented in a subsequent period. This chapter has not attempted to evaluate all outcomes nor judge which ones were affected by the historical conjuncture and which were not. Future research might also then address what aspects of Indonesia can be explained by rupture and what aspects of politics have prevailed in Indonesia despite the historical conjuncture.

This chapter has undertaken a more modest task, namely to look at the historical conjuncture on its own terms and examine the way in which it emerged and how it has affected some key outcomes in Indonesia today. It has done so under the premise that critical junctures themselves are often under-examined in explanations for political change. With a close look at the Indonesian case study, this chapter has tried to deepen and broaden our understanding of this historical conjuncture and the way in which it affected Indonesia's transition.

Notes

1. Margaret Levi, *Consent, Dissent, and Patriotism* (Cambridge: Cambridge University Press, 1997).
2. P. Pierson, "Increasing Returns, Path Dependence, and the Study of Politics", *American Political Science Review* 94, no. 2 (June 2000): 263.
3. Ibid., p. 251.
4. Giovanni Capoccia, "The Study of Critical Junctures: Theory, Narrative, and Counterfactuals in Historical Institutionalism", *World Politics* 59, no. 3 (2007): 349.
5. Pierson, "Increasing Returns, Path Dependence, and the Study of Politics", p. 263.
6. James Mahoney and Dietrich Rueschemeyer, *Comparative Historical Analysis in the Social Sciences*, Cambridge studies in comparative politics (Cambridge: Cambridge University Press, 2003), pp. 507–8.

7. Capoccia, "The Study of Critical Junctures", p. 348.
8. Jacques Bertrand, *Nationalism and Ethnic Conflict in Indonesia*, Cambridge Asia-Pacific studies (New York: Cambridge University Press, 2004), p. 28.
9. Stephen Gould, *Punctuated Equilibrium* (Cambridge, MA: Belknap Press of Harvard University Press, 2007).
10. Barrington Moore, *Social Origins of Dictatorship and Democracy: Lord and Peasant in the Making of the Modern World* (Boston: Beacon Press, 1966); Dietrich Rueschemeyer, Evelyne Huber Stephens, and John D. Stephens, *Capitalist Development and Democracy* (Chicago: University of Chicago Press, 1992).
11. Edward Aspinall, "Indonesia: Transformation of Civil Society and Democratic Breakthrough", in *Civil Society and Political Change in Asia: Expanding and Contracting Democratic Space*, edited by Muthiah Alagappa (Stanford University Press, 2004), p. 76.
12. Edward Aspinall, *Opposing Suharto: Compromise, Resistance, and Regime Change in Indonesia*, Contemporary Issues in the Asia Pacific (Stanford: Stanford University Press, 2005).
13. Edward Aspinall, "Students and the Military: Regime Friction and Civilian Dissent in the Late Suharto Period", *Indonesia* 59 (1995): 31.
14. Max Lane, "Students on the Move", *Inside Indonesia*, 1989.
15. Liddle, "Indonesia in 1996: Pressures from Above and Below", *Asian Survey* 37, no. 2 (1997): 168.
16. Daniel Ziv, "Populist Perceptions and Perceptions of Populism in Indonesia: The Case of Megawati Soekarnoputri", *South East Asia Research* 9 (2001): 73–88.
17. Robert Hefner, *Civil Islam: Muslims and Democratization in Indonesia* (Princeton, NJ: Princeton University Press, 2000).
18. John Sidel, "Social Origins of Dictatorship and Democracy: Colonial State and Chinese Immigrant in the Making of Modern Southeast Asia", *Journal of Comparative Politics* (2008): 141.
19. Eva Bellin, "Contingent Democrats: Industrialists, Labor, and Democratization in Late-Developing Countries", *World Politics* (2000).
20. Hal Hill, *Indonesia's New Order: The Dynamics of Socio-economic Transformation* (Honolulu: University of Hawai'i Press, 1994), p. 4.
21. Ibid., p. 6.
22. Paul Smoke and Blane Lewis, "Fiscal Decentralization in Indonesia: A New Approach to an Old Idea", *World Development* 24, no. 8 (1996): 1283.
23. Ibid., p. 1284.
24. Andrew MacIntyre, "Business, Government, and Development: Northeast and Southeast Asian Comparisons", in *Business and Government in Industrializing Asia* (Ithaca, NY: Cornell University Press, 1994), pp. 1–22.

25. Judith Bird, "Indonesia in 1997: The Tinderbox Year", *Asian Survey* 38, no. 2 (1998): 175.
26. Kees van Dijk, *A Country in Despair: Indonesia Between 1997 and 2000* (Netherlands: KITLV Press, 2001), p. 154.
27. Bird, "Indonesia in 1997: The Tinderbox Year", p. 173.
28. William Liddle, "Soeharto's Indonesia: Personal Rule and Political Institutions", *Pacific Affairs* 58, no. 1 (1985): 78.
29. Ahman Habir, "Conglomerates: All in the Family?" in *Indonesia beyond Suharto: Polity, Economy, Society, Transition*, edited by Donald K. Emmerson (Armonk, NY: Sharpe, 1999), p. 192.
30. Dijk, *A Country in Despair*, p. 149.
31. Hefner, *Civil Islam*, p. 200.
32. Dijk, *A Country in Despair*, p. 151.
33. Judith Bird, "Indonesia in 1998: The Pot Boils Over", *Asian Survey* 39, no. 1 (1999): 29.
34. Dijk, *A Country in Despair*, p. 199.
35. William Case, *Politics in Southeast Asia: Democracy or Less* (Routledge, 2002).
36. Donald K. Emmerson, "Exit and Aftermath: The Crisis of 1997–98", in *Indonesia beyond Suharto: Polity, Economy, Society, Transition*, edited by Donald K. Emmerson (Armonk, NY: M.E. Sharpe, 1999), p. 298.
37. Harold Crouch, *Political Reform in Indonesia after Soeharto* (Singapore: Institute of Southeast Asian Studies, 2010), p. 6.
38. Bertrand, *Nationalism and Ethnic Conflict in Indonesia*, p. 42.
39. B. Smith, "The Origins of Regional Autonomy in Indonesia: Experts and the Marketing of Political Interests", *Journal of East Asian Studies* 8, no. 2 (2008): 213.
40. Dwight King, *Half-Hearted Reform: Electoral Institutions and the Struggle for Democracy in Indonesia* (Westport, CT: Praeger, 2003), p. 51.
41. Ibid.
42. Stephen Sherlock, *The 2004 Indonesian Elections: How the System Works and What the Parties Stand For: A Report on Political Parties*, edited by Stephen Sherlock (Australian National University, 2004), p. 8.
43. Damien Kingsbury, *Power Politics and the Indonesian Military* (RouledgeCurzon, 2003), p. 164.
44. Jamie Mackie and Andrew MacIntyre, "Politics", in *Indonesia's New Order: The Dynamics of Socio-Economic Transformation*, edited by Hal Hill (Honolulu: University of Hawai'i Press, 1994), p. 24.
45. Kingsbury, *Power Politics and the Indonesian Military*.
46. King, *Half-Hearted Reform*, p. 60.
47. Ibid., p. 61.
48. Leo Suryadinata, *Elections and Politics in Indonesia* (Singapore: Institute of Southeast Asian Studies, 2002), p. 9.
49. Ibid., p. 89.
50. Ibid.

51. Sherlock, *The 2004 Indonesian Elections*, p. 8.
52. Edward Aspinall and Mark T. Berger, "The Break-up of Indonesia? Nationalisms after Decolonisation and the Limits of the Nation-State in Post–Cold War Southeast Asia", *Third World Quarterly* 22, no. 6 (2001): 1003–24.
53. James Alm, Robert Aten, and Roy Bahl, "Can Indonesia Decentralise Successfully? Plans, Problems and Prospects", *Bulletin of Indonesia Economic Studies* 37, no. 1 (2001): 83–102.
54. Edward Aspinall and Greg Fealy, *Local Power and Politics in Indonesia Decentralisation and Democratisation*, Indonesia update series (Singapore: Institute of Southeast Asian Studies, 2003), p. 4.
55. Alm, Aten, and Bahl, "Can Indonesia Decentralise Successfully?"
56. Gustav Ranis and Frances Stewart, *Decentralization in Indonesia* (Yale University, Economic Growth Center, 1995).
57. Charles Tiebout, "A Pure Theory of Local Expenditures", *Journal of Political Economy* 64 (1956): 416–24.
58. The government did establish Aceh and West Papua as Daerah Istimewah and Daerah Otonomi Khusus, respectively, giving them a significant share of natural resource revenue and broad legal authority.
59. Ehito Kimura, "Provincial Proliferation: Vertical Coalitions and the Politics of Territoriality in Post-authoritarian Indonesia" (PhD dissertation, University of Wisconsin–Madison, 2006).
60. Carter Center, *Final Report of the Carter Center Limited Observation Mission to the April 9, 2009 Legislative Elections in Indonesia* (Atlanta, GA: Carter Center, August 2009).
61. M. Mietzner, *Military Politics, Islam, and the State in Indonesia: From Turbulent Transition to Democratic Consolidation* (Singapore: Institute of Southeast Asian Studies, 2009).
62. M. Mietzner, "Indonesia in 2009: Electoral Contestation and Economic Resilience", *Asian Survey* 50, no. 1 (2010): 148.
63. Dan Slater, "Indonesia's Accountability Trap: Party Cartels and Presidential Power after Democratic Transition", *Indonesia*, no. 78 (October 2004): 61–92.
64. Vedi Hadiz, *Localising Power in Post-authoritarian Indonesia: A Southeast Asia Perspective* (Stanford: Stanford University Press, 2010), p. 55.
65. Vedi Hadiz, "Indonesian Local Party Politics: A Site of Resistance to Neoliberal Reform", *Critical Asian Studies* 34 (2004): 615–36.

References

Alm, J., R. Aten, and R. Bahl. "Can Indonesia Decentralise Successfully? Plans, Problems and Prospects". *Bulletin of Indonesia Economic Studies* 37, no. 1 (2001): 83–102.
Aspinall, E. "Students and the Military: Regime Friction and Civilian Dissent in the late Suharto Period". *Indonesia* 59 (1995): 21–44.

————. Indonesia: Transformation of Civil Society and Democratic Breakthrough. In *Civil Society and Political Change in Asia: Expanding and Contracting Democratic Space*, edited by M. Alagappa. Stanford: Stanford University Press, 2004.

————. *Opposing Suharto: Compromise, Resistance, and Regime Change in Indonesia*. Stanford: Stanford University Press, 2005.

Aspinall, E. and M.T. Berger. "The Break-up of Indonesia? Nationalisms after Decolonisation and the Limits of the Nation-state in Post-Cold War Southeast Asia". *Third World Quarterly* 22, no. 6 (2001): 1003–24.

Aspinall, E. and G. Fealy. *Local Power and Politics in Indonesia: Decentralisation and Democratisation*. Singapore: Institute of Southeast Asian Studies, 2003.

Bellin, E. "Contingent Democrats: Industrialists, Labor, and Democratization in Late-developing Countries". *World Politics*, 2000.

Bertrand, J. *Nationalism and Ethnic Conflict In Indonesia*. New York: Cambridge University Press, 2004.

Bird, J. "Indonesia in 1997: The Tinderbox Year". *Asian Survey* 38, no. 1 (1998): 168–76.

————. "Indonesia in 1998: The Pot Boils Over". *Asian Survey* 39, no. 1 (1999): 27–37.

Capoccia, G. and D. Keleman. "The Study of Critical Junctures: Theory, Narrative, and Counterfactuals in Historical Institutionalism". *World Politics* 59, no. 3 (2007): 341–69.

Carter Center. *Final Report of the Carter Center Limited Observation Mission to the April 9, 2009 Legislative Elections in Indonesia*. Atlanta, GA: Carter Center, 2009.

Case, W. *Politics in Southeast Asia: Democracy or Less*. London: RoutledgeCurzon, 2002.

Crouch, H. *Political Reform in Indonesia after Soeharto*. Singapore: Institute of Southeast Asian Studies, 2010.

Dijk, K.V. *A Country in Despair: Indonesia between 1997 and 2000*. Leiden: KITLV Press, 2001.

Emmerson, D.K. "Exit and Aftermath: The Crisis of 1997–1998", in *Indonesia beyond Suharto: Polity, Economy, Society, Transition*, edited by D.K. Emmerson. Armonk, NY: Sharpe, 1999.

Gould, S. *Punctuated Equilibrium*. Cambridge, MA: Belknap Press of Harvard University Press, 2007.

Habir, A. "Conglomerates: All in the Family?" In *Indonesia beyond Suharto: Polity, Economy, Society, Transition*, edited by D.K. Emmerson. Armonk, NY: Sharpe, 1999.

Hadiz, V. "Indonesian Local Party Politics: A Site of Resistance to Neoliberal Reform". *Critical Asian Studies* 36, no. 4 (2004): 615–36.

————. *Localising Power in Post-authoritarian Indonesia: A Southeast Asia Perspective*. Stanford: Stanford University Press, 2010.

Hefner, R. *Civil Islam: Muslims and Democratization in Indonesia*. Princeton, NJ: Princeton University Press, 2000.

Hill, H. *Indonesia's New Order: The Dynamics of Socio-economic Transformation*. Honolulu: University of Hawai'i Press, 1994.

Kimura, E. "Proliferating Provinces: Territorial Politics in Post-Suharto Indonesia". *South East Asia Research* 18, no. 3 (2010): 415–49.

King, D.Y. *Half-Hearted Reform: Electoral Institutions and the Struggle for Democracy in Indonesia*. Westport, CT: Praeger, 2003.

Kingsbury, D. *Power Politics and the Indonesian Military*. London: RouledgeCurzon, 2003.

Lane, M. "Students on the Move". *Inside Indonesia* 19 (1989): 10–13.

Levi, M. *Consent, Dissent, and Patriotism*. Cambridge: Cambridge University Press, 1997.

Liddle, W. "Soeharto's Indonesia: Personal Rule and Political Institutions". *Pacific Affairs* 58, no. 1 (1985): 68–90.

———. "Indonesia in 1996: Pressures from Above and Below". *Asian Survey* 37, no. 1 (1997): 167–74.

MacIntyre, A. *Business, Government, and Development: Northeast and Southeast Asian Comparisons, Business and Government in Industrializing Asia*. Ithaca, NY: Cornell University Press, 1994.

Mackie, J. and A. MacIntyre. "Politics". In *Indonesia's New Order: The Dynamics of Socioeconomic Transformation*, edited by H. Hill. Honolulu: University of Hawai'i Press, 1994.

Mahoney, J. and D. Rueschemeyer. *Comparative Historical Analysis in the Social Sciences*. Cambridge: Cambridge University Press, 2003.

Mietzner, M. *Military Politics, Islam, and the State in Indonesia: From Turbulent Transition to Democratic Consolidation*. Singapore: Institute of Southeast Asian Studies, 2009.

———. "Indonesia in 2009: Electoral Contestation and Economic Resilience". *Asian Survey* 50, no. 1 (2010): 185–94.

Moore, B. *Social Origins of Dictatorship and Democracy: Lord and Peasant in the Making of the Modern World*. Boston: Beacon Press, 1966.

Pierson, P. "Increasing Returns, Path Dependence, and the Study of Politics". *American Political Science Review* 94, no. 2 (2000): 251–67.

Ranis, G. and F. Stewart. *Decentralization in Indonesia*, Yale University, Economic Growth Center, 1995.

Rueschemeyer, D., E.H. Stephens, and J.D. Stephens. *Capitalist Development and Democracy*. Chicago: University of Chicago Press, 1992.

Sherlock, S, ed. *The 2004 Indonesian Elections: How the System Works and What the Parties Stand For: A Report on Political Parties*. Canberra: Australian National University, 2004.

Sidel, J. "Social Origins of Dictatorship and Democracy: Colonial State and Chinese

Immigrant in the Making of Modern Southeast Asia". *Journal of Comparative Politics* 40, no. 2 (2008): 127–47.

Slater, D. Indonesia's Accountability Trap: Party Cartels and Presidential Power after Democratic Transition". *Indonesia* 78 (October 2004): 61–92.

Smith, B. "The Origins of Regional Autonomy in Indonesia: Experts and the Marketing of Political Interests". *Journal of East Asian Studies* 8, no. 2 (2008): 211–34.

Smoke, P. and B. Lewis. "Fiscal Decentralization in Indonesia: A New Approach to an Old Idea". *World Development* 24, no. 8 (1996): 1281–99.

Suryadinata, L. *Elections and Politics in Indonesia*. Singapore: Institute of Southeast Asian Studies, 2002.

Tiebout, C. "A Pure Theory of Local Expenditures". *Journal of Political Economy* 64, no. 5 (1956): 416–24.

Ziv, D. "Populist Perceptions and Perceptions of Populism in Indonesia: The Case of Megawati Soekarnoputri". *South East Asia Research* 9, no. 1 (2001): 73–88.

7

THE RESISTIBLE RISE OF THAKSIN SHINAWATRA
Crisis, Change and the Collapse of Thailand's Democracy

Federico Ferrara

The military made its move on the evening of 19 September 2006. Ominously foreshadowing that something big was about to go down, Thai television stations abruptly cut out of scheduled programming and played soothing, ready-made slideshows bearing still images of the royal family, at times accompanied by music composed by the King. Shortly thereafter, CNN reported that tanks were rolling through Bangkok in the direction of Government House. The capital city — a megalopolis of ten million people — was taken with derisive ease, in a matter of just minutes. A few tanks and a busload of special forces was all it took for the army to re-take control of the entire country. Prime Minister Thaksin Shinawatra, hours away from speaking to the United Nations General Assembly, feigned outrage and surprise. But he had long been forewarned.[1] Cheered in Bangkok and unencumbered by any hint of active popular opposition, the generals apologized for the "inconvenience" caused, promised to return the country to democracy within a year and, good measure, gave everyone a day off. The edicts that suspended the 1997 Constitution and banned all political activities were accompanied by the instruction that soldiers keep smiling in public.

Thailand is certainly no stranger to *coups d'état*. The putsch that ousted Thaksin, that is, is only the latest in a string of coups staged since the end of the absolute monarchy in 1932. But things were supposed to be different this time. At the turn of the new millennium, Thailand had been hailed as a success story, a beacon of freedom in a region where more or less oppressive, corrupt dictatorships are the rule. Among other things, the country had pulled through the deep financial crisis that enveloped much of Southeast Asia in 1997 without turning to military strongmen or extra-constitutional rule. The generals, for their part, had no longer seemed to pose much of a threat since the massacre of unarmed demonstrators in May 1992. At long last, moreover, a brand new constitution promised to usher in the hitherto elusive consolidation of the country's democratic institutions. And yet, in a tragic reversal, less than fifteen years after Thais from all walks of life had chased the military back to the barracks — at the peril and sometimes the expense of their lives — many of the same people now greeted the troops with flowers, cheerfully posing for the cell-phone cameras alongside tanks deployed to Bangkok's major landmarks.

Indeed, it was argued at the time that the army did not kill democracy. The generals had merely euthanized it, ending its long, painful agony by bringing Thaksin's "elected dictatorship" to a deservedly ignominious close. Thaksin, it was said, had already eviscerated democratic institutions, imposing a measure of repression and social control more reminiscent of an authoritarian regime than a representative government in a free country. In five years at the helm, Thaksin had systematically subjected dissenting voices to police brutality, legal harassment, and a relentless smear campaign that portrayed them as anarchists and enemies of the nation. He had revived repressive legislation granting the police expansive powers to search and interrogate suspects. He had moved to assert editorial control over the television channels owned by the state. He had routinely pressured the print media to give favourable coverage through threats of legal action and the manipulation of the advertising budget of state-owned enterprises. And he had vanquished independent bodies like the Election Commission, the National Counter Corruption Commission, and the National Human Rights Commission through carrots, sticks, and a wave of partisan appointments.

To make matters worse, hundreds of people had been killed in a flurry of extra-judicial executions during the "War on Drugs" launched by the government in 2003, while Thaksin's heavy hand did much to inflame long-dormant ethnic tensions in Thailand's Muslim-majority southern provinces of Pattani, Yala, and Narathiwat. Insurgent offensives that targeted army bases and government schools in the country's deep south in early 2004 were followed by the government's brutal reprisals. The military and the police were cited in a number of episodes of torture, kidnapping, and murder of activists and suspected insurgents. Voices of dissent like those of disappeared human rights advocate Somchai Neelaphaijit were forever silenced. On 28 April 2004, 113 people were killed in incidents that culminated with the massacre of 28 lightly armed men who had barricaded themselves inside the Kru Ze mosque in Pattani. The following October, the military caused the death by suffocation of 78 among the hundreds of people who had been loaded on to military trucks during a peaceful protest at Tak Bai. By 2006, what had once been effectively contained to a low-intensity conflict characterized by sporadic episodes of minor violence erupted into a full-scale insurgency, the daily attacks on the representatives and the symbols of the state leaving hundreds dead in their wake.

In light of Thaksin's troubling record, many in Thailand and abroad could sympathize with the argument made in support of what some observers labelled "the good coup".[2] In fact, Thaksin's removal from office had characteristically very little to do with restoring democracy, as advertised by the generals and their supporters. Much like Prime Minister Chatichai Choonhavan in 1991, Thaksin was done in less by his efforts to establish an "elected dictatorship" than by his attempt to dismantle the country's "network monarchy"[3] — the loose network of palace insiders, royal advisors, military officers, high level bureaucrats, judges, and business elites long led by Privy Council President Prem Tinsulanonda.

As he was readying his guns for entry into politics, Thaksin had been at least as keen to ingratiate himself with Thailand's unelected ruling class as he was apt to pummel the elected leadership of Prime Minister Chuan Leekpai and the Democrat Party. The network monarchy, at first, appeared rather satisfied with the new Prime Minister. In 2001, Prem saved Thaksin's job — pressuring the Constitutional Court to acquit Thaksin of corruption charges he had scarcely bothered denying. The Court obliged, acquitting Thaksin in a close, eight-to-seven ruling, albeit not without some of its more disgruntled judges complaining to the press, anonymously, about the interference.[4] But it did not take long for Thaksin to turn on those he had once sought to please — in all probability, not out of disrespect or ideological distaste for the old order, but out of a desire to project his government's power deep into institutions traditionally impervious to encroachments by elected officials.[5]

This chapter sheds light on the process that led to Thaksin's rise, his subsequent authoritarian turn, and his eventual removal. The reason why Thaksin could not be removed except via *coup d'état*, in particular, lies in the decisive streamlining that Thailand's once-fractious party system had undergone since the late 1990s — in Sartori's language,[6] the emergence of a "predominant" party from a situation of rather extreme fragmentation. After his bone-crushing victory in the 2005 elections, Thaksin was much too strong to be cajoled, bullied, or undermined through the relatively subtle, inconspicuous means the network monarchy had employed to keep many of his predecessors in check. At the same time, Thaksin's pursuit of manifestly illiberal (if wildly popular) policies offered the pretext for the coup, helping the generals make the forcible removal of a democratically elected government acceptable to both the international community and the urban middle class electorate, whose acquiescence is typically required for military coups to be smooth and bloodless.[7]

The aggregation of Thailand's party system, and the accumulation of an unprecedented measure of power in the hands of an elected prime minister, cannot be explained without reference to the extraordinary circumstances in which Thaksin's meteoric rise took place. The assertion of Thaksin's dominance, in particular, would have been eminently avoidable, were it not for the displacement of entrenched patterns of party competition ushered in by the 1997 Asian crisis. This chapter identifies the period spanning from the resignation of Chavalit Yongchyudh's government on 8 November 1997 and the general elections of 6 January 2001 a "critical juncture" in the development of Thai political parties. The "juncture" in question is described as "critical" not simply in the sense that it was "a period of significant change",[8] but in the sense that it opened up the *potential* for Thailand's political scene to undergo substantial change by creating conditions of instability and flux where random events and decisions made by major political actors become substantially more likely to set in motion self-reinforcing, path-dependent processes that lead to the emergence of new equilibria.[9] Thaksin's early seizure of opportunities created by the exogenous shock inflicted on the Thai political system by the 1997 financial crisis,[10] in particular, triggered a self-reinforcing, path-dependent process that rendered Thai Rak Thai's electoral hegemony increasingly unassailable and constitutional routes to government alternation increasingly impracticable. Ultimately, the country's military, bureaucratic, and aristocratic elites had little choice but to deploy the tanks on the streets of Bangkok in a desperate attempt to salvage what was left of their long-standing dominance over Thai politics and society.[11]

A "SEMI-STRUCTURED" PARTY SYSTEM

The vertiginous rise of Thaksin Shinawatra can only be understood for the momentous break with the past it genuinely marked when contemplated against the backdrop of Thailand's post-absolutist history — "antecedent conditions" distinguished by the seemingly intractable weakness that the country's political parties have exhibited since the inception of electoral competition. In turn, the endurance of an "unstructured", or perhaps better, a "semi-structured" party system[12] dominated by personalities and plagued by extreme levels of factionalism until the mid to late 1990s is rooted in the fitful, spasmodic pace of the country's democratic development — the repeatedly botched transitions, military takeovers, and abortive attempts to consolidate democracy for which the country is now notorious.

Whereas national legislative elections have been held in Thailand since 1933, it was not until much later that political parties were allowed to register, field candidates, and campaign for votes. The clique of military officers and high-ranking civil servants who overthrew King Prajadhipok's absolute monarchy on 24 June 1932 at one time described themselves as the "People's Party" (*khana ratsadorn*). But for a variety of reasons — not the least of which was the fear that a serious attempt to mobilize voters might have given rise to parties that might chase them out of office[13] — the People's Party never really sought to expand its power base beyond its hardcore in the military and civilian bureaucracy. Incidentally, the tutelage system introduced in the 1930s made strong electoral organizations rather redundant, as only half of the country's National Assembly was popularly elected back then. The "Promoters" of the 1932 coup therefore chose to do away with political parties altogether, holding elections in 1933, 1937, and 1938 as contests between formally unaffiliated candidates.[14]

The interest in building party organizations was rekindled after World War II. The government of Field Marshal Phibun Songkhram (hereinafter, Phibun) was jettisoned as Japan approached defeat. In the aftermath of the war, in 1946, a new constitution and a generally more liberal environment spawned the registration of political parties and the election of a new House of Representatives finally devoid of appointed deputies. Phibun, however, stormed back on to the scene in 1947, headlining a coup that abrogated the new constitution and invalidated the results of the election held the year before. A subsequent coup staged in November 1951 forced the reintroduction of an amended version of the 1932 charter and the disbandment of all political parties.

In 1955, Thailand's military-dominated government promulgated a skeletal Political Parties Act, which had been promised in constitutions dating as far back as 1932. The members of the governing triumvirate at the time — Phibun, Field Marshal Sarit Thanarat, and Police Director-General Phao Sriyanond — put together the Serimanankasila party, which disintegrated as a result of infighting in the wake of its fraudulent electoral victory in February 1957. Following Sarit's coup later that year, his faction — Sahaphoom (or Unionist Party) — was, unsurprisingly, the top vote getter in the hastily called December elections. Three days after the vote, the Sahaphoom was superseded by the National Socialist Party, but this organization too was banned in the aftermath of Sarit's *autogolpe* in 1958. When political parties were once again allowed to assemble, Sarit's successor — Field Marshal Thanom Kittikachorn — effectively exploited his control of the state bureaucracy to win the February 1969 elections under the banner of the United Thai People's Party (UTPP). Ultimately, though, his legislative coalition's scarce cohesion factored into Thanom's decision to disband all parties in 1971, as he staged another *autogolpe* that yet again dispensed with even the most perfunctory of democratic façades.

Whereas introducing, restoring, or otherwise saving democracy has been cited as a justification for many of the plentiful coups that have forcibly, if often bloodlessly, removed a succession of Thai governments since 1932, real democracy has rather more often come to Thailand after civilian blood was spilled on the streets of Bangkok. The first such incident was sparked by the repression of student demonstrations carried out in October 1973 by the "Three Tyrants" — Field Marshal Thanom Kittikachorn, Field Marshal Prapat Charusathien, and Colonel Narong Kittikachorn — two years after Thanom had dissolved the National Assembly and voided the results of elections he had himself "won" in 1969. By the time half a million people took to the streets on 13 October, the more immediate demands for the release of activists arrested a week earlier had grown into more sweeping calls for democratic change. On 14 October the military began firing into the crowds, gunning down up to a hundred unarmed demonstrators. Following King Bhumibol's public intervention, the Three Tyrants resigned and fled the country.

The elections organized in 1975 are generally recognized as the first genuinely competitive elections held in the country's history. Not only was competition in this round of voting not hamstrung by the stringent restrictions traditionally imposed on political speech, assembly, and association; this time, no "government party" was there to parlay an outsized financial advantage, and exclusive control of the machinery of the state, into an all too predictable triumph at the polls. If the on-again, off-again nature of Thai elections had effectively prevented the emergence of a durable establishment party, the groups most commonly excluded from government had suffered just as badly from the intermittent bans imposed on their activities. With each new ban came not only the revocation of a party's registration, but also the dismantlement of its organization and the confiscation of its assets.[15] Even when such groups revived the labels they had used in previous elections, the labels themselves were of little or no value. The scarce meaningfulness of national elections and the dominance of government parties had for the most part rendered vain any attempt to attract a reliable, committed following. And the successive bans on embryonic party organizations had prevented the opposition from consolidating whatever support it had earned in elections it was allowed to contest.

With no organization and no electoral base, little incentive existed for politicians to maintain any level of party discipline or cohesion. Besides, having only months to re-constitute in advance of new elections reinforced the dependency of parties on local notables, whose networks of power and influence could most effectively be leveraged in the short term to deliver votes in the provinces. As a result, as the restrictions on party activities were periodically lifted to suit the needs of the day's dictator, a flurry of new parties bound by little more than a big man's popularity and ambition proliferated wildly. Only one party — the Democrat Party — achieved a modicum of continuity during that period. Founded in 1946, it received between a fifth and a quarter of the seats in each of the elections held between 1955 and 1969. No other group proved nearly as resilient. Over a hundred "parties" were registered between 1946 and the mid-1970s.[16] Most did not survive the crackdowns that accompanied the intermittent suspension of parliamentary government.

Thailand's 1975 elections, then, bore all the hallmarks of the competition for contributors, candidates, and votes in an environment of "atomization" — in Sartori's definition,[17] a situation where the vote is so widely dispersed across a multitude of weak and ephemeral party alternatives that "the number of parties makes little difference". As it turns out, the 1975 elections did little but entrench the fragmentation and feebleness of Thailand's party system. Most of the 22 parties that won seats in the House of Representatives served as little more than the electoral vehicles of politicians with a strong local base. Even the largest parties — Democrats, Social Justice, and Chat Thai — were dominated by personalities whose parliamentary cliques added internal segmentation to the already extreme fragmentation of the House of Representatives. Ultimately, it fell upon Social Action Party leader Kukrit Pramoj to piece together a coalition government with a chance to survive a confidence vote. The painstaking process of accommodating so many different parties as well as the factions within them eventually resulted in the formation of a limp, 16-party executive. An elaborate system of quotas was introduced, whereby each party and faction would receive a share of portfolios and undersecretaries commensurate with its size.

Ockey[18] points out that this method of dividing the spoils of government — born of necessity — set the Thai political system on the path to the kind of extreme fragmentation and instability it has exhibited almost ever since. Most importantly, perhaps, it created an incentive for already independent-minded members of parliament to form factions that could trade their participation in the government's legislative majority for a Cabinet post. The most ambitious and resourceful representatives put together factions held together by their ability to bankroll the campaigns of less-affluent followers; once in government, the faction leader would use the office to recoup his investment. The logic by which both factions and parties operated, moreover, was such to generate high levels of instability at both levels. Within factions, individual MPs could shift their support to whomever would pay the highest price for it. And, within parties, because most factions commanded their own finances and electoral organizations, little pressure could be exerted on them to exhibit any level of party discipline. In fact, all that bound different factions together in a single party was the expectation that the party would be invited to join the government. Accordingly, a party out of power could well expect to break up, as its factions scrambled to find alternative routes to all-important executive posts.

Thailand's first real experience under a fully democratic regime ended much the same way it began — in tragedy and bloodshed. Barely a year into its term, Kukrit's government collapsed. New elections were held in April 1976, but the new assembly was only marginally less fractious than the one elected the year before. This time, 19 parties won seats in the House; the weak government formed by Democrat leader Seni Pramoj survived a mere six months. Though the democratic governments that ruled Thailand between 1973 and 1976 were not short of notable achievements,[19] their extreme fragmentation impeded decisive action on the most pressing issues of the day — among them, increasingly bitter labour disputes, a restive student movement in Bangkok, and the communist insurgency in the periphery. It did not help matters that royalist, civilian vigilantes and the military embarked on a sustained campaign of bombings and assassinations targeting rural activists and leftist politicians, undermining the public's confidence in the ability of a democratic government to keep the peace.

The return to Thailand of former strongman, Thanom Kittikachorn, in the fall of 1976, sparked a new wave of student demonstrations that were once again savagely repressed. In this instance, however, the troops largely stood by as royalist civilian volunteer forces such as the Red Gaurs and the Village Scouts massacred dozens of Thammasat University students and mutilated their corpses. The King said nothing publicly, but quickly endorsed the inevitable military coup that followed. The National Administrative Reform Council, as the new junta called itself, ruthlessly pursued leftists suspected of communist sympathies as well as any voice clamouring for a return to democracy. Thousands of students and intellectuals fled the country or retreated to the jungles — joining forces with the communist insurgency in the northeast. Hundreds more were arrested on trumped-up charges and some tried in military tribunals. The new strongman, Supreme Court judge Tanin Kraivichien, was empowered by the new constitution to exercise near-absolute rule, checked only by an appointed legislature of handpicked military and public administration officials. By 1977, Tanin had become so unpopular that the army deposed him in yet another bloodless coup.

In the decade that followed, Thailand was ruled by a hybrid regime dominated by the palace and the military but supported by democratically elected legislatures.[20] New elections were held in 1979 after the promulgation of the country's latest "permanent" constitution. Difficulties encountered by the new coalition government were ultimately overcome with the appointment of General Prem Tinsulanonda, who served as Prime Minister between 1980 and 1988. Though not terribly consequential to the exercise of real political power, elections held during that period were hotly contested, especially as the positions of Member of Parliament and Cabinet Minister became potentially more lucrative in a context of fast-paced economic growth. If, as of the 1970s, 75 per cent of the Members of Parliament were estimated to have received kickbacks from development projects or direct cash payments in return for their support of a party,[21] the use of public office for private gain was transformed into a booming cottage industry in the 1980s. One grim measure of the newfound competitiveness of national elections is offered by Benedict Anderson,[22] who notes that political assassinations in the 1980s were increasingly related to the races for parliamentary seats. Eliminating rival candidates became much more commonplace than it had been in the past. So did the practice of taking out canvassers or *hua khanaen* who hogged too many of the resources disbursed by candidates while failing to deliver a commensurate number of votes.[23]

The legislative elections of 1979, 1983, and 1986 further entrenched the patterns of party competition that had emerged in the mid-1970s (see Table 7.1). The number of parties was limited somewhat, thanks to the introduction of a Political Parties Act in 1981 that tightened requirements for party registration.[24] By the late 1980s, many parties commanded several times the minimum number of MPs required to earn the leader a Cabinet post and well in excess of the minimum levels of popular support and territorial coverage required by the 1981 act to maintain registration. But the only glue keeping such parties together was the prospect of being included in a coalition government, which Ockey[25] suggests was considerably better for large than it was for small parties. As such, their membership was extremely fluid. Groups of MPs were constantly "up for sale". Faction leaders routinely re-negotiated the terms of their membership in a political party, ready to move their contingents of legislators, financial backers, and canvassers to another party any time a better deal might be extended to them in the form of direct monetary incentives or appointments to more lucrative government posts.

Table 7.1
Thai Election Results, 1983–96: Seats Won by Party

	1983	1986	1988	1992	1992	1995	1996
Chat Pattana	—	—	—	—	60	53	52
Chat Prachathippatai	15	3	—	—	—	—	—
Chat Thai	73	63	87	74	77	92	39
Democrat Party	56	100	48	44	79	86	123
Ekkaphap	—	—	—	6	8	8	8
Kao Na	3	9	8	—	—	—	—
Kit Prachakhom	—	15	9	—	—	—	—
Muan Chon	—	3	5	1	4	3	2
Nam Thai	—	—	—	—	—	18	—
New Aspiration	—	—	—	72	51	57	125
Phalang Dharma	—	—	14	41	47	23	1
Phalang Mai	—	1	—	—	—	—	—
Prachachon	—	—	19	—	—	—	—
Prachakorn Thai	36	24	31	7	3	18	18
Prachaseri	1	—	—	—	—	—	—
Prachathai	4	—	—	—	—	—	—
Puang Chon Chao Thai	—	1	17	1	—	—	—
Rassadorn	—	18	21	4	1	—	—
Raengngan Prachathippatai	—	1	—	—	—	—	—
Ruam Thai	—	19	35	—	—	—	—
Samakkhitham	—	—	—	79	—	—	—
Sangkhom Prachathippatai	2	—	1	—	—	—	—
Seriniyom	—	1	3	—	—	—	—
Seritham	—	—	—	—	8	11	4
Siam Prachathippatai	18	38	5	—	—	—	—
Social Action Party	92	51	54	31	22	22	20
Tai	—	—	—	—	—	—	1
Independents	24	—	—	—	—	—	—
Total	324	347	357	360	360	391	393

After the 1988 elections, Prem declined to serve another term as Prime Minister and joined King Bhumibol's Privy Council. For the first time in over a decade, the results of the elections would matter to the formation of a new government. The prime ministerial post was assumed by Chatichai

Choonhavan, leader of Chat Thai — the largest party in the newly elected National Assembly. Propped up by neither the military nor the crown — both repeatedly expressed their displeasure with the Prime Minister — the new government was to survive entirely on its own power. But given the fragmentation of Thailand's legislature, Chatichai's only hope to put together a durable coalition was to indulge the seemingly limitless appetite for personal gain and political patronage characteristic of the main parties and factions. What might have seemed at first as the dawn of a new era of parliamentarism and democracy in Thailand — now finally ruled by a government whose authority derived exclusively from the mandate it won electorally — was brought to an abrupt end in February 1991. Citing the corruption of Chatichai's "buffet cabinet" and the presence of many "unusually wealthy" politicians in its midst, General Suchinda Kraprayoon and his National Peace-Keeping Council (NPKC) seized power, promising reforms, investigations, and a swift return to democracy. Meanwhile, the military wasted no time abrogating the constitution and dissolving the National Assembly — the customary measures called for by these familiar circumstances.

When democracy returned in 1992, after the requisite massacre of peaceful demonstrators on the streets of Bangkok, it found well-established patterns of party competition that had developed during Thailand's long years of pseudo-democratic competition. At least in the print media, the campaign for the September 1992 elections was portrayed as a fight between "angels" and "devils"[26] — the "angels" being the pro-democracy parties that had been behind the demonstrations (Democrats, Palang Dharma, and New Aspiration), the "devils" being the surviving parties among those that had supported Suchinda through the events of "Black May" — Chat Thai, Social Action, and Prachakorn Thai above all, plus the newly assembled Chat Pattana of deposed Prime Minister Chatichai. But for hype about angels and devils, the September 1992 elections were entirely analogous to those of years past. The legislature returned by the 1992 contests was just as fragmented and factionalized as it had been throughout the 1980s. The three angelic parties — Democrats, New Aspiration, and Palang Dharma, now joined by the smaller party Ekkaphap — won a narrow majority in the House, taking 185 seats. The remaining 175 seats were shared by 7 other parties, the largest of which were Chat Thai and Chat Pattana.

The horse trading that took place after the elections evinced a political landscape far more fluid than the apocalyptic terms in which the media described the campaign might have suggested. Democrat leader Chuan Leekpai formed a coalition government that included Social Action, the least devilish of the parties that had supported Suchinda through the massacres just four months earlier. Unsurprisingly, Chuan's government failed to serve out its term — forced to resign in 1995 after Palang Dharma withdrew its support in a vain attempt to avert an ultimately fatal internal split. By that time, Chuan's majority had already withstood the defection of General Chavalit Yongchaiyudh's New Aspiration Party.

When new elections were called in 1995, many factions and their MPs were characteristically on the auction block. The most successful at chipping away candidates from other parties were Chat Thai and the Democrats, who fielded a number of incumbent MPs in excess of the number of seats they commanded in the House. Reportedly, some candidates were offered upwards of ten million baht ($400,000 at that time's exchange rate) to switch parties.[27] The 1995 elections brought to power a government headed by Chat Thai's new leader Barnharn Silpa-archa and supported by a ragtag assemblage of former "angel" and "devil" parties, now united in their pursuit of the spoils of power. Barnharn's widely reviled "mafia cabinet" lasted a mere fifteen months. In advance of the elections held in 1996, it was New Aspiration that bought the most candidates on the open market, running as many as 61 incumbents from the ranks of other parties in addition to the 57 it could already count on.[28] Having precipitated the government's collapse, having forced the dissolution of parliament, and having subsequently managed to win a narrow plurality, it was now Chavalit's turn to form a new government.

(RE-)ENTER THAKSIN SHINAWATRA

It took a blend of choice and chance, purposeful design and unintended consequences to shake up long-standing patterns of political competition in the late 1990s. The first major change was in the country's institutional architecture. Following the 1996 elections, a compromise was reached on the procedural rules that would govern the complete overhaul of Thailand's constitution. Chavalit's government allowed a 99-member Constitution Drafting Assembly to be impaneled. The document it produced was approved by parliament the following year.

The 1997 constitution redesigned several of Thailand's key political institutions. The legislature was rendered more "democratic" by replacing the appointed Senate with an upper chamber whose members were to be elected at the provincial level on a non-partisan basis. The size of the House of Representatives was increased to 500 deputies. All candidates were now required to have bachelor's degrees to stand for election. Voting was made compulsory, while an independent Election Commission was given wide-ranging authority to investigate allegations of fraud and vote buying, disqualify candidates found to have committed the gravest infractions, and ban the most egregiously corrupt politicians from elected office. The constitution included the explicit recognition of forty human rights — many unsanctioned in previous charters — as well as provisions guaranteeing Thai citizens greater protection from warrantless searches and seizures. A number of independent agencies were instituted as a means to fight corruption, human rights violations, and other abuses of power.

If the new constitution reshaped the legal framework within which political competition took place, the financial crisis that brought Thailand's once-buoyant economy to its knees in 1997, quickly spreading to much of East and Southeast Asia, completely revolutionized the dynamics of political competition. Repeated promises to the contrary notwithstanding, Chavalit's government responded to sustained attacks on the Thai baht and the consequent depletion of the country's currency reserves by unpegging the national currency from its fixed, 25 baht for $1 exchange rate. In one year the baht lost over half of its value, destroying much of the wealth built during the expansion of the previous fifteen years. The banking sector collapsed. Companies that had accumulated significant foreign debt went bankrupt. Eight hundred thousand people lost their jobs as the unemployment rate tripled. The stock market plunged. Gross domestic product shrank by 10 per cent. And three million more people were now poor.[29]

The crisis dealt a severe blow to national leaders and organizations, creating opportunities for new ones to take their places. The flimsy coalition that supported Chavalit's government was the first casualty. Four months after floating the baht, Chavalit was forced to resign and was replaced by a new government headed by Chuan Leekpai. Though ultimately successful in engineering Thailand's economic recovery, Chuan and his Cabinet were deeply unpopular because of their association with the International Monetary Fund (IMF). Characteristically, the crisis had been blamed on the twin bogeymen of international capitalism and globalization, so the structural adjustment policies that the IMF attached as a condition for bailing out the Thai economy through a $17.5 billion loan were viewed as yet another unwanted imposition from the same actors responsible for the crisis. With the decline of New Aspiration and the Democrats, the party system of old was left in a shambles. And its reorganization was now to take place under a much different set of rules.

It is in this context of upheaval and growing mistrust of the country's elites that the stalled political career of Thaksin Shinawatra accelerated to meteoric speed.[30] Thaksin had risen to national prominence as a telecommunications magnate, having made a fortune by securing government concessions over the booming markets for mobile phones and pagers thanks to well-placed contacts in Chatichai's "buffet cabinet" (1988–91). By the early 1990s Thaksin had become inordinately wealthy; his firms were marvellously profitable and their value had multiplied several times over in the stock market. Thaksin's interest in politics was natural. Given that government concessions are typically awarded and renewed through an entirely political process, it is no surprise that Thaksin got involved when Thailand seemed destined to undertake the road to economic liberalization. Thaksin formally entered the fray in 1994, becoming Foreign Minister in the first Chuan government (1992–95) under the ministerial quota set aside for Palang Dharma.

Palang Dharma's subsequent disintegration took place largely as a result of Thaksin's involvement. The party had built its image as an incorruptible organization inspired by Buddhist principles and administered by people whose lifestyles appeared to embody that very ethos. Thaksin, by contrast, was the quintessential "crony capitalist", having made his money thanks to backroom deals and personal connections. His invitation to assume a Cabinet post split the party, resulting in Palang Dharma's withdrawal from the coalition and the consequent collapse of Chuan's government. Now leader of the party following Chamlong Srimuang's retirement, Thaksin was elected to the House in 1995 and was given the position of Deputy Prime Minister. Palang Dharma suffered a precipitous decline with Thaksin at the helm. The party had its legislative contingent slashed by half in 1995 and virtually disappeared from the scene in 1996.

While his party had gone down in flames, in a political world ruled by money Thaksin was uniquely primed for a comeback. Thaksin's companies, after all, had escaped the brunt of the economic crisis. Not only did his businesses recover quickly, most emerged from the crisis stronger than before thanks to the decimation of much of the competition. Even here, it was alleged, Thaksin benefited from his position in the government by receiving advance warning of the upcoming devaluation of the baht. The economic crisis, then, offered Thaksin the opportunity to deploy his vast financial means to build a new party that would ostensibly better protect Thailand in a globalized economy, offer an alternative to grey bureaucrats and "professional politicians", and transform Thai politics by rendering it more hopeful, creative, cooperative, and clean. In July 1998, Thaksin was joined by a small group of intellectuals and government officials for the launch of a new political party named Thai Rak Thai (literally, "Thais Love Thais"). At first, Thai Rak Thai courted big business leaders who had taken a beating in 1997 and sought a bigger role in politics. Then, Thaksin pandered to small business owners and the rural poor by portraying himself as a self-made man and a decisive leader who could protect Thailand's economy without neglecting the workers and entrepreneurs that Chuan and the IMF were supposedly selling out to foreign interests.

At the same time, the crisis presented the budding Thai Rak Thai — initially devoid of but the faintest programmatic pretense — with an obvious narrative in which a group of self-described "outsiders", however well-heeled, could ground their quest to challenge the country's political establishment. Thaksin himself noted that he applied "scientific thinking" to engineer the rise of Thai Rak Thai, enlisting consultancy firms and polling organizations to craft a compelling message. The result was what Pasuk and Baker[31] characterize as a "new nationalism" that vowed to defend Thailand from foreign dominance and emphasized the need for the country to integrate into the global economy on its own terms.[32] An economic recovery plan centred on government assistance to small and medium-sized enterprises was announced in 2000. Then Thaksin rode the wave of discontent in the provinces by putting together a rural platform that could appeal to upcountry voters, leaders, and social movements like the increasingly vocal Assembly of the Poor. The cornerstones of his rural programme were an agrarian debt moratorium, the establishment of a million-baht fund for every village, and a thirty baht per visit health-care plan. With the endorsement of prominent community organizations came millions of new members and a massive influx of MPs from other parties. At least 100 of them were bought or cajoled into joining Thai Rak Thai in advance of the 2001 elections.

The 2001 elections marked a sharp break with Thailand's recent past (see Table 7.2). Thai Rak Thai took 248 seats, just 2 shy of an absolute majority in the House of Representatives. Its candidates won 200 single-member district races; its national party list won 48 seats. Most overwhelming had been Thaksin's victory in the rural provinces to the north and east of Bangkok. Thai Rak Thai's sole surviving rival, the Democrats, came in a distant second; its 128 seats were won thanks to the party's dominance of the South. New Aspiration, now reduced to 36 seats, was swept away, while Chat Pattana's seat share was almost halved. And Chat Thai improved only marginally on its disastrous performance in 1996. But it did not stop there. Over the ensuing four years, Thaksin embarked on a successful effort to make Thai Rak Thai the dominant force in Thai politics — to destroy any chance of government alternation by co-opting the leaders, factions, and politicians of all major parties except the Democrats. Fresh rounds of elections in 2005 were a testament to the party's newfound supremacy. Thai Rak Thai won three-quarters of the lower house seats. The Democrats

Table 7.2
Thai Election Results, 2001–5 Seats Won by Party

	2001			2005		
	SMD	PR	Total	SMD	PR	Total
Thai Rak Thai	200	48	248	310	67	377
Democrat	97	31	128	70	26	96
Chat Thai	35	6	41	18	7	25
New Aspiration	28	8	36	—	—	—
Chat Pattana	22	7	29	—	—	—
Seritham	14	0	14	—	—	—
Mahachon	—	—	—	2	0	2
Rassadorn	2	0	2	—	—	—
Social Action	1	0	1	—	—	—
Din Thai	1	0	1	—	—	—
Total	400	100	500	400	100	500

Notes: The column "SMD" reports the number of Single-Member Districts won by each party. The column "PR" reports the number of seats won by each party's national list in the proportional component of the election.

were forced to retreat deeper into their strongholds on the Malay Peninsula. Of the other parties remained but the carcasses, desolately strewn outside of the halls of parliament.

In the space of less than a decade, Thailand's political scene had undergone a remarkable transformation. In 1996 the Thai party system could have been described, at the very best, as "semi-structured". Just a few years later, it had produced a "predominant" party, one that "governs alone, without being subject to alternation, as long as it continues to win, electorally, an absolute majority".[33] What were once little more than legal shells for a bewildering number of internally fluid parliamentary factions dominated by local notables had seemingly crystallized around two alternatives — one of which, by 2005, seemed increasingly implausible as a governing party. In addition, whereas Thai Rak Thai's growth, as measured in seat shares, attests to a reduction in the number of parties, these numbers fail to tell an equally important side of the story. Thai Rak Thai, that is, was much more of a "real" party than almost any of its predecessors. Its organizational structure was highly centralized; its parliamentary wing sternly enforced party discipline through tough hardball tactics. Local politicians remained important for mobilizing votes in the provinces, but they were no longer the locus of the party's financial and organizational resources. And while as many as fifteen factions operated within Thai Rak Thai, their power and autonomy were severely curtailed under Thaksin's leadership.[34]

CRISIS AND TRANSFORMATION

Thaksin's rise to power, and the rapid transformation of Thailand's party system accomplished as a result, have been the subject of considerable academic debate. Perhaps most prominently, Hicken[35] singles out provisions in the 1997 constitution as the catalyst, emphasizing the importance of reforms made to the electoral system and prime ministerial selection procedures. In a nutshell, Hicken argues that the 1997 constitution gave politicians the incentive to engage in greater coordination, both *within* and *across* districts. Within individual constituencies the shift to a single-member district system led to lower dispersion of votes away from the top finishers. More importantly, by stipulating that the Prime Minister must be drawn from the ranks of elected representatives, the new constitution brought into law the right of the leader of the largest party in the House of Representatives to form a government. The reform, therefore, gave politicians an incentive to coordinate into larger parties potentially better positioned to capture the ultimate prize, now sure to go to the top finisher.[36]

Though it is quite true that Thailand has a history of Prime Ministers who came into office after general elections without having (ever) been elected to (any) office (most recently, General Prem Tinsulanonda after elections in 1979, 1983 and 1986, and General Suchinda Kraprayoon after the March 1992 elections), the three elections that preceded the introduction of the 1997 constitution were held in contexts that rendered the appointment of an outsider a remote possibility. The election held in September 1992, for instance, came at a time when the military was so discredited that it could have hardly been expected to impose its own man. In advance of that election, as well as those that followed in 1995 and 1996, it was widely anticipated that the leader of the largest party would be nominated Prime Minister. Chuan, Banharn and Chavalit served in precisely that capacity. To be sure, the articles in the 1997 constitution that altered the relationship between the legislative and executive branches, protecting the position of the Prime Minister from the vagaries of Thailand's fragmented legislature (see below), were highly instrumental to the *preservation* and possibly the enhancement of Thai Rak Thai's dominance *after* the 2001 elections. But the new constitutional provisions were not strong enough to single-handedly *engineer* Thaksin's rise. Implicit to Hicken's argument, in particular, is the expectation that party aggregation would have happened as a result of the 1997 constitution *regardless* of the circumstances. This expectation overly discounts the importance of the economic crisis as well as Thaksin's own acumen and persona.[37]

With regard to Thailand's financial collapse, this argument can be assessed with a sort of counterfactual thought experiment that asks the following question: had the crisis not occurred, would the 1997 constitution have sufficed for the 2001 elections to produce anything like the actual results? It is hard to say for sure, but there are good reasons to conclude that the answer must be negative. It was the crisis that damaged parties like New Aspiration, the Democrats and Chat Pattana in such a way as to provide a new party — especially one with those financial means — an opportunity to lure so many sitting members of parliament away from the competition. Had the crisis not occurred, fewer incumbents would in all likelihood have been available to jump ship, and those who were would likely not have all ended up in the same party. Chambers[38] explains Thaksin's success in the enlistment of incumbents from other parties by focusing on his financial resources. Even here, however, the crisis helped Thai Rak Thai by damaging provincial notables in such a way as to increase their dependency on external support. Thaksin, who had suffered little from the crisis as a result of his companies' low exposure to foreign debt, was in an ideal position to benefit from the weakening of local sources of money and patronage. As a result, Thai Rak Thai absorbed a multitude of politicians whom other parties increasingly did not have the means to recruit due to the weakening of their provincial backers.[39] The Asian crisis, in other words, permitted the streamlining of Thailand's fractured political landscape by drastically reducing the popularity of the country's established political parties, as well as the resources available to the existing parties' factions, candidates, and financial backers.

It is also worth noting that Thai Rak Thai's success in the 2001 elections went well beyond the number of sitting Members of Parliament it was able to field thanks to its superior financial resources. In fact, Thai Rak Thai won two-and-a-half seats for each incumbent it signed on. In part, the party's resounding victory may be attributed to its electoral platform. Ironically, while former Prime Minister Thaksin Shinawatra is loathed by many in Bangkok on account of his penchant for "buying votes", his enduring popularity is much less a function of his ability to outbid the competition in the market for votes than it is the consequence of actual policies he put forth and then quickly implemented. As one of Thailand's richest men, Thaksin had plenty of money to spend, and enough ambition to gamble almost all of it away on his political career. But the real game-changer, not to mention his most unforgivable crime, was that Thaksin for the first time "nationalized" elections in the provinces by crafting a simple platform that resonated with voters well beyond the popularity, wealth, and stature of any local candidate. In the wake of the 1997 Asian crisis, that is, Thaksin effectively combined the old money politics with a programme unprecedented for its detail and its focus on long-neglected regions and social classes. As a result, Pasuk and Baker[40] point out, the 2001 elections had been more about *parties* than just about any general election ever held in Thailand before — and that, especially in northeastern constituencies, members of prominent local families were defeated soundly by Thai Rak Thai candidates.

The aggregation of Thailand's party system beginning with the 2001 elections suggests a number of important considerations about the process of party formation and development in new or otherwise unfledged democracies. First, Thaksin's rise underscores the difficulties of engineering a measure of meaningful party aggregation in the context of a semi-structured party system. Thai Rak Thai's success may be owed to its resources and ideas, but it is unlikely that either would have mattered to the same extent had the economic crisis not weakened actors and organizations that had traditionally dominated Thailand's electoral arena. The advantage conferred by money would not have been quite as insurmountable without the concurrent depletion in both the resources available to local notabilities and the political capital of some of the main national parties. No party, in turn, could have made the kinds of inroads Thai Rak Thai made through its simple rural programme without the prior weakening of faction leaders and financiers. Without the crisis, Thai Rak Thai would never have been able to recruit quite as many incumbents. Without the incumbents making the party a real contender, it would not have been able to advertise its policies quite so widely and effectively. At the same time, Thaksin's reputation for decisiveness and managerial prowess may not have been quite as valuable an asset as it proved to be in a time of crisis.

It should be pointed out, however, that the 1997 Asian crisis merely rendered Thaksin's rise *possible*. In other words, whereas the exogenous shock that perturbed highly entrenched patterns of party competition was a necessary condition to the subsequent aggregation of Thailand's party system, the profound transformation observed thereafter was not the inevitable by-product of the crisis. In fact, the aftermath of the crisis meets the definition of a "critical juncture" not because it was determinative of any outcome, but rather because of the process' newfound openness to alternative, self-reinforcing developmental paths. Thaksin's rise, in this sense, illustrates how initial power asymmetries, produced in this case by an event, like an economic crisis, whose occurrence has a strong element of chance, may be quickly parlayed into an effectively insurmountable advantage. As the literature on path dependence and increasing returns suggests, an early competitive edge may give rise to "coordination effects" and "adaptive expectations"[41] that benefit prospectively more viable parties beyond their actual electoral strength.

Pierson[42] defines "coordination effects" as arising when "the benefits an individual receives from a particular activity increase as others adopt

the same option". This logic applies especially well to party elites, for
whom the benefits of affiliation with a given political party increase as
the party becomes larger, more powerful, and more cohesive. Recruiting
quality candidates and wealthy contributors, that is, increases the appeal
of the existing parties to other quality candidates and wealthy contributors
— joining the party becomes more advantageous as more of them join
because each new recruit increases the party's likelihood to score a victory
at the polls at the expense of its competitors. "Coordination effects" at
the elite level, in turn, help voters distinguish parties that are viable from
those that are not. At the same time, the visibility and financial resources
accumulated through the successful enlistment of candidates and donors
allows the party to further distinguish itself from the pack by broadcasting
its electoral appeal more forcefully and more widely.

In the electorate, once the mere expectation that the party will be
successful has emerged, voters are likely to make that expectation self-
fulfilling by rewarding alternatives perceived to be viable over those that
appear to be more of a long shot. Anticipating that parties with the fewest
resources and the fewest quality candidates will be defeated, short-term
instrumentally rational voters — who may not want to waste their ballot
on a hopeless party — maximize expected utility by coordinating on the
least disliked among the options perceived to be viable. This is the logic
said to characterize the widely studied issue of strategic voting.[43] What
is more, the attention of other, perhaps less strategic voters may simply
gravitate towards parties whose message they have heard most frequently,
whose prospects are discussed most insistently in the media, and whose
campaign efforts they have witnessed firsthand. Either way, in a typical
case of "adaptive expectations", expectations about the future behaviour
of others lead voters "to adapt their actions in ways that help to make
those expectations come true".[44] In other words, voters winnow out the
field in a manner consistent with their initial expectations about the parties'
relative viability; in the process, parties considered "viable" are rewarded
with more votes than they would have garnered in the absence of widely
available cues about their prospective electoral strength.

As the existing parties become electorally stronger and financially
more powerful, in turn, their attractiveness to ambitious politicians and
contributors increases further, as does their advantage in the battle for
votes. And, as their control of government and the state grows firmer, so
does their ability to manipulate the rules of the game in a way that protects

their dominance, prevents the entry of new competitors, or otherwise makes the task so difficult that most will be discouraged from trying in the first place. Donors can be rewarded with the policies and regulations they want. Prominent Members of Parliament can be kept happy with Cabinet appointments, committee assignments, financial support, and lavish perks. Depending upon their tastes and needs, key segments of the electorate can be satisfied with a varying mixture of patronage, pork, and popular legislation. Party financing laws can be tinkered with to benefit the parties that are already in power and drown out the voices of those that are not. And the electoral rules can be manipulated to cripple existing alternatives and discourage the entry of successful new ones. The early edge that grants some parties access to political power, in other words, triggers positive feedback mechanisms that render existing asymmetries of power increasingly wider. Over time, the resulting entrenchment of the existing parties gradually narrows opportunities for meaningful change.

Whereas the 2001 elections already marked a stunning success for Thaksin, not to mention a dramatic departure from the chronic fragmentation exhibited by Thailand's party system ever since the inception of democratic competition, Thaksin knew better than to rest on his laurels. After all, as of 2001, Thai Rak Thai was still little more than a collection of factions precariously held together by the personal popularity and resources of its leader. The propensity of such factions to switch between alternative coalitions had doomed many of Thaksin's predecessors.

Once he was sworn in as Prime Minister, Thaksin took a novel approach to consolidating his position and power. His predecessors Chuan, Banharn, and Chavalit had sought to build "minimum winning coalitions",[45] with some padding, that would maximize the share of benefits and Cabinet positions available for apportionment to their support-cast of parties and factions.[46] Minimum winning coalitions, however, were unstable because the parties and factions included in the majority had a clear incentive to withdraw their support and join the parties currently in the opposition whenever they sensed an opportunity to get a better deal by forming a different government. For various reasons, Chuan, Banharn, and Chavalit had been done in by their governments' inter- and intra-party divisions. Thaksin went at it a completely different way. Rather than leave his coalition vulnerable to the defection of small parties and factions, he endeavoured to put together a super-majority that could withstand any such desertion. Parties like New Aspiration and Seritham dissolved themselves into Thai

Rak Thai, while Thaksin also secured the participation in the governing alliance of all other parties except the Democrats. In the process, Thaksin had greatly reduced the power of factions within his own government. Now endowed with a super-majority, any party or faction that pulled its support would accomplish nothing but lose whatever positions it currently controlled. Thaksin had effectively killed the cycle of instability in the House of Representatives by forming a *predominant party*.

The question remains, however, why the parties and factions that saw their influence and independence shrink with every merger and the addition of every new coalition member did not desert Thaksin and put together a government that would guarantee them a larger share of the pie. In this regard, it certainly helped that Thaksin paid his MPs rather handsomely for their support — somewhere in the neighbourhood of $5,000 per month plus a bonus of at least $20,000 awarded during various festivities and millions of baht for their campaigns.[47] Even more significant is the assistance that Thaksin was offered by provisions in the 1997 constitution. First, given that Cabinet ministers had to resign their legislative seats, exiting the coalition would now amount to leaving elected office altogether. Any such defection was therefore costly. Second, the Prime Minister could now call elections at forty-five days' notice, but the new rules required each candidate to have been a member of a party for at least ninety days prior to the elections. Factions that would desert the government, precipitating the dissolution of the House, would be left out in the cold for an entire legislative cycle. As Thaksin added more components to his party and his coalition, the stability of his government increased and the possibility of having the tables turned on him vastly diminished. In turn, as the ability of the opposition to lure coalition members out of the government was neutralized, the pressure intensified for the remaining opposition parties to join the government themselves. More and more parties jumped on Thaksin's bandwagon, even at the cost of sacrificing much of the independence they once enjoyed.

Shrewdly enough, Thaksin capitalized on the stranglehold he had over factions within Thai Rak Thai and its main allies through the swift implementation of his trademark policies. And while these policies proved highly controversial because of the way the government paid for them as well as their dubious effectiveness, they were immensely popular with provincial voters and the urban working class. The popularity of these programmes, in turn, allowed Thai Rak Thai to "take credit for improvements in the lives of villagers, at the expense of the provincial and local notables who had previously characterized such resource allocation as personal rather than party patronage".[48] In so doing, Thaksin further solidified his electoral support and enhanced the power of Thai Rak Thai's central administration over provincial politicians. Whereas parties had once depended on notables to win provincial races, it was now local politicians who could hardly envision being re-elected without Thai Rak Thai's endorsement. By 2005 Thaksin had cannibalized virtually every component of his alliance.

It was precisely Thaksin's ability to reverse the long-standing fractionalization and instability of the Thai party system that gave him the mandate to pursue illiberal policies responsible for the severe deterioration of Thailand's democracy. To be sure, at the height of his power Thaksin was different things to different people. Some voters probably believed his government's half-hearted denials of any involvement in the extra-judicial killings and the muzzling of the media. Others, who no doubt understood quite well what the government was doing, might simply have taken the good with the bad — having deemed Thaksin's authoritarian turn the acceptable cost of his populist platform. But to many among Thaksin's supporters, the government's heavy-handedness in dealing with protesters, journalists, drug dealers, and presumed insurgents was simply the natural extension of his leadership and management style. As such, these policies were widely applauded. The War on Drugs was found to have the backing of as much as 90 per cent of the Thai electorate. And, at least initially, the wave of nationalist fervour sparked by the southern violence enabled Thaksin's hard-line approach to counter-insurgency, despite the growing criticism levelled against the government by activists and intellectuals.[49]

Once again, the overwhelming popular support that Thaksin's most illiberal policies enjoyed can only be understood with reference to the context in which his ascent took place. In the midst of a devastating economic crisis, the Chuan government was seen as weak and indecisive, paralysed by internal dissension and subservient to foreign interests. Splintered, factionalized, and porous as they were, the existing political parties presented no alternative to get Thailand out of its rut. As least as much as his ideas, it was Thaksin's biography, his projection of strength and decisiveness, and his brash, in-your-face style that offered something really new. Power-hungry politicians with no mission in politics but their own enrichment and little to show for their work but an endless cycle of defections, re-shuffles, and no-confidence motions seemed incapable of confronting the serious challenges the country was facing. Thaksin promised to do so; the aggressiveness with which he subsequently rammed his agenda through what had once been a fractious, do-nothing legislature demonstrated he very well could.

At the same time, if the economic crisis had given rise to a wave of "chauvinist resentment"[50] that Thai Rak Thai's brand of nationalism appropriated and then further inflamed, it was in his self-appointed role as the country's strenuous defender from a host of malevolent outsiders that Thaksin successfully recast his opponents as the country's enemies. It was thus that his critics in the media and civil society were accused of "damaging the country".[51] It was thus that those killed during the orgy of violence of the War on Drugs were branded "scum" and "threats to society", that those investigating the killings were slandered as being on the drug cartels' payroll, or that those who condemned the administration were labelled a menace to Thailand's independence.[52] It was thus that the southern youths who were massacred by the army and police came to be referred to as "beasts".[53] By the time of the coup of 19 September 2006, Thailand had developed a form of "democracy" with a much stronger "delegative" than "representative" or "liberal" flavour.[54]

IMPLICATIONS

The events of the past, tumultuous decade in Thailand's process of political development illustrate the severity of challenges that democracies new, transitional, and unfledged must overcome for a chance to build political parties that are at once strong enough to make democracy work and not so strong that they might subvert it. By the mid-1990s, the weakness of Thailand's party system was so deeply entrenched that it took a rather extraordinary set of circumstances to trigger a transformation — in the specific case, the effects of a new constitution combined with an exogenous shock that displaced established players and reconfigured asymmetries of power and resources, as well the presence of a political entrepreneur capable of seizing opportunities opened up in the aftermath of the Asian crisis. Far from resolving the issue, the rise of Thaksin Shinawatra highlights the vulnerability of democracy to a variety of existential threats, in the presence of "unstructured" or "semi-structured" party systems. On the one hand, if weak, splintered, territorialized, personality-based parties minimize accountability, produce gridlock and corruption, and deprive voters of a real choice, populist politicians who offer drastic alternatives may prove especially appealing when the going gets rough. On the other hand, whereas a weak party system had long allowed unelected institutions such as the palace, the military, and the bureaucracy to call the shots behind the scenes, the rise to power of a politician openly contemptuous of democratic values and procedures is what gave Thailand's "invisible hand" of generals and meddlesome courtiers the necessary cover to roll out the tanks and the special forces, formally taking power for a period long enough to write a new constitution capable of insulating them from the nuisance posed by elected officials.

In the ensuing years of political instability and upheaval, the actions of Thailand's royalist establishment at one point appeared to have succeeded in breaking Thaksin's coalition. The dissolution of Thai Rak Thai ordered by the courts in the wake of the coup, the banning of over a hundred of its executives from elected office, and the opposition of the military junta kept Thai Rak Thai's successor, the People Power Party, from winning a majority in the elections held in December 2007. When the People Power Party and two of its coalition partners were themselves disbanded by the courts a year later, the defection of powerful factions persuaded by senior establishment figures to jump ship and support a new government led by the Democrat Party's Abhisit Vejjajiva seemed to harbour a return to the fragmentation, factional politics, and instability of the mid-1990s.[55] The results of elections held on 3 July 2011 were for this reason all the more jarring. Pheu Thai, a party led by Thaksin's youngest sister, Yingluck Shinawatra, took 265 of the available 500 seats, scoring the second-best election result of any political party in the history of Thailand, going some way towards replicating Thai Rak Thai's success in the 2005 election. By building on these results, Thaksin may yet manage to put his old coalition back together. If that is ultimately allowed to take place, without triggering a new military coup, one can only hope that Pheu Thai's electoral dominance will be exercised in a more judicious, responsible, and liberal manner than Thai Rak Thai's. There can be no democracy without majority rule, but Thailand can do better than a merely "delegative" or "plebiscitarian" democracy.

Notes

1. Two months before the coup, Privy Council President Prem Tinsulanonda — a retired general, former Prime Minister, and now King Bhumibol's most senior advisor — was reported to have publicly reminded a group of graduating cadets that the loyalty of the military should rest with the King, not the elected

government (See *The Nation*, 15 July 2006). In a country with Thailand's history, the meaning of Prem's words could not be lost on the Prime Minister.

2. See Noi Chang (pseud.), "The Persistent Myth of the 'Good' Coup", *The Nation*, 2 October 2006.
3. See Duncan McCargo, "Network Monarchy and Legitimacy Crises in Thailand", *Pacific Review* 18 (2005): 499–519.
4. McCargo, *"Network Monarchy"*, p. 513.
5. For a more detailed analysis, see Federico Ferrara, *Thailand Unhinged: The Death of Thai-Style Democracy* (Singapore: Equinox, 2011).
6. See Giovanni Sartori, *Parties and Party Systems* (New York: Cambridge University Press, 1976).
7. For instance, see Laothamatas Anek, "A Tale of Two Democracies: Conflicting Perceptions of Elections and Democracy in Thailand", in *The Politics of Elections in Southeast Asia*, edited by Robert H. Taylor (Cambridge: Cambridge University Press, 1996), pp. 201–23.
8. See Ruth Berins Collier and David Collier, *Shaping the Political Arena: Critical Junctures, the Labor Movement, and Regime Dynamics in Latin America* (Princeton, NJ: Princeton University Press, 1991), p. 29.
9. Pierson (2004, p. 66) notes that "junctures are 'critical' because they place institutional arrangements on paths or trajectories, which are then very difficult to alter". On that basis, Capoccia and Keleman (2007, p. 348) define critical junctures as *"relatively* short periods of time during which there is a *substantially* heightened probability that agents' choices will affect the outcome of interest", where "the duration of the juncture must be brief relative to the duration of the path-dependent process it instigates" and "the probability that agents' choices will affect the outcome of interest must be high relative to that probability before and after the juncture".
10. Accounts relying on "path dependence" have been criticized for relying excessively on "exogenous shocks", and ignoring more endogenous, incremental forms of institutional change (see Streeck and Thelen 2005). The criticism is certainly warranted, as are the correctives that have been suggested (see Mahoney and Thelen 2009). The nature and destructive force of the Asian crisis, however, makes the focus on exogenous shocks appropriate in this case.
11. See Thitinan Pongsudhirak, "Thailand Since the Coup", *Journal of Democracy* 19 (2008): 140–53.
12. Sartori (1968, p. 294) deems a party system to be structured if "the major parties are more 'solid' and more 'real' than the personalities". Structuring requires that voters give allegiance to parties rather than to local notables or "chieftains" and that they perceive the party system itself as a "natural channeling system". Sartori (1968, p. 293), moreover, equates anything short

of a national party system to one that is "weak" and "unstructured". In the case of Thailand, the fragmentation, territorialization, and levels of electoral volatility exhibited by the party system until the 2001 elections, as well as the role played by personalities, factions, and local cliques within most political parties (see Nelson 2005), rendered the party system far short of "structured". At the same time, as McCargo (1997) pointed out, it would be a mistake to dismiss political parties as altogether irrelevant during that time. As a result, it is perhaps more accurate to use the term "semi-structured" — a characterization that Sartori (1994, p. 51) himself has applied to a case like India.

13. See Kramol Tongdhamachart, *Toward a Political Party Theory in Thai Perspective* (Singapore: Institute of Southeast Asian Studies Occasional Paper No. 68, 1982), pp. 8–9.

14. The largely abortive development of Thai political parties between 1932 and 1945 is chronicled in Murashima (1991).

15. James Ockey, *Making Democracy: Leadership, Class, Gender, and Political Participation in Thailand* (Chiang Mai: Silkworm Books, 2004), p. 24.

16. Kramol, *Toward a Political Party*, p. 5.

17. Sartori, *Parties and Party Systems*, p. 125.

18. Ockey, *Making Democracy*, p. 26.

19. For instance, Benedict Anderson, "Elections and Participation in Three Southeast Asian Countries", in *The Politics of Elections in Southeast Asia*, edited by Robert H. Taylor (Cambridge University Press, 1996), p. 18.

20. See Clark D. Neher, "Thailand in 1987: Semi-Successful Semi-Democracy", *Asian Survey* 28 (1988): 192–201; and Chai-Anan Samudavanija, "Thailand: A Stable Semi-Democracy", in *Democracy in Developing Countries*, edited by Larry Diamond, Juan Linz, and Seymour Martin Lipset (London: Lynne Rienner, 1990).

21. Pasuk Phongpaichit and Sungsidh Piriyarangsan, *Corruption and Democracy in Thailand* (Chiang Mai: Silkworm Books, 1994), p. 3.

22. Benedict Anderson, "Murder and Progress in Modern Siam", *New Left Review* 181 (1990): 33–48.

23. Alan Klima, *The Funeral Casino: Meditation, Massacre, and Exchange with the Dead in Thailand* (Princeton, NJ: Princeton University Press, 2004), p. 96.

24. Duncan McCargo, "Thailand's Political Parties: Real, Authentic and Actual", in *Political Change in Thailand: Democracy and Participation*, edited by Kevin Hewison (London: Routledge, 1997), p. 166.

25. Ockey, *Making Democracy*, p. 27.

26. See David Murray, *Angels and Devils: Thai Politics from February 1991 to September 1992 — A Struggle for Democracy?* (Bangkok: Orchid Press, 1996).

27. See David Murray, "The 1995 National Elections in Thailand: A Step Back for Democracy?" *Asian Survey* 36 (1996): 361–75.

28. David Murray, "The Thai Parliamentary Elections of 1995 and 1996", *Electoral Studies* 16 (1997): 384.
29. Pasuk Phongpaichit and Chris Baker, *Thailand's Crisis* (Chiang Mai: Silkworm Books, 2000).
30. Much of the historical detail discussed in this section on Thaksin's career in business and politics is drawn from Pasuk and Baker (2009).
31. Pasuk Phongpaichit and Chris Baker, *Thaksin* (Chiang Mai: Silkworm Books, 2009).
32. Pasuk and Baker, *"Thaksin"*, pp. 76–80.
33. Sartori, *Parties and Party Systems*, p. 127.
34. See Paul Chambers, "Evolving Toward What? Parties, Factions, and Coalition Behavior in Thailand Today", *Journal of East Asian Studies* 5 (2005): 514.
35. Allen Hicken, *Building Party Systems in Developing Democracies* (New York: Cambridge University Press, 2009), pp. 127–36.
36. Hicken (2009, p. 132) echoes the argument in Cox (1997), who focuses on the competition for the office of the chief executive as a key institutional explanation for the relative fragmentation exhibited by a country's party system at the national level. Cox (1997, p. 189), specifically, hypothesized that the more valuable the "ultimate prize" — that is, the more presidents or prime ministers resemble "elected dictators" — the greater the pressure to aggregate into national parties. Whether they are popularly elected presidents or indirectly elected prime ministers, chief executives are generally invested with considerable powers. Consequently, parties seeking to maximize their chances to win a legislative majority and/or the presidency have an obvious incentive to forge (or strengthen) cross-district linkages.
37. In response to a similar argument about the importance of the "Thaksin effect" (see Nelson 2007), Hicken (2007) concedes that Thaksin Shinawatra's presence on the scene at the time, and the resources at his disposal, were a necessary condition to the streamlining of Thailand's party system, but would not have been enough to bring it about without the 1997 constitution. The argument made here is that the 1997 constitution mattered less to the success of Thai Rak Thai in the 2001 elections than it did to the preservation of its dominance after the elections.
38. Chambers, *Evolving Toward What?* p. 496.
39. Ockey, *Making Democracy*, pp. 45–46.
40. Pasuk and Baker, *Thaksin*, p. 88.
41. Paul Pierson, *Politics in Time: History, Institutions, and Social Analysis* (Princeton, NJ: Princeton University Press, 2004).
42. Ibid., p. 24.
43. See Gary W. Cox, *Making Votes Count* (New York: Cambridge University Press, 1997).
44. Pierson, *Politics in Time*, p. 24.

45. William H. Riker, *The Theory of Political Coalitions* (New Haven, CT: Yale University Press, 1962).
46. Chuan's first government, formed after the 1992 elections, was supported by a coalition commanding 207 seats out of 360 (57.5 per cent); Banharn's government after the 1995 elections was supported by a coalition commanding 215 seats out of 391 (55 per cent); Chavalit's government after the 1996 elections was supported by a coalition commanding 221 seats out of 393 (56 per cent). By contrast, the coalition government put together by Thaksin Shinawatra after the 2001 elections was initially supported by 67 per cent of the House of Representatives.
47. Pasuk and Baker, *Thaksin*, p. 192.
48. Ockey, *Making Democracy*, p. 50.
49. Duncan McCargo, *Rethinking Thailand's Southern Violence* (Singapore: NUS Press, 2007), pp. 56–61.
50. Maurizio Peleggi, *Thailand: The Worldly Kingdom* (London: Reaktion Books, 2007), p. 127.
51. Pasuk and Baker, *Thaksin*, p. 157.
52. Pasuk and Baker, *Thaksin*, p. 164.
53. McCargo, *Rethinking*, p. 66.
54. "Delegative democracies" are characterized by O'Donnell (1994, p. 59) as "highly majoritarian" democracies resting "on the premise that whoever wins election to the presidency is thereby entitled to govern as he or she sees fit, constrained only by the hard facts of existing power relations and by a constitutionally limited term of office". Though not an elected president, the insulation that Thaksin enjoyed from the legislative branch as a result of new constitutional provisions gave him more or less the authority to "govern as he saw fit, constrained only by the hard facts of existing power relations and by a constitutionally limited term of office".
55. Federico Ferrara, *Thailand Unhinged: The Death of Thai-Style Democracy* (Singapore: Equinox, 2011), pp. 84–90.

References

Anderson, Benedict. "Murder and Progress in Modern Siam". *New Left Review* 181 (1990): 33–48.
———. "Elections and Participation in Three Southeast Asian Countries". In *The Politics of Elections in Southeast Asia*, edited by Robert H. Taylor. Cambridge: Cambridge University Press, 1996.
Anek Laothamatas. "A Tale of Two Democracies: Conflicting Perceptions of Elections and Democracy in Thailand". In *The Politics of Elections in Southeast Asia*, edited by Robert H. Taylor. Cambridege: Cambridge University Press, 1996.
Capoccia, Giovanni and R. Daniel Keleman. "The Study of Critical Junctures:

Theory, Narrative, and Counterfactuals in Historical Institutionalism". *World Politics* 59 (2007): 341–69.

Chai-Anan Samudavanija. "Thailand: A Stable Semi-Democracy". In *Democracy in Developing Countries*, edited by Larry Diamond, Juan Linz, and Seymour Martin Lipset. London: Lynne Rienner, 1990.

Chambers, Paul. "Evolving Toward What? Parties, Factions, and Coalition Behavior in Thailand Today". *Journal of East Asian Studies* 5 (2005): 495–520.

Chang Noi (pseud.). "The Persistent Myth of the 'Good Coup'". *The Nation*, 2 October 2006.

Collier, Ruth Berins and David Collier. *Shaping the Political Arena: Critical Junctures, the Labor Movement, and Regime Dynamics in Latin America*. Princeton, NJ: Princeton University Press, 1991.

Cox, Gary W. *Making Votes Count*. New York: Cambridge University Press, 1997.

Ferrara, Federico. *Thailand Unhinged: The Death of Thai-Style Democracy*. Singapore: Equinox, 2011.

Hicken, Allen. "Omitted Variables, Intent, and Counterfactuals: A Response to Michael H. Nelson". *Journal of East Asian Studies* 7 (2007): 149–58.

———. *Building Party Systems in Developing Democracies*. New York: Cambridge University Press, 2009.

Klima, Alan. *The Funeral Casino: Meditation, Massacre, and Exchange with the Dead in Thailand*. Princeton, NJ: Princeton University Press, 2004.

Kramol Tongdhamachart. *Toward a Political Party Theory in Thai Perspective*, Occasional Paper No. 68. Singapore: Institute of Southeast Asian Studies, 1982.

Mahoney, James and Kathleen Thelen. "A Theory of Gradual Institutional Change". In *Explaining Institutional Change: Ambiguity, Agency, and Power*, edited by James Mahoney and Kathleen Thelen. New York: Cambridge University Press, 2009.

McCargo, Duncan. "Thailand's Political Parties: Real, Authentic and Actual". In *Political Change in Thailand: Democracy and Participation*, edited by Kevin Hewison. London: Routledge, 1997.

———. "Network Monarchy and Legitimacy Crises in Thailand". *Pacific Review* 18 (2005): 499–519.

———. *Rethinking Thailand's Southern Violence*. Singapore: NUS Press, 2007.

Murashima, Eiji. "Democracy and the Development of Political Parties in Thailand 1932–1945". In *The Making of Modern Thai Political Parties*, edited by Eiji Murashima, Nakharin Mektrairat, and Somkiat Wanthana. Tokyo: Institute of Developing Economies, 1991.

Murray, David. *Angels and Devils: Thai Politics from February 1991 to September 1992 — A Struggle for Democracy?* Bangkok: Orchid Press, 1996.

———. "The 1995 National Elections in Thailand: A Step Back for Democracy?" *Asian Survey* 36 (1996): 361–75.

———. "The Thai Parliamentary Elections of 1995 and 1996". *Electoral Studies* 16 (1997): 379-85.

Neher, Clark D. "Thailand in 1987: Semi-Successful Semi-Democracy". *Asian Survey* 28 (1988): 192–201.

Nelson, Michael H. "Analyzing Provincial Political Structures in *Thailand: Phuak, trakun,* and *hua khanaen*". Southeast Asia Research Centre Working Paper Series No. 79. City University of Hong Kong, 2005.

———. "Institutional Incentives and Informal Local Political Groups (Phuak) in Thailand: Comments on Allen Hicken and Paul Chambers". *Journal of East Asian Studies* 7 (2007): 125–47.

O'Donnell, Guillermo. "Delegative Democracy". *Journal of Democracy* 5 (1994): 55–69.

Ockey, James. *Making Democracy: Leadership, Class, Gender, and Political Participation in Thailand*. Chiang Mai: Silkworm Books, 2004.

Pasuk Phongpaichit and Chris Baker. *Thailand's Crisis*. Chiang Mai: Silkworm Books, 2000.

———. *Thaksin*. Chiang Mai: Silkworm Books, 2009.

Pasuk Phongpaichit and Sungsidh Piriyarangsan. *Corruption and Democracy in Thailand*. Chiang Mai: Silkworm Books, 1994.

Peleggi, Maurizio. *Thailand: The Worldly Kingdom*. London: Reaktion Books, 2007.

Pierson, Paul. *Politics in Time: History, Institutions, and Social Analysis*. Princeton, NJ: Princeton University Press, 2004.

Riker, William H. *The Theory of Political Coalitions*. New Haven, CT: Yale University Press, 1962.

Sartori, Giovanni. *Parties and Party Systems*. New York: Cambridge University Press, 1976.

———. "Political Development and Political Engineering". In *Public Policy Vol. XVII*, edited by John D. Montgomery and Albert O. Hirschman. Cambridge, MA: Harvard University Press, 1968.

———. *Comparative Constitutional Engineering: An Inquiry into Structures, Incentives and Outcomes*. New York: New York University Press, 1994.

Streeck, Wolfgang and Kathleen Thelen. "Introduction: Institutional Change in Advanced Political Economies". In *Beyond Continuity: Institutional Change in Advanced Political Economies*, edited by Wolfgang Streeck and Kathleen Thelen. Oxford: Oxford University Press, 2005.

Thitinan Pongsudhirak. "Thailand Since the Coup". *Journal of Democracy* 19 (2008): 140–53.

8

THE MARCH 2008 GENERAL ELECTION IN MALAYSIA AS A HISTORICAL CONJUNCTURE

Johan Saravanamuttu

This chapter argues that the twelfth general election of 8 March 2008 in Malaysia was a watershed political event, which may be appreciated as a historical conjuncture, following Ganesan.[1] Certainly, 8 March altered significantly the political parameters of electoral politics and, as I have argued elsewhere, constituted or at least contributed to a reconfiguration of the political landscape in Malaysia.[2] In terms of electoral politics, it may be suggested that 8 March created a de facto and perhaps a *de jure* two-party (or two coalition) system if one considers both the parliamentary and state levels of governance. The character of Malaysian federalism may have paradoxically allowed for such a development.

The event saw the ruling National Front (Barisan Nasional) government lose its two-thirds share of seats in parliament which it had held since Malaysia became independent in 1957. The opposition parties, later formalized as the People's Alliance (Pakatan Rakyat),[3] won a total of 82 out of the 222 seats up for contest. The National Front barely won 50 per cent of the 7.9 million ballots cast, demonstrating that the electorate was virtually split down the middle. Furthermore, five state governments fell to opposition hands, unprecedented in Malaysian history. This essay argues that the political moment creating a two-party system in Malaysia was reinforced by several subsequently held by-elections after 8 March. The outcome of these by-elections indicates that the momentum and the factors that explain the 8 March result continue to drive current political developments. Factors driving Malaysia's new politics are both a function of its political transformations which have disembedded political legacies since arguably the 1980s and certainly after Anwar Ibrahim's sacking and incarceration in 1998. I suggest that while ethnicity remains a crucial variable in Malaysian politics, cross-ethnic voting represents the driver of Malaysia's new politics. Citizens across the board are now more informed of universal issues such as corruption and minority rights.

The path-dependency notion of "increasing returns" could be usefully applied to the 8 March conjuncture in that the series of nine by-elections held up until the end of 2009 saw seven won by the People's Alliance. This provides "diachronic" validation to the fact that the event of 8 March was no political fluke. Contrariwise, the increasing returns argument could well be applied to the ruling coalition, Barisan Nasional, with "first mover advantage" in electoral politics for decades, given its copious political and economic investments in institutions which reproduce ethnicized political structures. The fact that path dependency was dented on 8 March suggests to this author that a new path dependency based on a radically altered mode of political mobilization may have taken root in the Malaysian political system. This need not mean a departure from ethnicized politics, but a political shift in the direction of more universalist, participatory politics. This argument will be developed in the course of this chapter and in the conclusion.

An important theoretical point has been raised by O'Shannassy, who sought to answer the question of whether 8 March represented a "truly progressive moment, one that is long-term and structural, or is this instead a short-term, regressive, "restorative" moment?"[4] Invoking a Gramscian perspective, O'Shannasy seems to suggest that the jury is still out on this question although certain transformative elements of politics seem to have surfaced with 8 March. The view taken here is that such a Gramscian analysis probably understates significant political developments of an electoral sort which are closer to reformist rather than "revolutionary" developments in Malaysian politics. We will return to this question in the conclusion of this chapter.

The chapter begins with a section contextualizing the 8 March event and its outcome examining the *reformasi* movement and the emergence of new politics in Malaysia. It argues that the 8 March outcome was driven mainly by domestic political developments with little or no external impetus. A second section of the paper delves into the character of Malaysian ethnic politics and examines the significance of cross-ethnic voting on 8 March. The third section of the paper analyses the outcomes of by-elections after 8 March as well as other political developments.

CONTEXTUALIZING MARCH 2008 AS HISTORICAL CONJUNCTURE

The 8 March historical conjuncture needs to be contextualized by the rise of "new politics" in Malaysia, which was an outcome of the *reformasi* movement.[5] The movement was in turn sparked by the Anwar Ibrahim imbroglio, which saw the erstwhile Deputy Prime Minister and deputy leader of the ruling United Malays National Organisation (UMNO) incarcerated for what many have alleged to have been fabricated charges of political corruption and sexual misdemeanour. The Prime Minister Mahathir Mohamad, who saw Anwar as a political threat, was instrumental in bringing about the Anwar episode. Driven by and spearheaded by Malay reformist groups, the *reformasi* movement went well beyond the demand for Anwar's release and Mahathir's resignation to valorize such issues as "the rule of law", "participatory democracy" and "justice for all". Specifically the reforms[6] called for the removal of the Internal Security Act (ISA), for "accountancy" and "transparency" in decision-making and the eradication of "corruption, cronyism and nepotism". The formation of two civil society driven umbrella organizations called Gagasan Rakyat and Gerak was evidence that a large sector of the Malay middle class was involved in reform politics, which was then insitutionalized in the form of the Barisan Alternatif (BA), comprising the PKN (Parti Keadilan Nasional, the predecessor of the PKR, or People's Justice Party), PAS (Parti Islam Se-Malaysia) and DAP (Democratic Action Party). Writing on the significance of the *reformasi* movement, Weiss has argued that it represented a major shift in Malay politics and was distinctive in terms of its coherent aims, its innovative tactics of mobilization and organization and its substantive significance in terms of institution building. She further argues that it was distinctive because "the movement reflected the long-term demographic and ideational shifts, including the development of a multiracial 'new' middle class and gradually rising support for social issues".[7] This "new politics" as explained by Loh and Saravanamuttu[8] was characterized by the fragmentation of Malaysia's ethnic communities and by that token a devaluation of ethnicism coupled with the rise of participatory politics:

> [That] ethnicism no longer overwhelms the other discourses of Malaysian politics as it used to, at least not to the same predictable extent. For a large multi-ethnic middle-class coalition now exists in Malaysia, factions of which have become increasingly critical of the BN government, not just its resort to the politics of ethnicism but also its authoritarianism and economic policies increasingly riddled with cronyism.[9]

Most importantly, Weiss talks about how the institutional development of the *reformasi* changed from a collection of largely inchoate protestors into the broad based Gagasan and Gerak formations and then into the BA. She argues that the BA was the logical extension of the *reformasi* into Malaysian coalition politics, with four key institutional developments:

- First, the BA's commitment to displacing race as the central organizing principle of political contestation, all BA parties being non-racial ones, contra those of the BN;
- The BA's principle of opposing patronage politics, i.e., objective of eliminating corruption, cronyism and nepotism;
- The BA's contempt for "politics as usual" and debunking of old-style money politics and that politics should not just be left to politicians;
- The role of civil society agents (CSAs) which clearly laid claim to a niche in BA politics, whether working directly with political parties or as candidates endorsing particular policy positions.[10]

The outcome of the 1999 general election showed that new politics had gained traction perhaps more with Malays than with non-Malays at that stage. The BN's landslide win in the 2004 general election saw a swing against a waning opposition front weakened by a lack of leadership because of Anwar's imprisonment and the squabbling over the issue of an Islamic state which caused the departure of the DAP from BA. The electoral performance of the BN under Abdullah Badawi in 2004 has also been attributed to his hijacking of *reformasi* agendas by the ruling coalition.

For these reasons, it is thus argued here that the March 2008 electoral outcome as a natural development of new politics produced a necessary historical rupture and thus spurred the onset of a new path-dependent trajectory in Malaysian politics. However, it should be noted that the event may not be of the same order of a "critical juncture" of the sort alluded to by Collier and Collier,[11] namely, that it produces a distinctly new legacy by ending an old one, such as demolishing an *ancien régime*. In my reckoning, there would continue to be important continuities in politics after the 2008 general election. Secondly, the critical junctures identified by the Colliers in Latin America spanned periods of nine to twenty-three years.[12] March 2008 was but about ten years after the antecedent event of *reformasi* which generated the reform politics alluded to above. Its electoral antecedent was the 1999 general election which is acknowledged to have been "underwhelming" certainly when compared with what happened later in 2008. Nonetheless, the argument is that path dependence was created from 1999 which had valorized democracy, the discourse of social justice and participatory politics. Malaysian politics has changed palpably and radically but perhaps not to the extent implied by Collier and Collier and much will depend on further developments in the years following 2008.

THE 8 MARCH DECISION

There is little denying that the year 2008 will be remembered as a watershed in Malaysian electoral politics. The then Malaysian Prime Minister Abdullah Badawi already had more than his fair share of problems to deal with even before his tenure headed into 2008. After the 25 November 2007 rally on the streets of Kuala Lumpur involving some 30,000 Indians, five Hindu Rights Action Force (HINDRAF)[13] lawyers were detained under the draconian Internal Security Act (ISA) that allows for detention without trial, while one was at large. The V.K. Lingam video exposé in September and the Royal Commission of Inquiry of January 2008 remained much in the public consciousness,[14] so too the Mongolian model Altantuya's murder trial which implicated Najib Razak and had dragged on from 2007. Interfaith fractures, which had surfaced since 2005, remained largely unresolved along with internal squabbles within the ruling coalition parties. Most sensationally, the MCA (Malaysian Chinese Association) Minister of Health had to resign because of the circulation of a sex video by his detractors. Finally, the economy was not in great shape with petrol prices and inflation spiking and former premier Dr Mahathir still sniping Abdullah from the sidelines. Yet speculation was rife by early 2008 that an early election would be called presumably to salvage the premier's beleaguered situation, more than one year in advance of the mandatory five years. In a CNN interview Abdullah did admit that a fresh mandate was necessary for him to address a host of new issues and to make good his unfulfilled anti-corruption agenda.

During the event, parliament and state assemblies, with the exception of Sarawak, were dissolved on 13 February 2008. The Election Commission called for nominations on 24 February for the 12th General Election of Malaysia to be held on 8 March 2008. An unusually long period of thirteen days was given for campaigning and some 222 parliamentary seats were in contention along with 505 state seats. Two days before election day, Malaysian analysts (including me) speaking at a seminar were not prepared to concede that the Barisan Nasional (BN) would lose its two-thirds majority in parliament, let alone four more state governments.[15]

THE ELECTION OUTCOME

The outcome of the 8 March 2008 general election has been dubbed a "political tsunami" that some have argued brought about a tectonic shift to the Malaysian political landscape. The other hyperbole used was "a perfect storm".[16] But veteran political analyst Khoo Boo Teik strikes a more cautious note:

> The metaphors may be excessive. A true tsunami, say, would have swept the BN out of office. A perfect storm would not have bypassed Sabah and Sarawak.[17]

This observation notwithstanding, the three major ethnic communities — Malays, Chinese and Indians — and almost all the Peninsular states[18] swung decisively in favour of opposition parties as shown in Table 8.1 and deprived the ruling coalition of its all-important two-thirds majority in parliament, thus dealing a heavy blow to its ethnic power-sharing formula. However, more sceptical analysts may suggest that basically Malaysian politics remained pivoted on ethnic mobilization, symbolized by the still successful, if slightly frayed, formula of racially constituted political parties at its helm. The already growing literature on electoral politics in Malaysia has generally weighed in on the proposition that ethnicity

Table 8.1
Results of Parliamentary Election, 2008

Party	Votes	%	Seat	%
Barisan Nasional	4,090,670	50.14	140	63.1
UMNO	2,381,725	29.19	79	35.6
MCA	849,108	10.41	15	6.8
MIC	179,422	2.20	3	1.4
Gerakan	184,548	2.26	2	0.9
Others	495,867	6.08	41	18.5
Pakatan Rakyat	3,786,399	46.41	82	36.9
DAP	1,107,960	13.58	28	12.6
PAS	1,140,676	13.98	23	10.4
PKR	1,509,080	18.50	31	14.0
Others	28,683	0.35	0	0
Independents	63,960	0.78	0	0
Spoilt votes	175,011	2.14	–	–
Unreturned votes	41,564	0.51	–	–
Total	8,159,043	100	222	100

Source: Computed from Election Commission data.

or racial motivations have always driven Malaysian electoral politics. Implicitly or explicitly, writers would take their point of departure from the two classic studies by Ratnam and Von Vorys on "communalism" in Malaysia.[19] Not totally rejecting this paradigm, this essay suggests that a sensibility to universal values such as human rights and even class or bread-and-butter issues have become increasingly germane to an understanding of election results.[20]

It is now recognized that the 8 March general election in terms of enduring political outcomes has surpassed the 1969 watershed general election which triggered the outbreak of riots in Kuala Lumpur on 13 May.[21] The 2008 outburst of election rallies throughout the campaign period by opposition parties was oddly reminiscent of May 1969, but perhaps eclipsing the 1969 campaign by the sheer numbers that attended such rallies throughout the country.[22] One large rally in Penang saw some 50,000 in attendance, a turnout that was clearly unprecedented.[23]

Despite the ruling BN coalition losing its hold on the two-thirds majority of seats, no untoward events occurred after 8 March, speaking well for the fact that Malaysian society had arrived at a political threshold where violence as an instrument of change was eschewed.

What then are the salient facts of the 2008 outcome? The BN government arguably suffered its worst defeat in history with a loss of its two-thirds majority of seats. As shown in Table 8.2, the BN government also just about lost the popular vote in Peninsular Malaysia, including the loss of four state governments while one continued to be in opposition hands. There was a vote swing away from the BN government in every state in the Peninsula.

Table 8.3, based on estimates, shows that Chinese and Indian voters clearly preferred the opposition parties while Malays still had a preference, but a reduced one, for the BN parties. The most significant swing came from Indians, who evidently abandoned the ethnically constituted Malaysian Indian Congress (MIC). The Chinese voters also swung palpably in the direction of ostensibly non-Chinese parties, dealing the Malaysian Chinese Association (MCA) its poorest showing since 1969.

Most significant, I would argue, was that Malaysia edged towards a formal parliamentary two-party system and in fact instituted a two-party system at the state-level of governance. Let us now turn briefly to the

Table 8.2
Percentage of Votes for Opposition Candidates, Parliament, 1995–2008

State	1995	1999	2004	2008	Change 2004–8
Perlis	31.5	43.8	36.3	39.9	+3.6
Kedah	35.3	44.2	40.2	53.2	+13.0
Kelantan	56.7	60.9	48.7	55.0	+6.3
Terengganu	45.4	58.7	43.6	44.7	+1.1
Penang	39.0	48.4	43.2	63.0	+19.8
Perak	31.7	44.1	40.5	53.3	+12.8
Pahang	28.4	42.6	32.3	40.5	+8.2
Selangor	24.7	44.8	34.0	55.4	+21.4
KL	41.1	49.4	41.2	62.0	+20.8
Putrajaya	—	—	11.7	24.4	+12.7
N. Sembilan	29.7	40.8	30.1	45.1	+15.0
Melaka	31.7	43.4	28.8	42.6	+14.3
Johor	20.5	27.1	20.4	34.7	+14.3
Pen. Malaysia	33.4	44.4	36.2	50.2	+14.0

Source: Khoo, *Aliran Monthly* 28, no. 3 (2008): 4.

Table 8.3
The Malay, Chinese and Indian Vote for BN, per cent[24]

	1995	1999	2004	2008	Change 2004–8
Malay	69	53	63	58	5
Chinese	56	62	65	35	30
Indian	96	75	82	47	35

Source: Straits Times, 11 March 2008.

election results, a summary of which is found in Table 8.1. Some of the salient outcomes of 8 March could be said to be the following:

- The BN barely got half (50.1 per cent) of the 7.9 million ballots cast nationwide and lost the popular vote on the Peninsula, garnering only 49 per cent of the ballots.
- The BN lost its two-thirds majority in parliament, winning 140 federal seats and 307 state seats; the opposition took 82 and 198 respectively.
- The BN lost the state governments of Selangor, Penang, Perak and Kedah, while Kelantan remained in opposition hands. (In its worst performances of the past, BN had failed to capture only two state governments, Kelantan and Terengganu, in 1959 and 1999).
- BN casualties included the Women, Family and Community Development Minister, Shahrizat Abdul Jalil, Information Minister Zainuddin Maidin, the presidents of the Malaysian Indian Congress, S. Samy Velu, People's Progressive Party (PPP), M. Kayveas, and Gerakan, Koh Tsu Koon.
- Parti Islam Se-Malaysia (PAS)'s women's wing chief Lo' Lo' Mohd Ghazali became the second woman from the party to win a parliamentary seat (the first was Khadijah Sidek in 1959).

One of the more significant aspects of 2008 in contrast to previous general elections, was the comprehensive vote swing of all major ethnic communities away from the BN parties. Political scientist Ong Kian Ming has estimated that some 30–35 per cent of non-Malay voters swung to the opposition parties, compared with the popular vote in the previous election of 2004. Although the overall corresponding swing for Malays was only about 5 per cent, Ong has argued the following:

It is important to highlight that these vote swings are not uniformly distributed. For example, the Malay vote swing in the West Coast states, especially in Penang, Selangor and Kuala Lumpur was higher than the estimated 5% and was closer to 10% or even higher in certain constituencies like Balik Pulau, Gombak and Lembah Pantai. It would not have been possible for the opposition, PKR in these cases, to win without a sizeable swing in the Malay vote.[25]

Nationwide, in mixed seats where the electorate formed 40–60 per cent of Malay voters, the BN won 28 seats and the opposition 26 seats, showing that the alternative Pakatan had become a veritable contender to the BN and in some sense was emulating BN's model of electoral success.[26] It could well be argued that cross-ethnic voting accounted for a significant number of victories of the Pakatan and, had the pattern of cross-ethnic voting which occurred in the Kelang Valley been replicated in states like Pahang, Malacca, Negeri Sembilan and Johor, the BN government might well have been toppled on 8 March.[27]

A TWO-PARTY SYSTEM

The fact that Malaysia may have become a *de jure* two-party system at the state level can be attributed to the stunning victories of the Pakatan coalition of forces led by Anwar Ibrahim as shown in Figure 8.1. In fact some analysts have pointed out that the sixth state to fall was the federal territory of Kuala Lumpur, where all but one parliamentary seat out of 12 seats went to the Pakatan.[28] Anwar further reinforced the 8 March outcome by sweeping the Permatang Pauh by-election with a majority of well over 15,000 votes on 26 August and was subsequently officially anointed as Leader of the Opposition in Parliament.

First, it must be stressed that the major change in the political landscape is the still nascent, two-party (or two-coalition) system at the state level, where Pakatan governments initially ran five governments, namely, Selangor, Penang, Perak, Kedah and Kelantan.[29] In these states the BN found itself in the unfamiliar role of opposition, except in Kelantan where this had been the case for about two decades. One could well argue that Malaysian democracy has perhaps arrived at a new threshold and that citizens could now have the opportunity to judge four alternative state governments and choose to re-elect or reject them the next time around. As such, the formalization of the Pakatan coalition as an alternative coalition to

Figure 8.1
Malaysian Election 2008: Distribution of Seats Won in Each State Legislature

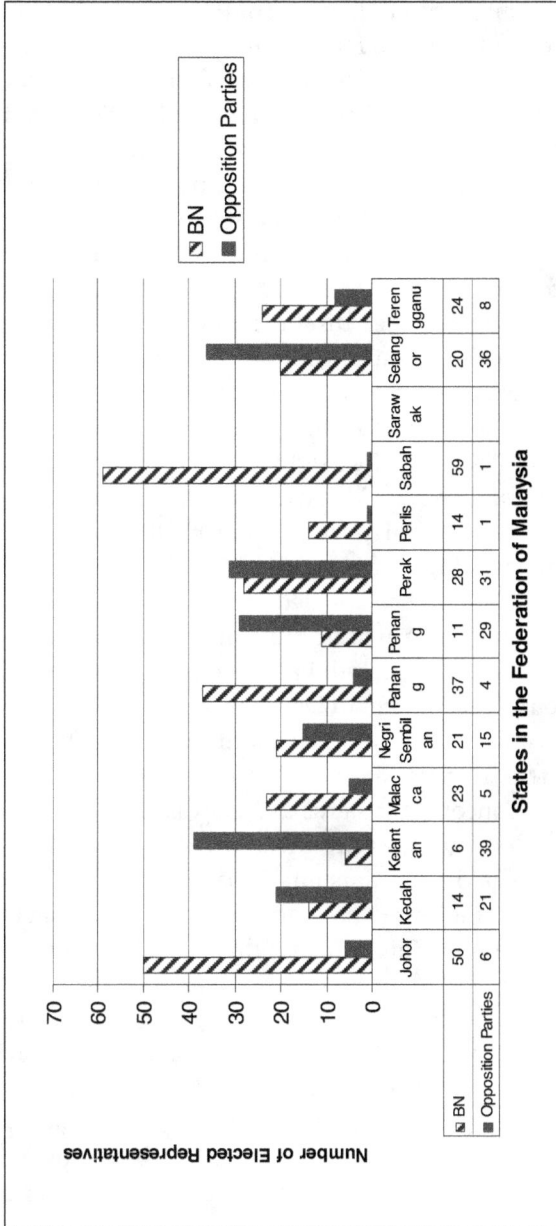

	Johor	Kedah	Kelant an	Malac ca	Negri Sembil an	Pahan g	Penan g	Perak	Perlis	Sabah	Saraw ak	Selang or	Teren gganu
BN	50	14	6	23	21	37	11	28	14	59		20	24
Opposition Parties	6	21	39	5	15	4	29	31	1	1		36	8

States in the Federation of Malaysia

Source: Computed from Election Commission data.

the National Front appears to be fait accompli. Unlike its predecessor, the Alternative Front (Barisan Alternatif) of 1998–99, the Pakatan governmental presence seems guaranteed for some time to come by virtue of state power. By late 2009, the Pakatan had announced a common political manifesto and agreed to a common logo, like the BN. Its registration awaits the approval of the Registrar of Societies at the time of writing.

Second, the obverse trend may be true for the BN coalition. This long-standing coalition is clearly in a state of flux if not turmoil. Already one component party, the Sabah Progressive Party (SAPP) has left the BN coalition (on 17 September 2008) while the Gerakan and even the MCA have noted their deep disaffection with UMNO politics. These two Chinese-based component parties are themselves in a state of political reinvention, spurning an earlier suggestion of merger. After the 8 March result, one senior woman leader and her supporters left the MCA and joined Anwar's party.[30] Most significantly, former UMNO law minister Zaid Ibrahim and former MCA vice president Chua Jui Meng became members of the PKR.[31] The suggestion by the Gerakan President Koh Tsu Koon to have direct membership in the BN and to turn it eventually into a multiracial party is a veiled critique of the current poor formula of racial power sharing within the National Front today. The leader of Sabah's native-based United Pasokmomogun Kadazandusun Murut Organization (UPKO), Bernard Dompok, has also expressed grave concern about the failure of the National Front government to deal with three urgent matters, namely, the unequal exchange of economic benefits to Sabah and its concomitant status as Malaysia's poorest state, the issue of religious freedom and the unresolved problem of the influx of more than one million illegal immigrants into Sabah.[32]

However, not all was necessarily rosy for the Pakatan governments in the aftermath of 8 March. Taking the instance of Penang, the DAP-led government may have weathered a number of UMNO-generated political storms and self-inflicted faux pas but the going has been tough, admitted as much by Chief Minister Lim Guan Eng.[33] Similarly, the PKR-led Selangor government also had its fill of challenges but it seems to be holding firm. The most outrageous development was the power grab by the BN of the Perak state government in February 2009 (to be discussed further later). The PAS-led government of Kedah also has its own political hiccups.

At the federal level, the formation of a strong parliamentary opposition with 82 seats seems to be having a noticeable impact on the BN, even without a no-confidence vote against the government.[34] The Malaysian budget for 2009 was made somewhat irrelevant by the global financial crisis in October 2008, with the new Finance Minister introducing new measures such as the injection of a RM7 billion ringgit stimulus package for the economy.[35] By the end of 2008, UMNO appeared to have re-established itself under its new leader, Najib Razak, whose actions (at the time of writing) have been partially successful in checking the negative effects of the 8 March outcome for the ruling coalition while managing damage control in BN politics up to a point.

ETHNIC AND CROSS-ETHNIC VOTING ON 8 MARCH

In trying to comprehend the nature of ethnic voting patterns in 2008, the overall swing in popular votes deserves deeper analysis which we will now undertake. As can be seen from Table 8.3, a minor swing in popular votes could produce significant seat changes in the first-past-the-post electoral system of Malaysia but the comprehensive character of the BN's slippage in 2008 cannot be denied. The 2008 election is comparable to the 1969 result when the Alliance government coalition lost the popular vote for the entire country. In 2008 the BN barely scraped through and showed even poorer performance in terms of the percentage of parliamentary seats secured.

Below are three scatter plots (Figures 8.2, 8.3 and 8.4) showing parliamentary seats won by the main parties in Peninsular Malaysia in terms of the ethnic proportionality of the seats. As we are using the data provided by the Election Commission (EC), the parties of the ruling coalition have been collapsed into the BN while the individual parties of the opposition are displayed. Ethnic proportionality in terms of Malay, Chinese and Indian votes is measured by simple percentage as again provided by the EC data. Our scatter plots reveal some interesting facts about the 2008 election. The first point to be made is that Malaysian political parties are still predominantly ethnic in their electoral politics, or put differently, UMNO and PAS tend to be successful in predominantly Malay constituencies while the DAP is particularly successful in predominantly Chinese constituencies. The exception tends to be the PKR which has performed with great success in mixed constituencies. Paradoxically, we could extrapolate from the scatter plots that UMNO non-Malay partners also find their electoral success in mixed constituencies despite their ethnic

Figure 8.2
Proportion of Malay Voters for Each Seat Won by Political Parties

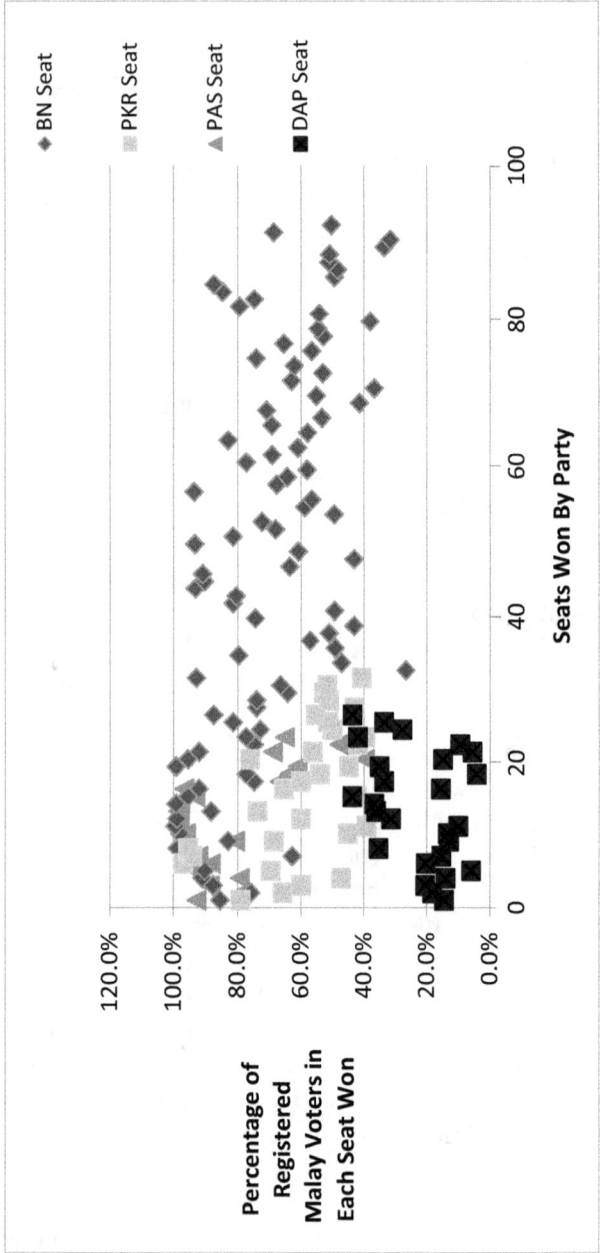

Figure 8.3
Proportion of Chinese Voters by Seats Won

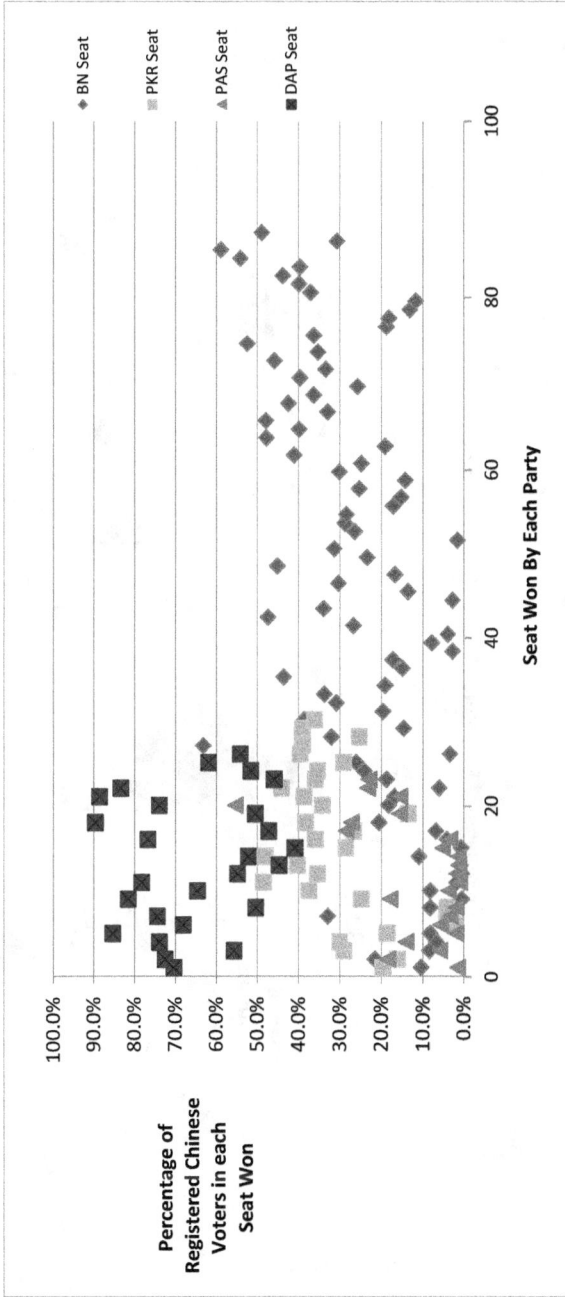

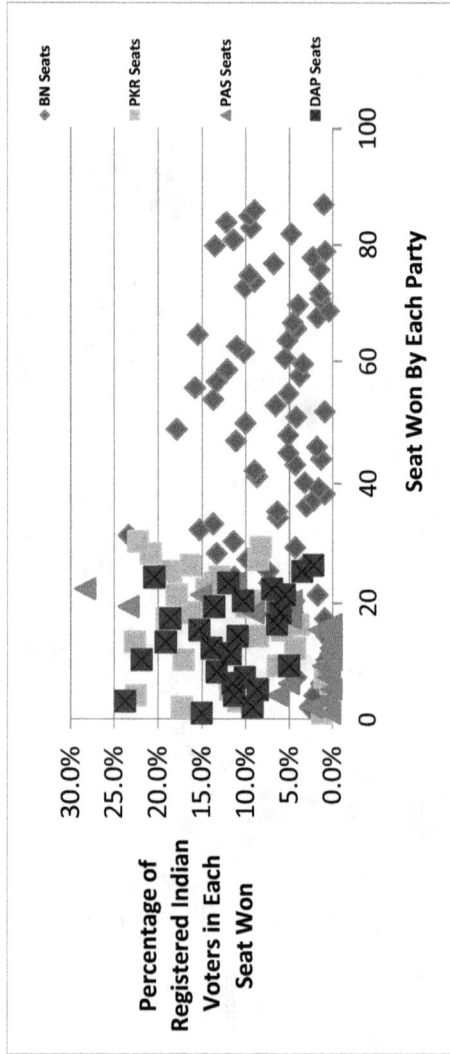

Figure 8.4
Percentage of Registered Indian Voters by Seats Won

orientation.[36] Let us examine each of the scatter plots for more specific observations.

In Figure 8.2, we can clearly see PAS and DAP at two extreme ends of the Malay racial continuum, PAS winning in high-density Malay constituencies while DAP takes low-density Malay seats. The PKR plays the perfect role of winning the mixed seats and thereby holding the PR coalition together. Figure 8.3 shows the obverse position vis-à-vis Chinese high-density constituencies. The PKR coalition again holds the middle ground. When looking at the BN's performance which unfortunately is not broken down into that of its component parties, it can still be deduced that UMNO won the high-density Malay constituencies. A much larger proportion of high to middle density Malay constituencies are won by the BN suggesting that its component parties also can do well in Malay majority constituencies. A clear rejection of BN parties in Chinese high-density constituencies is indicated in the second scatter plot, and implied in the first. This should definitely be of concern to Chinese-based BN parties, the MCA and Gerakan.

Turning to the Indian vote as shown in Figure 8.4, the first thing to note is that the PKR has performed very well along with the DAP with two PAS outliers seemingly securing high Indian votes. Since there are no real high-density Indian constituencies, with 30 per cent as its uppermost limit, one could extrapolate that winning seats above the 15 per cent margin is a good indicator of Indian support. This being the case, the BN parties have fared poorly in securing the Indian vote, with barely four wins in that category.

CROSS-ETHNIC VOTING IN KUALA LUMPUR AND SELANGOR[37]

As can be seen in Table 8.4, the BN received a severe thrashing in Kuala Lumpur in 2008. This is explained by a massive swing of Malay, Chinese and Indian votes in the direction of PAS, DAP, PKR. Even in the constituency of Putrajaya, where civil servants constitute the electorate, the PAS candidate gained some 12.7 per cent more votes than in 2004. In total the Pakatan won 61.6 per cent of the votes in Kuala Lumpur and most significantly won all the mixed constituencies except for Setiawangsa. The top performing Teresa Kok of the DAP won a 19.4 per cent swing of votes in Seputeh, garnering a stunning 36,500 votes, which was 82 per cent of the total. However, perhaps the most significant result came in the mixed

Table 8.4
Ethnic Composition and Seats Won in Kuala Lumpur, Putrajaya, 2004 & 2008

	Malay %	Chinese %	Indian %	2004	2008
Kepong	4.1	89.5	6.0	DAP	DAP
Batu	42.9	39.6	16.3	Gerakan	PKR
Wangsa Maju	51.1	39.0	8.5	UMNO	PKR
Segambut	34.9	50.4	13.6	Gerakan	DAP
Setiawangsa	56.4	31.3	10.0	UMNO	UMNO
Titiwangsa	65.0	22.9	11.1	UMNO	PAS
Bukit Bintang	14.7	73.9	10.3	DAP	DAP
Lembah Pantai	52.8	25.3	20.8	UMNO	PKR
Seputeh	5.4	88.9	5.5	DAP	DAP
Cheras	9.3	83.3	7.0	DAP	DAP
Bandar Tun Razak	51.7	39.1	8.3	MCA	PKR
Putrajaya	93.5	1.5	4.2	UMNO	UMNO

Source: Adapted from Ooi, Saravanamuttu and Lee (2008, p. 93).

constituency of Lembah Pantai, where Nurul Izzah, Anwar Ibrahim's daughter, up-ended three-term incumbent and Women's Minister Sharizat Abdul Jalil. The 22.2 per cent in the voter swing saw Nurul win by a 2,895 majority, an impressive result by any measure for a rookie candidate. As pointed out by Ooi, Saravanamuttu and Lee,[38] Nurul's win came from the sizeable Chinese and Indian vote since these communities make up 25.3 and 20.8 per cent of the constituency respectively.

We now turn to the state of Selangor. Selangor registered the largest vote swing of about 21 per cent for the Pakatan in both parliamentary and state contests winning the coalition some 55 per cent of the total votes. Most impressively, Pakatan won 18 of the 22 parliamentary seats and left the BN with only 3 out of the 18 mixed constituency seats. A comparison of parliamentary seats won in 2004 and 2008 in Table 8.5 shows the comprehensive character of the BN's defeat in 2008 in the most developed state of Malaysia.

The DAP and Pakatan swept the four constituencies where Chinese made up the majority or largest plurality, namely in Petaling Jaya Utara, Klang, Serdang and Petaling Jaya Selatan. DAP also won in the mixed seat of Puchong which had a Malay plurality. PAS candidates defeated UMNO counterparts in other mixed Malay plurality seats in Shah Alam, Kuala Selangor and Hulu Langat. It is clear from the above results that the Pakatan won most of the middle ground in Selangor. As suggested by Ooi,

Table 8.5
Seats Won in Selangor by Ethnic Composition

Parliamentary Constituency	Malay %	Chinese %	Indian %	2004	2008
Sabak Bernam	81.30	13.60	5.10	UMNO	UMNO
Sungai Besar	67.90	30.30	1.80	UMNO	UMNO
Hulu Selangor	53.90	26.70	19.00	MIC	PKR
Tanjong Karang	72.10	16.70	11.10	UMNO	UMNO
Kuala Selangor	61.00	15.60	23.30	UMNO	PAS
Selayang	44.80	38.24	16.23	MCA	PKR
Gombak	76.00	13.50	9.90	UMNO	PKR
Ampang	56.20	34.20	8.90	UMNO	PKR
Pandan	49.34	45.04	5.15	MCA	BN
Hulu Langat	39.50	55.30	4.70	UMNO	PAS
Serdang	36.60	52.10	10.90	MCA	DAP
Puchong	43.60	40.80	15.30	Gerakan	DAP
Kelana Jaya	41.90	38.70	17.90	MCA	PKR
Petaling Jaya Selatan	39.60	44.10	14.50	MCA	PKR
Petaling Jaya Utara	15.40	76.70	6.40	MCA	DAP
Subang	50.00	35.90	13.50	MIC	PKR
Shah Alam	68.80	15.50	15.10	UMNO	PAS
Kapar	51.40	35.40	13.00	MIC	PKR
Klang	33.50	47.10	18.60	MCA	DAP
Kota Raja	47.80	23.20	28.30	MIC	PAS
Kuala Langat	55.30	29.10	18.50	UMNO	PKR
Sepang	58.70	23.30	17.90	UMNO	UMNO

Source: Adapted from Ooi, Saravanamuttu and Lee (2008, p. 105).

Saravanamuttu and Lee,[39] had the pattern of cross-ethnic voting in Kuala Lumpur and Selangor held for the rest of Peninsular Malaysia, the Pakatan may have won the majority of the parliamentary seats on the Peninsula. However, the older ethnic voting pattern continued to prevail in the states of Pahang, Malacca, Negri Sembilan, and particularly in Johor.

BY-ELECTIONS AFTER 8 MARCH

Remarkably, sixteen by-elections and a state election in Sarawak have been held since the March 2008 general election up until mid-2011. The threshold period for by-elections expired at the two-and-a-half year mark post-March 2008. This section will attempt to briefly review and analyse the results of most of these by-elections and related political developments. On 26 August 2008, as noted above, Anwar Ibrahim won a landslide victory in his old parliamentary constituency of Permatang Pauh after his wife Wan Azizah stepped down to let him contest the seat. While this was largely predictable, Anwar's political comeback meant that the Pakatan as a coalition was further strengthened given his pivotal role as its leader. The second by-election came in Kuala Terengganu on 17 January 2009 with the death of UMNO's deputy education minister Razali Ismail. On this occasion, the PAS candidate Abdul Wahid Endut won 51 per cent of the vote with a comfortable margin of 2,631 votes. This was a major blow to the faltering UMNO leader Abdullah Badawi and also his deputy Najib who was responsible for the campaign. At the end of the day, Abdullah turned out to be a major casualty of the 8 March political tsunami with the Kuala Terengganu result propelling his departure from the political stage.

Then came the triple by-elections of 7 April 2009 in Bukit Gantang, Perak, Bukit Selamabau, Kedah, and Batang Ai, Sarawak, all state seats. The Batang Ai result, which saw the Barisan Nasional win convincingly by garnering some 66 per cent of the votes of mostly Ibans, confirmed that the overall 8 March trend did not really penetrate into East Malaysia. However, the outcome in Perak and Kedah proved the opposite. As I have argued elsewhere,[40] the new dynamics of politics were reinforced by the double whammy defeats delivered to the BN in the two "bukits".

Let me begin with Bukit Gantang, the more significant of the two Peninsular by-elections, a parliamentary constituency with an electorate of 55,471 voters, lying on the outskirts of Taiping town. A former stronghold of UMNO, it slipped into PAS's grip in the 8 March General Election, the Islamic party capturing a credible majority of 1,566 votes. The death of the PAS assemblyman forced the 7 April outcome which saw the charismatic Nizar Jamaluddin take on UMNO's local boy, Ismail Safian. Nizar, the erstwhile Menteri Besar (MB — Chief Minister) of Perak took the seat with an increased majority of 2,789, this despite the fact, PAS would admit, that he lost the Malay votes. An analysis by PAS showed that Nizar may have won only 43 per cent of the Malay votes. The results showed that the more rural areas of Trong gave UMNO a majority of votes while the more urbanized regions around Sepang, Bukit Gantang proper and Kuala Sepetang gave Nizar sizeable majorities.

Nizar won the seat by capturing a sizable portion of the Malay votes, but in Malaysian politics today, this is a necessary but not a sufficient condition for success. Nizar had to win the non-Malay votes by a good margin and he did. Thus, the non-Malay electorate has become kingmakers whenever the Malay vote is split more or less down the middle. It was crystal clear that Nizar swept the non-Malay, mostly Chinese, votes sometimes to the tune of 80 per cent. At the DAP contribution dinner at Simpang, Bukit Gantang, on 5 April, Nizar arrived to speak to the tumultuous roar of approval of thousands of Chinese supporters.[41] A field trip to Kuala Sepatang (formerly Port Weld), gave me the distinct impression that the Chinese fishing community seemed totally supportive of this man, who in his short tenure as MB had legalized Temporary Occupation Lease (TOL) land to Chinese farmers and other tenants.

Nizar had called the by-election a "referendum" on the BN government, particularly the action of new premier Najib Razak in seizing power from his (Nizar's) government in February 2009. The Perak Assembly was hung with Nizar mounting a legal challenge to newly minted UMNO MB Zambry Abdul Kadir after three Pakatan legislators crossed the floor to the BN. The by-election result was seen not only as indictment of Najib Razak's action but also that of Sultan Raja Azlan Shah who speedily anointed Zambry as MB without a vote of confidence in the Assembly, while rejecting Nizar's request to dissolve the Assembly for fresh elections after the three Pakatan members hopped out of the coalition.

Let me now turn to the Bukit Selambau by-election outcome. S. Manikumar of the People's Justice Party's (PKR) won by a large majority of 2,403 votes, adding a thousand votes to the previous win. This happened despite a lineup of fifteen contenders, something quite unprecedented in Malaysian political history. The PKR win was a major blow to Najib and, in particular, the Malaysian Indian Congress (MIC). Bukit Selambau, with 30 per cent of Indian voters, is a barometer of MIC's popularity among Indians. MIC's more experienced S. Ganesan lost to newcomer Manikumar even though six other Indians, along with six Malays, were there to split the PKR vote. The campaign had become acrimonious when MIC Youth kicked up a ruckus at a *ceramah* (prayer meeting) and the Federal Reserve Unit (FRU) had to intervene and stop the event before its allotted time. To my mind, the outcome shows that Anwar Ibrahim, leader of the Opposition, who campaigned vigorously in the constituency, effectively deployed a multi-ethnic coalition mode of politics. Additionally, Indian voters prefer to support PKR candidates rather than those from the MIC. The corollary of this is that the BN has lost an important plank in its platform and along with it support of the Indian voters. Furthermore, as shown above, the Chinese have also evinced great support for even PAS candidates like Nizar. The Chinese party, MCA, was conspicuous by its absence in campaigning for both by-elections.

Three subsequent by-elections followed. On 14 July, PAS retained the Kelantan seat of Manek Urai by a wafer-slim 65 votes. PAS was clearly on the back foot after the exposé and open altercations over "unity talks" with UMNO which implicated their top leadership. By 25 August PAS regained its ground in Permatang Pasir, in the state of Penang, defeating UMNO by capturing some 65 per cent of the 14,832 votes. The PAS candidate of Pakatan routed the UMNO candidate of BN by 4,511, just 882 votes shy of the previous victory on 8 March 2008. A drop in voter turnout from 82.6 per cent to 73.1 per cent could account for this margin of difference. More interestingly, PAS won in both Malay and non-Malay polling stations according to ground reports and the Chinese areas evinced even more comprehensive support. It appeared then that Pakatan remained the choice for Malaysian voters after seven Peninsular Malaysia by-elections. The other by-election on 31 May in the Penang state seat of Penanti saw a no contest on the part of UMNO and was easily retained by PKR's Mansor Othman. Three other independent candidates lost their deposits.

The BN finally stemmed the tide of by-election losses by a landslide victory in the state seat of Bagan Pinang on 11 October 2009, when former UMNO Negri Sembilan supremo, Mohd Isa Abdul Samad roundly defeated his PAS opponent by a majority of 5,435 votes. Certainly, the Bagan Pinang outcome augurs well for the new Prime Minister Najib and his government and commentators opined that it had stemmed the tide of the 8 March 2008 political tsunami. What was interesting was the large non-Malay swing towards BN, in particular the Indian vote, which constituted some 21 per cent of that constituency. However, the actual breakout of fights between UMNO and PAS supporters in this instance showed the intensity of intra-Malay politics.

The Bagan Pinang result seemed to seal a north-south divide in Peninsular Malaysian politics which is likely to remain for most of 2010 and beyond. Put differently, states south of Selangor seem to remain firmly under the BN wing. The Perak situation remained muddled until a conclusion came about when the Federal Court, on 9 February 2010, with a full panel of five judges, unanimously ruled that the UMNO leader Zamry Abdul Kadir was the rightful MB.[42] However, conditions in Penang, Kedah

and Selangor have largely firmed up with the Pakatan well in place at
the time of writing. Kelantan on the East Coast is likely to be PAS terrain
for a long time to come. On the other hand, the East Malaysian states of
Sabah and Sarawak seemed destined to remain as BN territory perhaps
until a political change occurs in the centre. In short, Malaysia's nascent
two-party system is set to remain in place until the next general election.
This is despite the fact that both the BN and the Pakatan coalitions are
facing internal problems.

After the Bagan Pinang result, an important contest came on 25 April
2010 by way of the tenth by-election for the parliamentary seat of Hulu
Selangor which was a two-way contest between the MIC (BN) and the PKR
(Pakatan). In 2008 the seat was won by the PKR's candidate by a whisker-
thin margin of 198 votes. The new Pakatan heavyweight, Zaid Ibrahim, the
former UMNO Minister, was clearly affected by pork-barrel politics and
character assassination tactics against the BN's candidate. The 7,000 FELDA
dwellers in the constituency were targeted with an RM1,000 handout and
the promise of another RM49,000 should the BN win, while a Chinese
school was promised RM3 million after the election. To compound the PKR
problems, there were suggestions of internal differences in Zaid's choice
as a candidate. In the event, the BN candidate, MIC's P. Kamalanathan,
defeated Zaid by 1,725 votes. The BN's win was still a far cry from their
14,483 majority of 2004.

A famous victory for the Pakatan came in the parliamentary
constituency of Sibu in Sarawak on 16 May. Taking up the cudgels for
the Pakatan, the DAP candidate Wong Ho Leng defeated his SUPP
opponent Robert Lau by a 398 vote margin in this predominantly Chinese
seat (Chinese 66.7 per cent, Iban 22 per cent, Melanau/Malay 10.5 per
cent). While slim, the Pakatan victory demonstrated a serious erosion of
Chinese and possibly even of Iban support for the BN in its stronghold
state of Sarawak. Most importantly, from the analytical stance of this
essay, the trajectory of Pakatan electoral strength in Chinese-dominant
constituencies appears to have remained stable two years after March
2008 and, indeed, was further demonstrated in the 16 April 2011 Sarawak
state election.[43] The outcome of the Sarawak state election showed that
twin-coalition electoral politics has found traction in this East Malaysian
state, particularly that the Pakatan has made major inroads into the non-
bumiputera constituencies of Sarawak.

Let us now examine the Tenang by-election held on 30 January 2011,
which saw the third consecutive by-election victory of the Barisan Nasional

(BN) since the March 2008 general election.[44] This fourteenth by-election witnessed a resurgence of voter support for the ruling coalition but fell short of the 5,000 vote majority that the BN had expected. UMNO took the seat by a majority of 3,707, some 1,200 more than it won during 2008 with a voter turnout of 9,833, which is only 67 per cent of the electorate. Massive flooding in the constituency during voting day accounted for this low voter turnout. Tenang practically exhibits the Peninsular template of Malay-Chinese-Indian distribution (49-38-12, and 1 per cent "others") and its result could well be seen by some as a barometer of the state of play in Malaysian electoral politics. The electoral result shows that the UMNO candidate Azahar Ibrahim swept more than 80 per cent of the Malay vote. The PAS challenger Normala Sudirman evidently won the Chinese vote, but the numbers had shrunk somewhat since 2008. This was thought to be because of the low voter turnout among the Chinese. She was able only to win a majority in the 95 per cent Chinese polling area of Labis Tengah but lost in Labis Timor and in Labis Station, which had lower Chinese percentages. The DAP claim is that she still picked up the majority of Chinese votes. DAP publicity chief Tony Pua suggested that Umno's Azahar Ibrahim received 83.3 per cent of Malay votes, up four percentage points from 2008. This was helped by an 81 per cent showing of Malay voters. The Indian vote also went to BN but the community had a low 40 per cent turnout. The flood situation meant that more assistance was given to UMNO voters to get to polling stations. The Tenang by-election result was already predictable before voting day and only the margin of victory was at issue. As such, the interesting points to be made are about the different styles, tactics and approach to by-elections of Malaysia's twin coalition system. The BN clearly optimized on a strategy of using its copious resources and electoral machinery with great effect. The Pakatan on the other hand often floundered under the weight of BN power and its monopoly of state resources.

What then were the new political dynamics that the Peninsular by-elections and the Sarawak state election have re-established? *First*, the momentum of 8 March 2008 establishing a two party (or two-coalition) system had not abated; indeed, the symmetrical by-election results of eight wins seem to reinforce the trend. Moreover, the Sarawak state election of April 2011 exhibited a clear traction of the opposition coalition politics of the Peninsula, with the DAP's strength established in the urban areas, PKR and PAS making important inroads in rural and semi-urban areas. *Second*, the BN formula for capturing cross-ethnic votes appears to have become less effective, again following the trend of 8 March, while the opposite is true for the Pakatan forces which have largely succeeded where the BN has continued to fail. *Third*, the Islamic party, PAS, despite some internal hiccups, appears to be superseding UMNO as the voice of the Malays and, furthermore, as the putative Malay voice to non-Malays. I hasten to add that this last point comes with two caveats, namely that the process is still ongoing and has been the case for many years. But only now, West Coast states like Perak and Kedah have increasingly evinced such a trend while in the past this may only have been evident in East Coast states like Kelantan and Terengganu. The second caveat is that UMNO retains strong support among the older generation of voters and among highly rural constituencies.

CONCLUDING REMARKS

Several important points should be made about considering 8 March as a historical conjuncture in this essay. First, it may not be fully of the order such as a "critical juncture" of the sort alluded to by Collier and Collier,[45] namely, that it produces a distinctly new legacy by ending an old one, such as demolishing an *ancien régime*. In my reckoning, there would be important political continuities in politics after the 8 March conjuncture. The critical junctures identified by the Colliers in Latin America spanned periods of 9 to 23 years. At the time of writing, the outcome of the March 2008 election has surpassed three years while the antecedent event to which we alluded was *reformasi* of the 1998–99 years, which was about 13 years ago. My argument is that politics has been putatively changed but perhaps not as radically as implied by Collier and Collier. As Malaysia prepares itself for the thirteenth general election, which is expected to be held in early 2013, the two-coalition political system laid down in 2008 remains well in place.

In addressing the profundity of change question, the thesis in this essay is that the political moment of 8 March basically had its antecedent in the *reformasi* movement of 1999 in disembedding certain legacies of Malaysian politics. The Anwar episode of 1998–99 generated a post-Mahathirism politics which, coupled with the failure and ineptitude of the short-lived Abdullah Badawi government, created the conditions for the 8 March moment. However, I may not go as far as to argue that "[s]ince March 2008, Malaysia's political landscape has changed forever"[46] but that new path dependencies are now palpable and if reinforced by events and "increasing returns" could generate a genuine political shift in the character of politics. This may not take the form of a Gramscian moment of organic change but it could drive the political system away from what one writer has termed "electoral authoritarianism".[47] The same writer avers that 8 March was a "landmark event" with the suggestion that a sort of political liberalization may be occurring.[48] Again such a change may depend greatly on whether the incipient two-party takes firm root.

A second point is that 8 March does indeed represent a moment of political crisis. In a broad sense, UMNO and the BN faced a legitimacy crisis in which the former could no longer stand its ground firmly as a consociational party representing Malays and non-Malays. This legitimacy crisis runs deep also because of its egregious corruption and money politics of the political regime under the BN. Political parties such as UMNO, with its particular form of "party capitalism", have lost legitimacy like parties in Taiwan and Japan.[49] It could be argued that UMNO's cronyism could eventually be its Achilles heel. The Malay vote is now split almost evenly between UMNO and its two rivals PAS and PKR, but more so PAS has assumed its role as the putative voice of the Malay-Muslims. The PKR, on the other hand, since the 1999 election, has established the importance of cross-ethnic voting and clearly broke the mould of the old pattern of ethnic voting on 8 March.

Thirdly, 8 March also created a legitimacy crisis for the BN non-Malay component parties by Pakatan sweeping the middle ground of electoral politics — the mixed constituencies. The question that remains moot is whether this Pakatan formula can be effective in the East Malaysian states of Sabah and Sarawak. The Klang valley's pattern of cross-ethnic voting could hold as long as the Pakatan continues to fashion a common political platform and succeeds in formalizing itself as a political entity like the BN. However, as I have argued elsewhere, because of its prevalent discourse and practices of Islamism, the PAS could be the spoiler in the Pakatan coalition. So far, however, the pact has held firm and appears (at the time of writing) to be on the path of constituting itself as a formal body in preparation for the next general election.[50]

Finally, we return to the point made earlier that 8 March sees a culmination thus far of the "new politics" as articulated by Loh and Saravanamuttu and generated by the *reformasi* movement of the late 1990s. This was a politics which valorized participatory democracy and the engagement of civil society forces directly in the electoral process. It was also one which set reformist agendas aimed at eroding a power bloc embedded in a form of highly corrupt, ethnicized politics. The trajectory of new politics, while remaining ethnic in sensibility and in terms of political mobilization, nonetheless favours cross-ethnic or multi-ethnic political coalitions which have as their objects a reformed political economy not anchored on race. I would argue that the reflexivity of such a new path dependency has produced a changed trajectory of Malaysian politics possibly for some decades to come.

Notes

1. Ganesan (2010) cites Pierson (2004) who sees a historical conjuncture as the conjoining of "distinct causal sequences" at particular points of time. He states further: "Conjunctures are moments in time that offer the possibility of evolving path dependent decisions."
2. The narrative of 8 March, its outcome and ramifications draw considerably on these earlier pieces of writing of mine but further updating and analytical points have been added in this chapter. See Johan Saravanamuttu, "The 12th General Election in Malaysia", *Opinion Asia*, 15 February 2008; "Malaysia: Political Transformation and Intrigue in an Election Year", *Southeast Asian Affairs 2009*, edited by Daljit Singh; and Ooi Kee Beng, Johan Saravanamuttu, and Lee Hock Guan, *March 8: Eclipsing May 13* (Singapore: Institute of Southeast Asian Studies, 2008).
3. Also known as "People's Pact", hereinafter, also as "Pakatan" for short.
4. See Michael O'Shannassy, "Beyond the Barisan Nasional? A Gramscian Perspective of the 2008 Malaysian General Election", *Contemporary Southeast Asia* 31, no. 1 (2009): 89.
5. Francis Kok Wah Loh and Johan Saravanamuttu, eds., *New Politics in Malaysia* (Singapore: Institute of Southeast Asian Studies, 2003).
6. Loh and Saravanamuttu, "*New Politics*", p. 10.
7. Meredith L. Weiss, *Protest and Possibilities: Civil Society and Coalitions for Political Change in Malaysia* (Stanford: Stanford University Press, 2006), p. 164.
8. Loh and Saravanamuttu, "*New Politics*".
9. Ibid., p. 278.
10. Weiss, *Protest and Possibilities* , pp. 174–75.
11. Ruth Berins Collier and David Collier, *Shaping the Political Arena: Critical Junctures, the Labour Movement, and Regime Dynamics in Latin America* (Notre Dame: University of Notre Dame Press, 2002).
12. Ibid., p. 32.

13. HINDRAF, a coalition of Hindu NGOs, was formed in 2005 and declared illegal by the government in 2008.

14. The video clip showed lawyer V.K. Lingam allegedly speaking to former Chief Justice Fairuz Abdul Halim about his appointment as Chief Justice of the Federal Court. A commission of inquiry found the video to be authentic but till date no action has been taken on the matter.

15. Most pundits couldn't see the opposition winning more than 40 seats. At a pre-election seminar at the Institute of Southeast Asian Studies, two days before polling day, main speaker Dato' Dr Michael Yeoh of the Malaysian think tank ASLI and other speakers were confident that the BN would retain its two-thirds majority.

16. See Stephen Gan's editorial in the Internet paper, Malaysiakini, 19 March 2008.

17. See Khoo Boo Teik, "The Monkeys Strike Back: The 12th General Election and After", *Aliran Monthly* 28, no. 2 (2008).

18. The exceptions were Terengganu, Perlis and Pahang, but even these states swung in single digit percentage points. See Table 8.1.

19. K.J. Ratnam, *Communalism and the Political Process in Malaya* (Singapore: University of Malaya Press, 1965); and Karl von Vorys, *Democracy without Consensus: Communalism and Political Stability in Malaysia* (Kuala Lumpur/ Singapore: Oxford University Press, 1976).

20. Loh and Saravanamuttu in *New Politics in Malaysia* (Singapore: Institute of Southeast Asian Studies, 2003) in particular have tried to show that a "new politics" which transcended ethnicity, which was sparked by the *reformasi* movement, valorized non-racial campaign issues while driving the participation of civil society in the 1999 election. This development adversely affected UMNO's performance. For studies that put the accent on race as the primary factor driving electoral politics, see, for example, K.J. Ratnam and R.S. Milne, *The Malaysian Parliamentary Election of 1964* (Singapore: University of Malaya Press, 1967); Raj Vasil, *The Malaysian General Election of 1969* (Singapore: Oxford University Press, 1972); Chandra Muzaffar (Chandrasekaran Pillay), *The 1974 General Elections in Malaysia: A Post-Mortem* (Singapore: Institute of Southeast Asian Studies, 1974). The volume by Puthucheary and Noraini Othman entitled *Elections and Democracy in Malaysia* (Bangi: Penerbit Universiti Kebangasaan Malaysia, 2005) examines the electoral process from the perspective of democracy, with authors attempting to steer discussion away from ethnicity to the direction of electoral reform.

21. In the 1969 general election, the Alliance took only 48.5 per cent of the ballots while the opposition captured 51.5 per cent of the total vote. The Alliance lost its two-thirds majority in Parliament and the elections in Sarawak and Sabah were postponed. Both Perak and Selangor were also on the balance

in terms of seats held, Perak virtually lost, but the opposition was split and had no electoral pact. See von Vorys (1976, pp. 297–98) and Harold Crouch, *Government and Politics in Malaysia* (Ithaca: Cornell University Press, 1996), p. 74. For a broad discussion of the implications of 8 March in contrast to 1969, see Chapter 1 of Ooi, Saravanamuttu and Lee (2008).

22. This observation is based on personal experience as I was present in May 1969 as a journalist in Kuala Lumpur and I also observed the 2008 event in Kelantan and Penang.

23. See Ooi's "The Opposition's Year of Living Demonstratively" for an account of the extraordinary events in Penang in Ooi et al. (2008), pp. 17–20.

24. The sources cited by the *Straits Times* were Ong Kian Ming, *The Star*/Asia News Network and Election Commission. In fact, political scientist, Ong Kian Ming, made the calculations. Ong, in an article for Malaysiakini (11 March 2008), has explained that he used a certain statistical method called ecological inference, theorized by Gary King, who is a professor of government and statistics at Harvard University. On his figures, Ong says the following: "It is important to highlight that these vote swings are not uniformly distributed. For example, the Malay vote swing in the West Coast states, especially in Penang, Selangor and Kuala Lumpur was higher than the estimated 5 per cent and was closer to 10 per cent or even higher in certain constituencies like Balik Pulau, Gombak and Lembah Pantai. It would not have been possible for the opposition, PKR in these cases, to win without a sizeable swing in the Malay vote."

25. Ong Kian Ming, "Making Sense of the Political Tsunami", Malaysiakini, 11 March 2008.

26. See Maznah Mohamad, "Malaysia — Democracy and the End of Ethnic Politics?" *Australian Journal of International Affairs* 62, no. 4 (December 2008): 46.

27. This is the thesis proffered by Lee in Ooi Kee Beng, Johan Saravanamuttu, and Lee Hock Guan, *March 8: Eclipsing May 13* (Singapore: Institute of Southeast Asian Studies, 2008), pp. 113–14).

28. See Lee's analysis of the Kuala Lumpur voting, ibid., pp. 92–103.

29. Perak was lost to the BN after three Pakatan legislators crossed over in February 2009. Two were from the PKR, one the deputy speaker from the DAP. See my discussion further below.

30. On 17 July 2008, MCA former women's wing deputy chief and former cabinet minister, Dr Tan Yee Kew, quit her party and in August joined the PKR with 1,700 supporters <http://anilnetto.com/malaysian-elections/tan-yee-kew-and-1700-mca-members-cross-over-to-pkr/>.

31. Zaid wrote an open letter on 30 September 2008 which condemned the draconian actions of the Abdullah government in using the ISA and also upbraided it for its failure of law reform for which he was held responsible. See Saravanamuttu, "Malaysia: Political Transformation and Intrigue", pp.

183–84. However, Zaid subsequently left the PKR soon after losing the Hulu Selangor by-election and formed his own political party, KITA, in January 2011.

32. Dompok raised these issues in a twenty-one-page keynote policy address at his party's twelfth triennial meeting in October 2008. See "Dompok: Tide against BN in Sabah", Malaysiakini, 12 October 2008.

33. See Lim's statement in Malaysiakini.com, 21 December 2008 <http://www.malaysiakini.com/news/95227> (accessed 29 December 2008). By October 2009 another major issue was the Kampong Buah Pala episode which saw forty-odd Indian families dislodged for a housing scheme. The state government was however successful in negotiating adequate compensations for these families.

34. The threat of crossovers remains possible although Opposition leader Anwar Ibrahim appears to have dropped the idea, as suggested in the section below.

35. Najib made this announcement on 4 November. The government had earlier also announced that there would be an injection of RM5 billion into the Malaysian Bourse, the money being sourced from the Employees Provident Fund (EPF). *Malaysian Insider*, 4 November 2008 <http://www.themalaysianinsider.com/index.php/malaysia/11792-najib-epf-loan-to-valuecap-is-guaranteed-by-government> (accessed 29 December 2008).

36. The scatter plots do not show the seats won by UMNO, the MCA, MIC and Gerakan or other component parties of BN. I have made my inferences by examining the information given on candidates' ethnicity given in the detailed results provided by the Election Commission.

37. I draw the data and analysis from the penetrating study of Lee (Chapter 3) in Ooi, Saravanamuttu and Lee (2008).

38. Ibid., p. 101.

39. Ibid., p. 113.

40. Saravanamuttu, "More of a Double Blow Than Status Quo", *Straits Times*, 15 April 2009.

41. I was there to witness the immense popularity of this man who was greatly liked by Chinese and Indian voters.

42. See the *Star* online, 9 February 2010 <http://thestar.com.my/news/story.asp?file=/2010/2/9/nation/20100209091318&sec=nation> (accessed 26 February 2010). The decision has been criticized by civil groups and legal experts as having overturned a legal precedent that a vote of no-confidence is required if a head of government does tender his resignation. The judges ruled that the Perak Sultan's decision to appoint a new MB was valid despite the lack of a no-confidence vote in the state assembly.

43. The elections saw the BN winning 55 seats, with the PBB, Taib's party, winning all 35 seats contested, the PRS winning 8, the SPDP winning 6 and the SUPP

6. The BN more than retained its two-thirds majority, with the PR winning 15 seats in total, one going to an independent. Within the BN coalition, SUPP crashed with the defeat of its leader George Chan and deputy Tiong Thai King and retained only two Chinese seats. Its nemesis was the DAP which was the biggest winner on the opposition side, taking 12 of 15 seats it contested. The PKR faired poorly in terms of seats, contesting 49 and winning only 3. However, Baru Bian, land rights champion and leader of the PKR won his seat in Ba'kelalan, so too another prominent land rights lawyer, PKR's See Chee How in Batu Linatang. One other seat in the Miri area (Senadin) was won by the BN by a mere 58 votes. While PAS lost all 5 seats contested, it came within 391 votes of winning the predominantly Malay-Melanau seat of Beting Maro. Most importantly, the Pakatan as a whole won some 41 per cent of the popular vote and established itself, for the first time, as the opposition in the state of Sarawak. See Saravanamuttu and Rusaslina, *ISEAS Viewpoints* (2011).

44. BN went on to win two other by-elections on 6 March 2011 in Malacca, namely, in the state seats of Merlimau and Kerdau, previously held by UMNO.

45. Collier and Collier (2002).

46. See James Chin and Wong Chin Huat, "Malaysia's Electoral Upheaval", *Journal of Democracy* 20, no. 3 (2009): 70–85.

47. See Thomas B. Pepinsky, "The 2008 Malaysian Elections: An End to Ethnic Politics", *Journal of East Asian Studies* 9, no. 1 (2009): 115.

48. The caveat is whether UMNO "hard-liners" (Najib) or "soft-liners" (Abdullah) have the upper hand in politics, to wit: "For the 2008 Malaysian elections to yield true liberalization, the BN's soft-liners must come to believe that liberalization holds the key to their political survival, while hard-liners must be contained" (ibid., p. 117). Abdullah's fall and Najib's ascendancy must then cast a gloomy shadow on Malaysian political liberalization, going by this argument. I don't entirely agree. See my conclusion.

49. See my analysis of *Party Capitalism in Southeast Asia: Democracy's Bane?* Ishak Shari Memorial Lecture 2007 (Asia in the Twenty First Century), Bangi: IKMAS, Universiti Kebangsaan Malaysia.

50. The Anwar Ibrahim "Sodomy II" trial and its outcome may prove to be an important factor affecting the Pakatan's fortunes. Pakatan insiders have indicated that PKR president Wan Azizah will take up the mantle from Anwar should he be imprisoned again.

References

Boo Teik, Khoo. "The Monkeys Strike Back: The 12th General Election and After". *Aliran Monthly* 28, no. 2 (2008).

Chin, James and Wong, Chin Huat. "Malaysia's Electoral Upheaval". *Journal of Democracy* 20, no. 3 (July 2009): 70–85.

Collier, Ruth Berins and David Collier. *Shaping the Political Arena: Critical Junctures, the Labour Movement, and Regime Dynamics in Latin America*. Notre Dame: University of Notre Dame Press, 2002.

Crouch, Harold. *Government and Politics in Malaysia*. Ithaca, NY: Cornell University Press, 1996.

Ganesan, N. "Conjunctures and Continuities in Southeast Asian Politics". Revised paper originally prepared for the workshop on critical conjunctures in Southeast Asian politics, 3–5 October 2009, Royale Bintang Hotel, Kuala Lumpur, Malaysia.

Loh, Kok Wah Francis and Johan Saravanamuttu, eds. *New Politics in Malaysia*. Singapore: Institute of Southeast Asian Studies, 2003.

Mohamad, Maznah. "Malaysia — Democracy and the End of Ethnic Politics?" *Australian Journal of International Affairs* 62, no. 4 (2008).

Muzaffar, Chandra (Chandrasekaran Pillay). *The 1974 General Elections in Malaysia: A Post-mortem*. Singapore: Institute of Southeast Asian Studies, 1974.

O'Shannassy, Michael. "Beyond the Barisan Nasional? A Gramscian Perspective of the 2008 Malaysian General Election". *Contemporary Southeast Asia* 31, no. 1 (2009) : 88–109.

Ong Kian Ming. "Making Sense of the Political Tsunami". Malaysiakini, 11 March 2008.

Ooi, Kee Beng. *Lost in Transition: Malaysia under Abdullah*. Petaling Jaya: Strategic Information and Research Development Centre; Singapore: Institute of Southeast Asian Studies, 2008.

Ooi, Kee Beng, Johan Saravanamuttu, and Lee Hock Guan. *March 8: Eclipsing May 13*. Singapore: Institute of Southeast Asian Studies, 2008.

Pepinsky, Thomas B. "The 2008 Malaysian Elections: An End to Ethnic Politics". *Journal of East Asian Studies* 9, no. 1 (2009): 87–120.

Pierson, Paul. "Increasing Returns, Path Dependence, and the Study of Politics". *American Political Science Review* 94, no. 2 (2000): 251–67.

———. *Politics in Time: History, Institutions, and Social Analysis*. Princeton, NJ: Princeton University Press, 2004.

Puthucheary, Mavis and Noraini Othman, eds. *Elections and Democracy in Malaysia*. Bangi: Penerbit Universiti Kebangasaan Malaysia, 2005.

Ratnam, K.J. *Communalism and the Political Process in Malaya*. Singapore: University of Malaya Press, 1965.

Ratnam, K.J. and R.S. Milne. *The Malaysian Parliamentary Election of 1964*. Singapore: University of Malaya Press, 1967.

Saravanamuttu, Johan. "The 12th General Election in Malaysia". *Opinion Asia*, 15 February 2008.

————. "Malaysia: Political Transformation and Intrigue in an Election Year". In *Southeast Asian Affairs 2009*, edited by Daljit Singh. Singapore: Institute of Southeast Asian Studies, 2009.

————. "More of a Double Blow Than Status Quo". *Straits Times*, 15 April 2009.

————. "The Spoiler in Malaysia's Two-Party Politics". *Opinion Asia*, 30 August 2009.

————. *Party Capitalism in Southeast Asia: Democracy's Bane?* Ishak Shari Memorial Lecture 2007 (Asia in the Twenty First Century), Bangi: IKMAS, Universiti Kebangsaan Malaysia, 2009.

Saravanamuttu, Johan and Rusaslina Idrus. "The Sarawak Polls of 2011: Implications for Coalition Politics in Malaysia". *ISEAS Viewpoints*, 4 May 2011.

Vasil, R.K. *The Malaysian General Election of 1969*. Singapore: Oxford University Press, 1972.

von Vorys, Karl. *Democracy Without Consensus: Communalism and Political Stability in Malaysia*. Kuala Lumpur/Singapore: Oxford University Press, 1976.

Weiss, Meredith L. *Protest and Possibilities: Civil Society and Coalitions for Political Change in Malaysia*. Stanford: Stanford University Press, 2006.

9

CONCLUSION
Conjunctures and Continuities
in Southeast Asia

N. Ganesan

The case studies from Southeast Asia examined in this book appear to indicate that there have been a large number of developments that can be considered critical conjunctures in the last two decades or so. The country experts that were selected for this project obviously appear to think so and go on to offer compelling reasons on why particular events constitute the equivalent of conjunctures. In line with the requirements of the project, authors were tasked to trace antecedent conditions prior to the occurrence of a conjuncture. Similarly, they were then required to describe the changes that had been brought about by the said conjuncture. Particularly important in this regard is the appearance of contingent conditions that allow for the unfolding of various possibilities. Similarly, authors were also tasked to identify how a chosen course of action resulted in path-dependent outcomes that were subsequently replicated and acquired a certain trajectory that then became embedded over time. Other important questions pertain to the types of triggers for the conjuncture and the importance of structural and agency reasons for the path-dependent consequences. This concluding chapter ends the book with a discussion of broader theoretical concerns and trends that the book has highlighted.

BROADER TRENDS AND OBSERVATIONS

There are a number of important theoretical considerations that arise from these case studies. One of the major ones would be whether a conjuncture was made possible by external developments and if so whether the nature of such a development was broad-based or not. The preliminary evidence suggests that the Asian financial crisis served just such a function and was responsible for the downfall of the Soeharto regime in Indonesia and the meteoric rise of Thaksin Shinawatra in Thailand. Both countries were severely affected by the crisis and the Indonesian and Thai case studies indicate how post-crisis developments eventually led to the unfolding of a conjuncture. It may be remembered that both countries were recipients of international financial assistance made available by the World Bank and the International Monetary Fund that came with conditionalities that included broad structural changes to the economy.

In the Indonesian case, the structural economic reforms mandated by international donor agencies resulted in food riots and political violence that eventually unseated the Soeharto regime. And Habibie's decision to take the democratic route after the conjuncture led in turn to path-dependent developments. In the case of Thailand, Thaksin, who was relatively insulated from the crisis, was able to take advantage of his immensely disproportionate wealth and cobble together a populist political party with tremendous nationalist appeal. The introduction of populist policies that were attractive to the rural poor ensconced his appeal and subsequent political consolidation through the strengthening of his Thai Rak Thai party. His determination to create a predominant political party that aggregated the unstructured party system in Thailand also enabled significant structural change in the local political landscape that displaced the traditional elite from power. In fact his power was such a threat that the only way to dislodge him was through extra-constitutional means.

The popularity of Thaksin's party and policies inspired a successor party — Palang Prachachorn (People Power Party) — that was banned by the courts as well. The two Prime Ministers who led the post-Thaksin government — Samak Sundaravej and Somchai Wongsawat — were also forced to resign. The Thai conjuncture led to the formation of two social movements at either end of the political spectrum — the People's Alliance for Democracy (PAD, Yellow Shirts) that represented the traditional establishment and the United Front for Democracy Against Dictatorship (UDD, Red Shirts). The tensions unleashed by the conjuncture were so significant that the stalemate was eventually resolved through the use of force in April and May 2010. Nonetheless the structural problems attendant on Thailand's political economy have neither abated nor been resolved by the violence. In this regard, Thaksin's actions will have lasting consequences for national politics and the new political culture that emerges from it. The unwillingness of the Democrat-led Abhisit government to hold an early election was understandable since his parliamentary majority was only obtained through the defection of a pro-Thaksin faction in parliament. And the Pheu Thai Party's Yingluck Shinawatra scored an astounding victory in the 2011 polls returning Thaksin supporters and sympathizers to power with all the attendant dangers for the traditional establishment that includes the monarchy and the military. The devastating floods of October 2011 and Thaksin's attempts to arrange for a pardon or judicial review early on in his sister's term continue to augur dangers for the new administration.

Two more of the case studies appear to have benefitted at least in part from external stimuli. The first of these is the Four Eights movement in Myanmar. Tin argues that a major source of inspiration for the movement was the broad international developments favouring democracy following the resistance to communism in Eastern Europe. The intellectual fascination with democracy is also likely to have inspired students and intellectuals during this period. In fact there is evidence that the protest movements against Soeharto in Indonesia and Mahathir in Malaysia against corruption, collusion and nepotism were equally inspired by these broader developments. Additionally, developments in both countries appear to have had a demonstration and interactive effect on each other. And Saravanamuttu's assertion that the 2008 conjuncture derived its impetus from the *reformasi* movement allied with Anwar appears to suggest that the conjuncture may have been a long lasting one that slowly played itself out and culminated in the events of 2008.

The contingent condition that writers on conjunctures refer to appears to have been most observable in the Myanmar case where a wide range of decisions could have been and indeed were made. Although the type of regime that obtained after the conjuncture did not vary substantially from the previous regime type, the 1988 incident did have profound effects on the state. In this regard, not all conjunctures yield regime change. The Vietnamese case points to a similar situation although the antecedent conditions were rather drawn out and *doi moi* was actually the culmination of a reform process that began much earlier.

Choices were also widely available in the Indonesian and Thai cases when important decisions were made. Those that were acted on clearly had path-dependent conditions that triggered increasing returns, leading to the onset of the conjuncture. Yet, path-dependent conditions can also be reversed by a sustained series of decisions to stem the process as was the case with the military government in Myanmar. The Malaysian government is equally engaged in various attempts to wrest power away from the political opposition and has already succeeded in regaining the state of Perak. In this regard, incumbent governments, even in democratic regimes, have tremendous structural power and resources to attempt to alter the course of what might otherwise have been path-dependent trajectories.

On the question of developments that trigger the onset of conjunctures, it may be argued that the outbreak of violence, especially by the state and its enforcement agencies, often trigger the onset of a conjuncture. This observation is clearly borne out in the Indonesian and Myanmar cases. Inflamed passions and mass emotive responses also appear to augur the potential for conjunctures. The nationalist rhetoric of Thaksin and the charged atmosphere in Malaysia that led to the formation of the *reformasi* movement were moments in time that eventually led to conjunctures.

The Cambodian case stands out for its exceptionalism in this study. Ramses Amer's hypothesis that there have indeed been four recent conjunctures in the country is certainly different from all the other case studies. He does however go on to add that the ouster of Norodom Sihanouk in 1970 led in turn to the developments of 1975 and 1978/79. This assertion augurs the possibility of treating the first three conjunctures as a single drawn-out conjuncture that culminated in the Vietnamese invasion and occupation of Cambodia. The only problem with such an interpretation is his assertion that all three events were contingent situations themselves with their own path-dependent developments and increasing returns. Consequently, such bundling appears problematic.

Finally, while dealing with conjunctures it must be remembered that important continuities are likely to obtain as well. Well-entrenched patterns of behaviour are not likely to dissipate very quickly. Such deep changes require more increasing returns spread out over a long period of time. And important continuities may well reappear in different forms and require considerable investigation to be uncovered. The case studies in this book offer ample examples of just such continuities and a few examples will serve to prove the point. In the case of Indonesia, an important continuity is the continued territorial deployment of the military that allows it significant autonomy and power as noted by Kimura. Similarly, the process of administrative decentralization has created provincial elite that are able to liaise with national elite and entrench themselves within a corruption-prone and nepotistic relationship. And in the case of Thailand, even Thaksin was unable to escape the pervasiveness of factions and faction leaders. The parliamentary coup staged by the Abhisit-led Democrat Party was only possible owing to the defection of a pro-Thaksin faction leader. Similarly, the manner in which the pent-up tensions were resolved through violence harkens to an important continuity in Thai politics. Equally, the dissolution of pro-Thaksin parties and the ban on political activities of his supporters and sympathizers may well return Thailand to its previous legacy of unstructured parties.

Important continuities in the Malaysian case are continued ethnic patterns of voting in the more rural areas and the general continuation of party aggregation and formation along ethnic lines too notwithstanding the cross-ethnic polling in its favour. It is the broadly welded coalitions, both in the government and the opposition, that is keeping the parties together. In the Myanmar case, the pre-eminent role of the military in domestic politics continues to obtain and the new constitution is certain to entrench this dominance structurally as Tin has argued. Likewise, Ramses Amer points to the all important personality of Norodom Sihanouk and the constant role that he had played in Cambodian politics at all critical conjunctures from 1970 onwards. In light of these developments, it is worth noting that conjunctures notwithstanding, their path-dependent trajectories and increasing returns are likely to coexist alongside important continuities. Hence both phenomena are not mutually exclusive in any sense of the words. It is likely that richer and much more detailed case studies will yield even higher levels of such coexistence.

The presence of contingent conditions during a conjuncture brings us to the question of not just widespread choices and possibilities with different path-dependent trajectories but also the importance of conscious decision-making. In the case studies examined, there are clearly pivotal figures whose decisions have placed the country and its politics on a different course. Such personalities deserve much greater scrutiny in conjunctural studies. After all, such opportunities if not appropriated in a timely fashion, may not have led to the changes discussed in this book. There is a general tendency in the field of comparative politics to distinguish between structural and agency factors, with the latter referring to conscious decision-making on the part of specific individuals. It may well be worthwhile to examine the contributions of such pivotal figures more closely. After all, states do not determine politics; statesmen do.

CONCLUSION

Historical conjunctures and legacies are important concepts in that they offer an important methodological framework to uncover and document changes that have significantly altered the political template of a country. Southeast Asia has clearly undergone its fair share of historical conjunctures in the last two decades. Since such events are meant to be a major break with past practices, there is a sense in which they are easy to locate and identify. Cataloguing legacies that are structural or legal in nature tends to be far easier than documenting those that are softer and centre on state-society relations or the political economy of a state. Identifying the latter is also complicated by the extended nature of their reproduction since social relations and practices often take much longer to change. Importantly, there is also the risk that such patterns of behaviour may be exhibited in different ways and effectively constitute continuity rather than an abrupt rupture as demanded by conjuncture theorists.

Conjunctures are most easily identified when the rupture involves regime change rather than a simple change of government. The Philippine case in 1986 and the Indonesian case in 1998 are easily identifiable as conjunctures in part because they replaced military authoritarian regimes. The conjunctures and their path-dependent trajectories in terms of the strengthening of democracy and the prevention of a return to previous practices are more easily documented. This change also made the Cambodian case far easier to catalogue. The Thai case demonstrates that it is equally possible for a conjuncture to reverse previous political gains although the general trajectory of regional political developments is the movement away from authoritarianism and towards democratic norms.

The location of a conjuncture where systemic and structural changes are not forthcoming is invariably much more difficult to identify. Nonetheless, as the Myanmar, Vietnamese and Thai cases demonstrate, major shifts in state-society relations are recognizable. The previous rules of the game appear to have been changed with little possibility of a return to the status quo ante. Although both Myanmar and Thailand do not practise democracy as popularly understood, changes of enduring value in the calibration of state-society relations have taken place. In the Vietnamese case it was initiated by the state and in the case of Myanmar there was an implosion of the previously constituted government. The latter allowed for the usurpation of space by civil society elements that have continued to obtain in the face of severe repression. The ruling junta's loss of legitimacy in the outcome of the 1990 elections and the severe regional and international criticisms have in turn forced it to acquire more acceptable norms of political legitimacy.

The Malaysian case is actually the most problematic in its classification as a historical conjuncture. On the one hand it may be viewed simply as the case of an incompetent government that has effectively lost its political mandate to rule. Although the extent of the loss was beyond the expectations of most watchers there were indications of unhappiness with the government among the minority ethnic communities. The high levels of violence and corruption were also beginning to alienate the urban electorate and the political opposition capitalized on these misgivings and cobbled together a successful coalition and strategy. The social movements and political parties that spawned before and after the elections do appear to indicate a major shift in state-society relations. The incumbent government's losses in most of the by-elections called since then also indicate a tectonic shift. Yet, the government is continuously attempting to regain lost ground through various manipulations. These efforts are clearly intended to prevent the increasing returns necessary to sustain the conjuncture. This constant tug of war between the opposition and elements of civil society on the one hand, and the federal government on the other, has also made the situation more fluid. In this regard it is likely that developments are still unfolding and likely to take much more time to crystallize. It is however important to remember that the Barisan coalition may well perform far better in the future. Such an outcome will not change the conclusion that a historical conjuncture has occurred if there is a reordering of state-society relations. In this regard the Malaysian case is not unlike the Myanmar case where a historical conjuncture has occurred notwithstanding the government's attempts at resisting or preventing it. It is also worth remembering that it is often easier to trace antecedent conditions after the onset of a conjuncture rather than attempting to predict one. *Ex post facto* judgements are far more easily substantiated than clairvoyancy, for which social scientists have a poor track record.

Index

www.ingramcontent.com/pod-product-compliance
Lightning Source LLC
Chambersburg PA
CBHW050419280326
41932CB00013BA/1920